ELECTRIFIED VOICES

STUDIES OF THE WEATHERHEAD EAST ASIAN INSTITUTE,
COLUMBIA UNIVERSITY

STUDIES OF THE WEATHERHEAD EAST ASIAN INSTITUTE,
COLUMBIA UNIVERSITY

The Studies of the Weatherhead East Asian Institute of Columbia University were inaugurated in 1962 to bring to a wider public the results of significant new research on modern and contemporary East Asia.

For a list of titles in this series, see pages 279–81

ELECTRIFIED VOICES

HOW THE TELEPHONE,
PHONOGRAPH,
and
RADIO SHAPED MODERN
JAPAN, 1868–1945

KERIM YASAR

Columbia University Press
New York

Columbia University Press
Publishers Since 1893
New York   Chichester, West Sussex
cup.columbia.edu
Copyright © 2018 Columbia University Press
All rights reserved

Library of Congress Cataloging-in-Publication Data
Names: Yasar, Kerim, author.
Title: Electrified voices : how the telephone, phonograph, and radio shaped modern Japan, 1868–1945 / Kerim Yasar.
Description: New York : Columbia University Press, [2018] | Series: Studies of the Weatherhead East Asian Institute, Columbia University | Includes bibliographical references and index.
Identifiers: LCCN 2018012328 | ISBN 9780231187121 (cloth) | ISBN 9780231187138 (pbk.) | ISBN 9780231547024 (e-book) Subjects: LCSH: Japan—Civilization—1868–1945. | Japan—History—1868- | Communication—Social aspects—Japan—History. | Sound recordings—Social aspects—Japan—History. | Mass media and culture—Japan—History. | Nationalism—Japan—History.
Classification: LCC DS822.25 .Y3784 2018 | DDC 952.03—dc23
LC record available at https://lccn.loc.gov/2018012328

Cover design: Noah Arlow
Cover image: Takabatake Kashoe, *Natsukashi no mikoe* (Nostalgia of the real voice). Japan, 1920s. Courtesy of the Yayoi Museum

FOR MY MOTHER, AND FIRST
AND BEST TEACHER,
AZADE SEYHAN

CONTENTS

List of Illustrations ix
Acknowledgments xi
Note on Names xvii

INTRODUCTION: ALL THAT IS SOLID MELTS INTO SOUND   1

1. VOCAL CORDS AND TELEPHONE WIRES: ORALITY IN JAPAN, OLD AND NEW   22

2. SOUND AND SENTIMENT   52

3. THE GRAIN IN THE GROOVE: INSCRIBED VOICES, ECHOED TEMPORALITIES   83

4. IMAGINING THE WIRELESS COMMUNITY   114

5. GHOSTLIER DEMARCATIONS, KEENER SOUNDS: EARLY JAPANESE RADIO DRAMA   154

6. SOUND AND MOTION   192

CODA-*OKE*   225

Notes   229
Bibliography   253
Index   263

ILLUSTRATIONS

Figure 1.1 Postcard of Fukui Post Office Telephone Exchange. 49
Figure 1.2 Telephone switchboard, Kosaka Mining, Smelting, and Refining Works. 50
Figure 4.1 Subjects of the Japanese Empire listening to the Imperial Rescript on Surrender on August 15, 1945, in Yotsuya in Tokyo, Japan. 115
Figure 4.2 Postcard of JOBK in Osaka. 117
Figure 4.3 Cover of the NHK guidebook for radio exercise leaders, 1940 (in celebration of the putative 2,600th anniversary of the foundation of Japan). 119
Figure 4.4 Interior of the NHK guidebook for radio exercise leaders. 122–23
Figure 4.5 "Sports Sketch" recording of Keiō–Waseda Baseball Game announced by Matsuuchi Norizō, 1930. 132
Figure 4.6 Recording insert of Kasai Sansei's recording of the 800-meter relay at the 1936 Berlin Olympics. 141
Figure 4.7 Original disc of the Shōwa emperor's declaration of surrender, NHK Museum of Broadcasting. 153
Figure 5.1 Photo of Nagata Mikihiko, featured in *Musen to jikken* (Radio experimenter), June 1925. 159

ACKNOWLEDGMENTS

I led a peripatetic life during the writing of this book, living in many places and being affiliated with many institutions. The people named here all contributed something of value to the finished product, but its shortcomings are attributable to me alone.

Paul Anderer has been a generous and inspiring mentor, one who gives all of his students the freedom to pursue their intellectual passions while gently nudging them away from flying too close to the sun. We are as diverse a group as one could imagine coming from a single doctoral adviser, which speaks, I think, to his open-mindedness and genuine curiosity. Haruo Shirane gave me a rigorous grounding in the language and culture of premodern and early modern Japan, one that continues to inform the work that I do on later cultural production. Tomi Suzuki led me through some of the most difficult critical texts I have ever read in Japanese, a trial by fire that made everything that followed seem that much easier. James Schamus took time from his remarkably hyphenated career as producer-screenwriter-studio head-professor-scholar—and now, director—to teach me much of what I know about film theory and to support my research and career in other ways. Many other current and former Columbia University faculty have given generously of their time and expertise, including Carol Gluck, David Lurie, Gregory Pflugfelder, Wei Shang, Lening Liu, and Henry D. Smith. Just as important as my teachers were my fellow graduate students, who were and are dear friends and are all now exemplary scholars and teachers: Michael Berry, Torquil Duthie, Michael Emmerich, Linda Rui Feng, Sun-Chul Kim, Christina Laffin, Tom Mullaney, Se-Mi Oh, Gian Piero Persiani, Tomoko Sakomura, Satoru Saito, Satoko Shimazaki, and Weijie Song.

Toeda Hirokazu has mentored a long line of U.S.-based doctoral students at Waseda University, and I'm proud to boast that I was the first. He and Tanaka Hikari have been good friends and mentors over the years. Tsuge Gen'ichi, professor emeritus at the Tokyo University of the Arts, gave me my first opportunity to study in Japan, and for that I will always be grateful.

I took a hiatus from my graduate studies to work at Vertical, Inc., in New York City, an experience that, though removed from the academy, taught me much of what I know about contemporary Japanese literature and the inner workings of the culture industry more generally. Ioannis Mentzas, Hiroki Sakai, and Anne Ishii (also a classmate at Columbia) made that possible and made it fun.

My first academic job, at Boston University, was a delight, thanks largely to my colleague J. Keith Vincent, who is a brilliant scholar, a gracious host, and a gentleman nonpareil. I'm grateful to Sarah Frederick for hiring me to cover for her while she was away and to my other colleagues, Peter Joseph Schwartz, Sunil Sharma, William Waters, and Anna Zielinska-Elliott.

After that, I spent three idyllic years at Princeton University's Society of Fellows in the Liberal Arts. Mary Harper, the (now former) executive director of the society, was a peerless administrator and a fine scholar in her own right. Scott Burnham, the interim director during my first year, never failed to convey the joy of my first love (music) or to put a smile on my face. Susan Stewart, who served as director for the rest of my time there, is a poet and scholar with rare gifts who led the organization with aplomb. Thomas Hare in the Department of Comparative Literature was a consistently supportive mentor. David Bellos never missed an opportunity to support translators and translation. I'm also grateful to my colleagues there in the field of East Asian studies: Steven Chung, Martin Collcutt, Benjamin Elman, Sheldon Garon, David Howell (now at Harvard), Martin Kern, Paize Keulemans, David Leheny, Federico Marcon, Jerome Silbergeld, and Atsuko Ueda. I would also take this opportunity to honor the estimable memory of Richard Hideki Okada, who passed away during my last year at Princeton. Other people I met at Princeton, most of whom have moved on elsewhere, also made my time there wonderful. They include On Barak, Yulia Frumer, Scott Gregory, Russ Leo, Noriko Manabe, Nikos Panou, and Patrick Schwemmer. Last but certainly not least, I am grateful to Simon Grote, whom I only met well into my life's course, but who now feels like a lifelong friend.

During the summer of 2011, I was a visiting researcher at the Institute for Advanced Studies on Asia at Tokyo University. My thanks to Haneda Masashi, who was then director of the institute, for hosting me, as well as to Baba Norihisa for his help and friendship.

The year I spent at the University of Notre Dame was in many ways a transitional period, but it was a rich and productive time that I remember with great fondness. Lionel Jensen, my larger-than-life colleague, went out of his way to make me feel welcome from day one, while Julia Adeney Thomas and Michael Brownstein have continued to be supportive in ways that I hope to be able to repay one day. Thanks as well to East Asian studies librarian Hye-jin Juhn.

The Department of East Asian Languages and Literatures at Ohio State University was a singularly collegial and supportive professional home during the four years that I spent there. I'll always be grateful to my colleagues Mark Bender, Marjorie Chan, Kirk Denton, Naomi Fukumori, Meow-Hui Gou, Xiaobin Jian, Pil Ho Kim, Debbie Knicely, JJ Nakayama, Mari Noda, Danielle Pyun, Charlie Quinn, Shelley Quinn, Pat Sieber, Richard Torrance, Jim Unger, Galal Walker, Jianqi Wang, Zhiguo Xie, and Etsuyo Yuasa. I'm also deeply indebted to the now-retired Japanese studies librarian, Maureen Donovan, for building a collection that has breadth, depth, and character, and for supporting the collection of historical recordings. My thanks as well to Tommy Davis, Dave Filipi, Namiko Kunimoto, and Paul Reitter for their support and friendship.

I'm still something of a newcomer at the University of Southern California, but already my colleagues have been a source of inspiration and encouragement at this crucial stage in my career. I'm very grateful to Brian Bernards, David Bialock, Bettine Birge, Youngmin Choe, Brianna Correa, Géraldine Fiss, Hajime Hori, Namkil Kim, Sonya Lee, Audrey Li, Akira Lippit, Sunyoung Park, Brett Sheehan, Christine Shaw, and to the

Japanese studies librarian, Rachel Corbett. Thanks to Veli Yashin in the Department of Comparative Literature. Thanks are due as well to the USC Shinso Ito Center for Japanese Religions and Culture for crucial research support.

Other colleagues in the profession who have given generously of their time, advice, feedback, and friendship are almost too numerous to mention, but I'll try. I wish I could list in detail everything for which I feel indebted to them, but I hope if they see their names here they'll know that I, at least, remember: Jonathan Abel, Davinder Bhowmik, Giorgio Biancorosso, Michael K. Bourdaghs, Anthony H. Chambers, Rebecca Copeland, Ryan Cook, James Fujii, Joseph Hankins, Fusako Innami, Ken K. Ito, Earl Jackson, Seth Jacobowitz, Alexander Jacoby, Ken Kawashima, Seiji Lippit, Hoyt Long, Margherita Long, Ted Mack, Hiromu Boschee Nagahara, Miri Nakamura, Johan Nordstrom, Markus Nornes, Michael Raine, Ann Sherif, and John Treat.

I'm grateful to the Weatherhead East Asian Institute for including this book in its series and to Ross Yelsey for guiding it through that process. My profound thanks go to my editor, Philip Leventhal, and to the two anonymous reviewers for their close, thoughtful readings and constructive feedback. Noah Arlow designed the fabulous cover. Special thanks to Kristin Sivak for editorial help during the manuscript stage, Kathryn Jorge for guiding the book through production, Kjeld Duits for assistance with images, Margaret B. Yamashita for her careful editing, and the entire Columbia University Press team for all of the excellent work they do (and not just on this book). Do Mi Stauber made the index.

Other friends and mentors that I would be remiss not to mention are Neely Bruce, Michael Carrasco, John Gudelj, Ruth Hultengren, Francisco LaRubia-Prado, Wolfgang Lorenz, Roberto Pinheiro Machado, Russ Moench, Jacob Benjamin Morris, Jeff Peck, Roberta Ricci, Iraj Saniee, Kamron Saniee, Satō Ayaka, and, in memoriam, Dale Hultengren, Franklin D. Reeve, Donald Richie, and Marjan Saniee.

It is the convention to save family for last in acknowledgments because, well, they're the best. Many thanks to Selim Seyhan, Tülay Özkan Seyhan, Betül Yasar, Bülent Yasar, Erhan Yasar, Ilhan Yasar, Nadine Yasar, Ozan Yasar, and Zehra Dilek Yasar. My late grandparents, Hazime and Muvaffak Seyhan and Daniye and Sait Yasar, made everything possible. No person has sacrificed more to see this book come into the world than my mother, Azade Seyhan. I can only hope to leave a fraction of the mark that she has left through her scholarship and teaching. And Mengjun Li has been a best friend, an uplifting interlocutor, and a life partner. It's no coincidence that this book finally found completion only after she entered my life.

NOTE ON NAMES

With the exception of the names of authors cited whose texts were originally written in English or other European languages, or who use another convention in their professional profiles, all East Asian names follow the East Asian convention, in which family names precede given names.

ELECTRIFIED VOICES

INTRODUCTION

All That Is Solid Melts Into Sound

In 1876 Isawa Shūji (1851–1917), who was then studying at the Bridgewater Normal School in Massachusetts, visited the Centennial Exhibition at Philadelphia's Fairmount Park. He sought out the display of one Alexander Graham Bell (1847–1922). Isawa knew about Bell because in Massachusetts he had encountered a special alphabet, "Visible Speech," that Bell's father, Melvin, had devised to help mute persons learn how to speak. Isawa was curious about this alphabet because he was still struggling with English and believed that it might also help him with his English pronunciation.

Although Bell's new device for transmitting the human voice across a distance had become the talk of the exhibition, Isawa was more interested in Visible Speech, which included a series of diagrams of the mouth showing how to produce sound physically with one's lips, tongue, and teeth. Isawa's interest in pronunciation was especially strong because musical education, including singing, was an important part of the curriculum at Bridgewater, and Isawa was having trouble both with Western musical scales and the pronunciation of the English words he had to master in order to excel in these classes.

When he returned to Boston from the Centennial Exhibition, Isawa visited Alexander Graham Bell and asked him for lessons in proper pronunciation. At that time Bell was a professor of vocal physiology and elocution in Boston University's School of Oratory. He took Isawa on as a student and assistant, even though the sensation caused by his new device had made him a very busy man.

One day that same year—it is not recorded exactly when—Isawa invited his friends and fellow exchange students Kaneko Kentarō (1853–1942) and Komura Jutarō (1855–1911), both of whom were studying law at Harvard University, to visit Bell's laboratory to see Bell's invention. Many people, not having seen the invention or perhaps suspecting trickery, were still skeptical that the voice could really be transmitted from one place to another. Isawa had yet to try the device for himself, and Kaneko found the entire idea preposterous.

After a thorough presentation of the principles of telephony, Bell invited two of the young Japanese students to try the device for themselves. Bell handed Kaneko the receiver and then spoke into the other end: "Hello! Hello!"

Kaneko was astounded. Bell gave the handset to Isawa, who then proceeded to speak to Kaneko in English. Shocked that it was working, Isawa began to mumble to himself in Japanese.

"Isawa!" Kaneko cried. "This machine is incredible! It works in Japanese too!"

Japanese thus became the second language, after English, to be transmitted across a telephone line.[1]

The study of modernity has long favored the visual, which is understandable as so many of the representative forms of modern cultural production—photography, cinema, architecture—are largely, if not exclusively, visual in their appeal. Yet modernity was no less transformative of auditory culture than of visual culture, and arguably even more so. The reproduction and transmission of sound was phenomenologically unprecedented in human history—unlike, say, photography, which was new only in the sense that it was indexical; it could inscribe the physical reality of light in a form that could address our organs of perception in a way not all that different from light itself (making allowances, of course, for the lack of color, three-dimensionality, actual size, etc.). But photography was not new as a *frozen visible representation of the visible*. Representations of the audible had existed before sound recording, in the form of visual notations and oral mimicry, but both differed from sound reproduction in crucial ways: Whereas a painting or drawing is a visual representation of visual stimuli, written notation is a visual representation of audible stimuli. It is a translation across a sensory modality and not at all indexical. Oral mimicry, in contrast, is of a piece with the auditory phenomena it purports to represent, but it is a performance, not a reproduction, and is subject to the vagaries of the performer's memory, skill, and physical characteristics such as vocal cords, mouth, and chest cavity.

For the first time, sound recording and transmission allowed human beings to capture sound, reproduce it, replay it, and archive it. This was a transformative cultural and technological innovation of modernity, one whose importance has until recently been overlooked or downplayed, even by scholars of sound. Rather than thinking of sound *as sound*, a subtle yet persistent imperative, influenced perhaps by Derridean critiques of phonocentrism, is to look at sound recordings as inscriptions (which they are) rather than as reproductions (which they also are), as if the entire phenomenological dimension of sound must be disavowed lest it seduce us into the cardinal philosophical sin of phonocentrism.

There have also been, to be sure, ocularphobic and antivisual counternarratives, both ancient and modern. Martin Jay's magisterial *Downcast Eyes: The Denigration of Vision in Twentieth-Century French Thought*[2] charts the course of these counternarratives in a context that might be surprising given France's Cartesian legacy. That said, ocularphobic discourses are not the same as discourses that take auditory culture as their subject and describe its history and workings. Moreover, as sensitive and nuanced as Jay's readings are, he also cannot resist the temptation to privilege the visual, not only by providing the astronomical number of rods in each eye (120 million)[3] as proof of their unparalleled sensitivity to fine gradations, but also by pointing out that the eye "is also the most expressive of the sense organs, with the only competitor being touch."[4] Without denying the eyes' and hands' profound capacities for expression, surely the most expressive organ of all is the mouth, which besides being the sense organ for taste addresses the organ of hearing. The deeper problem, I submit, is a reflexive tendency toward hierarchical organization, which elicits the kind of one-upmanship I attempted in the last sentence to perform ironically.

I base my study on the postulate that sound occupies an important place in the economy of the human sensorium, one worthy of focused and sustained examination, nothing more or less. In making this assertion, I hope not to recapitulate, simply with another sense, the mistakes of traditions old and new that have placed vision at the apex of a hierarchy of the senses. It is also not my intention to privilege spoken language over written discourses on religious, philosophical, linguistic, or any other grounds. Written discourse is capable of forms of thought and expression that elude spoken language, just as spoken language and physical paralanguage are capable of forms of expression that elude writing. None of the senses is any more "base" or "noble" than another, and none is more "important" than another in any absolute sense, regardless of the number of fine gradations of which the sense is capable. To disabuse themselves of any such notions of hierarchy, those who prize vision or hearing above the other senses might want to have their sense of touch shut down pharmacologically for a time or, even worse, lose their sense of smell when somebody leaves the gas turned on.

Nonetheless, the tasks of culture have been parceled out among the senses in ways that address the particular textures, tonalities, and modalities that each affords. Because sound is so ephemeral and exists in a state of decay if it is to exist at all, it is particularly effective at pacing our sense of lived time and shaping our sense of time as a whole. Sound is movement by definition, and movement is time. It is this power to sculpt time that makes sound (chant, music, rhythm, sonic punctuation) so integral to ritual practices across human societies. Even a sound as brief and seemingly unmusical as the pounding of a magistrate's gavel serves a ritual function.

Among the infinite sounds that constitute human social and sonic environments, of special interest for the human subject is the human voice. The ability to reproduce and transmit not just any sounds, but the human voice in particular, is what rendered the nascent auditory technologies so transformative of the practice of culture. As Mladen Dolar argues, the voice is both the bearer of utterance and a material (non)residue that does not itself signify:

> If we speak in order to "make sense," to signify, to convey something, then the voice is the material support of bringing about meaning, yet it

does not contribute to it itself. It is, rather, something like the vanishing mediator (to use the term made famous by Fredric Jameson for a different purpose)—it makes the utterance possible, but it disappears in it, it goes up in smoke in the meaning being produced.[5]

Far from being a liability, this transience endows the voice with an auratic charge. Because the voice is always vanishing, because it cannot be stopped, fixed, and scrutinized, it always occupies a liminal, indeed ghostly, space of absent presence. Paradoxically, this auratic charge is often heightened by its mechanical reproduction. The acousmatic or disembodied voice is doubly absent, a vanishing mediator produced by an absent body. More than a century of ubiquitous sound reproduction has normalized this auratic charge, rendered it quotidian, but even today one can get a taste of it by listening to the radio at night with the lights turned off, or by listening to an audiophile stereo system with uncanny fidelity. Even the ubiquity of the technology cannot completely erase the eeriness of hearing voices that can't be traced back to bodies. One of the recurring themes of my study is how these acousmatic voices render their effects in the spectral economy of modernity where "all that is solid melts into air"—where all that is solid, in other words, becomes like the voice.

To reverse order, then, my study is rooted in the following axioms: Sound is central to social and ritual life, and the ability to reproduce and transmit sound has radically altered human beings' relationship to sound and thus to social life, including economic and political life.

The roles that sound is expected to play, the uses to which it is put, are also historically and culturally conditioned. Both church bells and the call of the Muslim muezzin employ sound, widely dispersed, for ritual religious purposes, but both vastly differ in the temporal regimes they follow (and enforce), as well as in their phenomenological textures and semiotic and semantic logic.

Every culture (and every sub- and microculture) has its own relationship to sound and the sonic environment (witness the dramatic diversity of musical cultures around the world), and another of this work's premises is that Japan is no exception to this rule. In other words, Japan's auditory culture(s) during the period I cover here are distinctive and deserving of sustained consideration. This first assertion is uncomplicated, but the question becomes more fraught when it comes to why this history would be of interest to non-Japanese.

The centrifugal motion of the study of modernity away from the usual Euro-American suspects over the past two decades has revealed that modernity takes many forms, that modernities are plural. These differences are not merely superficial. Japan presents an interesting test case for a number of reasons: a product of the greater Sinitic cultural realm, a civilization that (unlike Islam, for example) developed independently of Greco-Roman and Judeo-Christian currents, Japan furthermore is an island nation that, with some exceptions, lived up to the epithet "insular" until it was forced to open, at which point it became eager to absorb and assimilate everything that modernity's easily confused twin, technology, had to offer. Japan's leaders in the Meiji era (1868–1912) decided not just to emulate the West but to outdo it. They rushed to absorb technologies and institutions from the outside while simultaneously holding fast to cultural traditions that had endured for centuries and inventing others to construct a past that would underwrite a distinctive identity in modernity's catalog of nations.[6] Whereas the cultural practices that come under the sign of modernism were, in the West, a product of historical-dialectical motions that emerged in the wake of Romanticism and various forms of classicism, Japan in the late nineteenth century was jolted from the multifarious (indeed, proto-*post*modern) popular urban culture of the Tokugawa period (1603–1868) into the material and environmental realities of modern capitalism, industrialization, and proselytizing Christianity. It was jolted as well by the cultural forms that were transforming, before everybody's eyes, into the practices of modernism. Thus the cultural logic of Japanese modernity was the product of three contributing streams: a rapid immersion in the cultural history of the West stretching all the way back to antiquity but favoring the latest and newest; domestic cultural forms that were strategically repressed for the sake of modernization but that, with a millennium and a half of their own history, continually reasserted themselves, sometimes violently; and, finally, material and economic changes that were rooted in technologies and institutions imported from abroad but that could be deployed instrumentally without having to assent to all the cultural assumptions of the societies in which they developed.[7]

Although sound reproduction and transmission were symbols of the modern, their place in Japan's modernity was marked by a parallel and countervailing continuity with a traditional past. As I will show, premodern and early modern Japanese performing arts reserved a special place for storytelling and the narrative voice. Donald Richie termed this emphasis "presentational,"[8] in contrast to what he saw as the "representational" assumptions of theater in the West. I argue that this "residual orality" offered a fertile substrate in which the seeds of "technologized orality" (as Walter Ong called it) occasioned by auditory media could grow. Residual orality certainly wasn't unique to Japan, but it was distinctive for the role it played in folk and popular culture and in institutionalized and canonized cultural forms as well. It also had a special importance in Japan because of arguably unique tensions between the written and spoken languages of Japan well into the twentieth century.

Auditory technologies in Japan thus exemplify a modernity that is at once a sharp technological rupture with the past and a reformulation of the past's practices. Japan's oral performance traditions were not vanquished by modernity—on the contrary, they experienced a renaissance while concurrently metamorphosing into new genres across new media and distribution platforms. Japan's residual orality provided a climate receptive to the introduction of auditory technologies. Once those technologies had been introduced, residual orality became deeply imbricated in, and largely indistinguishable from, technologized orality. The recognition that modernity and modernism are indebted to traditional forms is not new.[9] Rather, what I wish to emphasize is how modern technologies, which have often been thought to go hand in hand with modern forms, became vectors for traditional arts and even for traditional lifeways and reactionary ideologies.[10]

What I hope becomes clear by the end of this book is that different media condition expression and communication in specific ways. Even a term like "technologized orality" is too broad, an umbrella for the very specific types of orality conditioned by the phonograph and telephone, and then later by radio, sound cinema, and the many different types of orality delimited by each at different moments in their technological development and reception (say, the difference between early radio and postwar stereophonic FM radio). My primary concern here is not with orality per se as a cultural or historical phenomenon. Instead, I hope to tease out the ways in which materiality matters, the ways in which the medium structures and textures the message while not really being the message itself (I would say Marshall McLuhan went too far). Languages, both spoken and written, are themselves media that limit and establish possibilities for communication and expression. When the medium of language is doubly mediated—when the media are thereby layered—those limits and potentials are subtly altered, and neither medium—neither language nor its material vector—is left unchanged by the encounter. Furthermore, because each language is a distinctive medium, each negotiates that encounter in a distinctive way.

The history I present here predates the rise to global prominence of Japanese audio electronics manufacturers such as Sony, Denon, JVC, Onkyo, and Pioneer, but it does show how the audiophile culture that helped set the stage for these later industrial achievements took root in Japan in the late nineteenth and early twentieth centuries. Needless to say, these industrial achievements were not limited to sound equipment, and they arose out of a confluence of historical conditions and capital flows that were determined both inside and outside the Japanese state, as well as by a culture of craftsmanship with antecedents in Japan's early modern period. Nonetheless, Japan's role in global auditory culture in the second half of the twentieth and the beginning of the twenty-first centuries, which included providing one of the largest markets in the world for recorded music (as of this writing, second only to the United States), cannot be denied. Like so much else in postwar Japanese history, this phenomenon had its roots in the prewar period.

The field I survey is broad, as it includes the major auditory technologies that were adopted in Japan between 1868 and 1945. I can therefore make no claims to comprehensiveness, as that would demand multiple volumes by multiple authors devoting lifetimes of study. My aim is, first, to provide an overview of this field, which has been sorely lacking in English-language scholarship, and to focus on specific episodes, historical actors, and texts that illustrate larger, recurrent issues.

Some of these issues have been objects of inquiry for interdisciplinary formations such as media studies and science, technology, and society (STS), which in turn draw from established disciplines ranging from history to sociology to literature. My own academic training began with the study of ethnomusicology and electronic/experimental music, transitioned to graduate work in literature and film studies, and then took a turn toward cultural history and media studies more broadly as the contours of this book took shape over a period of years. As a work of history, its orientation is primarily descriptive, but my interpretations of this history do carry theoretical implications. One of the clearest of these is that media and materiality do matter, that the materialities of media transform people, institutions, and societies. In its most simplistic forms, this argument is often pejoratively dismissed as technological determinism, a naive belief in technological teleology and technology's capacity to override human autonomy. The original corrective to naive technological determinism was a rigorous study of the ways in which technological developments and deployments were socially negotiated and mediated. The findings from this line of inquiry were tremendously valuable and put agency back where it belongs, in human subjects acting in social formations.

And yet, it is difficult to dispute that human agency operates within constraints. Physical and biological constraints are the most obvious of these, but equally important are the ways in which social life is composed of games (in the game-theoretical sense) that are both cooperative and competitive. The problem with the idea that social processes are "negotiated" is that this presumes a relatively consistent cooperative framework in social decision-making. In reality, many games are competitive and involve asymmetries of power and information that render decision-making exceedingly difficult and give some actors much greater say than others. At the same time, powerful actors are also constrained by the constantly shifting constellation of other actors and material realities that can defy their plans and intentions. The result is that although human intelligence is *at work* in these social processes, human intelligences do not in fact *guide* them, because actors and subjectivities are multiple. The processes are emergent properties of the games and relationships themselves, and change along with them. If human history seems like a continual parade of folly, one reason (along with actual folly) might be that we have yet to figure out how to be truly cooperative social actors. Another word for this phenomenon, of course, is politics.

One example that illustrates the constrained agency (and, therefore, folly) of human subjects in games is the Cold War arms race. The proliferation of nuclear weaponry during the postwar period, especially in the arsenals of the two superpowers, was not the product of negotiation or purely rational decision-making between the major actors but resembled, rather, two of the simplest of all games: Chicken and Prisoner's Dilemma. The best—certainly the most reasonable—possible course of action would have been for both sides to disarm; that would have been the safest and the least expensive option for both. But because both sides were locked in competitive antagonism, such negotiation was precluded in the absence of a spontaneous transition to a cooperative game. Both sides had to consider the possibility that the other side would continue to arm, which would in turn render vulnerable the side that chose to disarm. *Neither side designed or negotiated this state of affairs alone or together*; it was an emergent property of the course of events up to that point. In turn, those events were the product of other, prior games in which the choices of actors had been similarly constrained. The game transitioned to a more cooperative orientation (it has never actually "ended")[11] only when one side was forced by material circumstances (themselves the products of countless constrained decisions) to take the chance of making concessions that were potentially unfavorable to itself.

The sobering upshot of these dynamics is that technological development *usually* follows a logic of competitive escalation and almost mindless deployment. Nation-states and smaller social formations may elect not to use certain technologies or to use them in ways that deviate from evolving normative expectations, but such choices inevitably come with costs that a predictable majority of state and nonstate actors will elect to avoid. A measure of resistance and deviation will be observed and will in turn diminish as the costs of resistance and deviation grow with the calcification of norms.

This nonhuman logic is enabled and conditioned by the economic and social practices that we group under the sign of capitalism, but it is not necessarily confined to them, as the case of the Cold War implies. We could argue that the Soviet Union and the Eastern Bloc were exemplars of state capitalism rather than communism proper (and I agree with that characterization), but barring a return to a preindustrial economy and a unified world government, it is difficult to imagine all human groups electing together never to try to attain technological superiority over one another. The moment that one *did* attempt to secure that technological edge, the others would feel compelled to follow, and the competitive game would begin anew.

Media are an especially volatile component of material reality because they shape representation and constitute large stretches of lived experience. Mass media, in particular, give powerful actors a potent means of influencing the symbolic representations of less powerful actors. The materiality of the media shapes both the attentive *strategies* and the *capacities* of human subjects, whose neuroplasticity allows lived experience (which includes the experience of media) to refashion the brain's neural organization.[12] Because these changes occur slowly, often imperceptibly, across long stretches of time and because both the creators and consumers of media are usually unaware of the changes of subjectivity effected by those media, it is difficult, if not nonsensical, to speak of social negotiation in such cases. One cannot have "negotiation" in any meaningful sense without consent, and one cannot give informed consent to a consequence of which one is initially unaware.

Media are thus doubly potent, medium and message working sometimes in tandem, sometimes at cross-purposes, in ways that consuming and mediated subjects cannot always perceive or untangle. This is not to say that the consuming subjects are entirely passive. As Michel de Certeau made clear, subjects confront, evade, reject, and play with the cascading stimuli with which media inundate them.[13] Even the best surfers, however, eventually find themselves underwater because the initial costs of nonparticipation in the game are generally higher than the initial costs of participation.

What I propose, however, should not be construed as a form of hard technological determinism or an object-oriented ontology that assigns these technologies, much less sound itself, objecthood outside human social formations and human perceptions. To the extent that these technologies are not *entirely* subject to unilateral and willful human control and, furthermore, create their own constraints and incentives to some human actions and not others, they are not totally within the matrix of the social. At the same time, they cannot exist, or make any meaning at all, outside the social, outside what is made possible by human subjectivity, which is profoundly socially conditioned.

Sound is a particularly ineffable vector of the kaleidoscopic confusions of modernity. Its origins, contours, and next moves are marked by an indefinability and an unpredictability that leave us relatively defenseless. We can track the visual like hunters, but sounds leave us feeling like prey. While game-theoretical concepts provide useful reference points with which to understand how technological development and deployment unfold in modern nation-states, they are of little use in understanding how the materialities and modalities of audition function and feel. They also tell us little about how auditory technologies function ideologically. To address these latter questions, I have relied to a large extent on the body of thought produced by the scholars of the Ljubljana school, most conspicuously Slavoj Žižek and Mladen Dolar. In the modern philosophical and theoretical canon, only two major approaches address sound and the voice with any sustained theoretical rigor: phenomenology, and psychoanalytical thought influenced by the work of Jacques Lacan (1900–1981). While the work of phenomenologists is rich, variegated, and valuable in its own right, phenomenological approaches tend to be ahistorical and largely indifferent to cultural differences. The same could probably be said of Lacanian psychoanalysis in its purest form, but Žižek and his colleagues combine Lacan with Hegel and Marx in ways that illuminate vast stretches of history and its attendant ideological engines. Dolar's pioneering work, *A Voice and Nothing More*, is, in my opinion, the most important and interesting work on the ideological and psychoanalytical dynamics of the voice yet published.

That said, Žižek, Dolar, and other theorists influenced by Lacan arguably overstate the case for the immateriality of the voice. This is not to suggest that they deny vocal materiality altogether, simply that sonority per se—and its intimate connections with embodiment and other kinds of materiality—often get short shrift in favor of mapping psychoanalytical dynamics. For example, Dolar writes, "Is not the mother's voice the first problematic connection to the other, the immaterial tie that comes to replace the umbilical cord, and shapes much of the fate of the earliest stages of life?"[14] The casual reference to the mother's voice as "immaterial" (which, intentionally or not, activates secondary meanings like "trivial" and "unimportant") bespeaks a Lacanian indifference to materiality (which the Ljubljana school has balanced with Marxist materialism, and which they might in any case dispute with an appeal to Lacan's late meditations on the Real) and also reminds us of Lacan's "detethering"[15] of sexuality from the body of the mother. For all their startling and provocatively dialectical psychoanalytical insights, the Ljubljana theorists have less purchase, in my mind, when it comes to questions of materiality, embodiment, and gender. As we shall see, the uses and understanding of the voice have culturally and historically specific dimensions that are not captured by the often Eurocentric focus of European and American theorists.

The emerging field of sound studies has also provided a fertile field of inspiration, for obvious reasons. If I were to name the three works that cast the longest shadows over this book, they would be *Koe no shihonshugi* (Capitalism of the voice) by Yoshimi Shun'ya,[16] *The Audible Past* by Jonathan Sterne,[17] and *Noise: The Political Economy of Music* by Jacques Attali.[18]

In sum, insofar as labels mean anything, I would describe my approach as an impure deployment of the tactical and the dialectical, raiding the cabinets of Marxism and psychoanalysis, media and sound studies, actor-network and game theory, and historicisms old and new, in order to arrive at provisional and evolving understandings of specific and contingent phenomena in particular times and places. This is not a grand theory, just a collection of theoretical contraptions and an occasional insight out of the blue.

I have gone to some lengths to announce my theoretical and methodological coordinates here because I do not believe that there is a way to "do history," or "media studies," or any other form of inquiry that is normative, universally applicable, or free of philosophical assumptions. Some practitioners are aware of their models and articulate them clearly, and others are not or do not, accepting as normative approaches that are the products of historical, cultural, and institutional contingencies. While I anticipate that some readers will disagree with my choices of methodology, I hope that nobody can accuse me of being unaware of the assumptions and values that guide this inquiry.

In this book, I look at the beginnings of the telegraph, telephone, phonograph, radio, and sound film in Japan. I present a brief history of each technology's arrival and some of the representative popular and elite discourses that were generated during the process of adoption and assimilation. I then offer a theoretically inflected consideration of the nexus of cultural, social, and political practices into which the new technology was integrated, considering, for example, the roles that they played in language reform, literary and cinematic practice, subject formation, cultural memory, and nationalism.

This focus on "beginnings," on originary moments, is useful because it poses some of the most potent challenges to technological determinism and to what might be called technological universalism, the idea that technologies have a set of normative uses that will prevail everywhere in the same way. If there was a time when social negotiation was possible, it was during these early days when everything was provisional and tentative, before the interests of capital and political power had figured out exactly how to appropriate new technologies. As I suggest however, those interests eventually did figure out how to appropriate those technologies and did so in remarkably similar ways across national boundaries, largely because they mimicked one another along the lines of the competitive games just described.

In addition to these overarching arguments—namely, that sound reproduction and transmission were radically new material and technological arrivals that also, paradoxically, reanimated the oldest of oral performance traditions—I will try to show how these technologies became integrated with the larger media ecology. Whereas in chapters 1, 2, and 3 my emphasis falls more heavily on sound and orality per se, in chapters 4 and 5 I concentrate on describing how sound technologies partnered with other media (particularly print media) and how the innovations of radio, especially voice acting and sound effects, contributed to Japan's newly emergent sound cinema. The contribution of radio drama to one of Japan's most popular cultural exports—animated film—also demands greater recognition. The explicit focus of the final chapter is sound cinema and comes full circle by calling back the concerns of the first two chapters, language and music.

In chapter 1, I examine the ways in which two new technologies, the telegraph and telephone, reconfigured the relationship between orality and writing in Meiji Japan. For example, the telegraph was used to transmit a written language that until then had been written in a mixture of Chinese characters and syllabaries. The limits of the new technology dictated that the phonetic syllabary be used exclusively because this was much easier, and cheaper, than using Chinese characters. This material contingency reinforced a resurgent phonocentrism that arose from multiple sources, including Western conceptions of writing. I argue that these material constraints bolstered discourses of phonocentrism that guided efforts at language reform during the Meiji era; at the same time, I present evidence that a different phonocentric bias was in fact present in Japanese discourses of language dating far back into the early modern and premodern periods. In *Origins of Modern Japanese Literature*, Karatani Kōjin,[19] following Jacques Derrida's critique of phonocentrism, argues that the *genbun itchi* (unification of speech and writing) movement was the product of a distinctly Western phonocentrism. I maintain, in contrast, that the telegraph and telephone became vectors for the resurgence of a residual orality that was operative in Japanese culture long before any encounter with the technologies of the West. In other words, residual orality and technologized orality converged. I show how the telegraph conferred a new utility and, indeed, technological glamour upon the indigenous phonetic kana syllabaries. Later, the telephone and phonograph allowed the voice and spoken language to be transmitted and, perhaps more important, *inscribed* and *archived*, thus freeing spoken language from the dual constraints of spatial locality and temporal ephemerality, which in turn transformed the voice into a cultural-material artifact in its own right.

In this chapter I also explore some of the ways in which the telephone altered the social landscape of Meiji Japan. I identify an inversion of the common narrative of new technologies as labor- and time-saving devices and demonstrate that the telephone was a source of distraction, inefficiency, and annoyance when compared with other, cheaper and faster, means of communication. This inefficiency was exemplified by the practice of *yobidashi denwa*, a popular means of communicating by telephone even when one or both parties didn't own phones at home. The system involved summoning one's interlocutor to the post office with a telegraph in order to carry out a telephone conversation. I argue that despite the time and expense involved, the popularity of this service suggests that the telephone was appreciated less for its efficiency than for the pleasures of hearing another's voice, as well as for the opportunity to participate in prestigious forms of modernity even when these forms were economically out of reach and took more time than sending letters by post, as was the case in Tokyo, where intracity mail was at one point delivered ten times per day.

In chapter 2, I consider the urban soundscapes of the Meiji and early Taishō (1912–1926) periods, which were transformed not only by the telephone and the phonograph, but also by the sounds of industrialization and the importation of Western music. Music of all kinds took on new social and cultural roles when it became mechanically reproducible, and I reconstruct the transformation from a premodern soundscape of fulling blocks, geta, and shamisen music to a modern soundscape of machines, mechanically reproduced sounds, and Western and Westernized music. It was at this time that musical education in Japan's public schools became exclusively centered on Western-style music while traditional Japanese music was quarantined to the realms of hereditary profession or amateur pursuit. Government bureaucrats at the time believed that Western musical forms (particularly songs and marches) were more appropriate to the creation of a national subject identity. Drawing on the pioneering theoretical formulations of Jacques Attali as well as on the "earwitness" testimony of both Japanese and Western auditors, I outline the transitional period from Japanese music and preindustrial soundscapes to Western and Westernized music and modern urban soundscapes, and in the process examine what it means for an indigenous musical tradition to be made foreign on its own soil.

Chapter 3 turns to the history of the sonic archive. The introduction of the phonograph transformed sound into a preservable and archivable artifact. This carried considerable cultural significance in a culture that had inherited from China powerful assumptions about inscription and preservation as sources of value and prestige. Recorded sound could now become an object of study and preservation in its own right. I pay special attention to the intersection of recording history with the histories of two genres that illuminate different facets of the technology's cultural meaning and ramifications: kabuki and *naniwabushi* (also known as *rōkyoku*, storytelling accompanied by a shamisen). Kabuki helped demonstrate and, in a sense, legitimate the new technology by offering the voices of its most famous actors as the content for the earliest phonograph recordings, which were played publicly in Japan's urban centers around 1890. I also show how the gramophone returned the favor in the 1920s when kabuki faced its own period of testing.

Naniwabushi's role in the story of recording came later, and it was a very large role indeed because it launched the new technology into commercial viability. *Naniwabushi* performers in the 1910s such as Tōchūken Kumoemon and Yoshida Naramaru II became the first recording superstars, and they held that position until the advent of *ryūkōka*, popular songs and singers, in the 1920s. Although the story of *ryūkōka* is crucial, I will not discuss it here, both because it is in the able hands of others[20] and because it is the product of a relatively mature industry and not of the transitional and experimental periods that are the primary focus of this book. Instead, I consider the role of recordings in changing ideas of authorship and copyright, changes that had a profound effect on the subsequent production and commodification of reproductive cultural artifacts into the present day.

In the late Taishō and early Shōwa (1926–1989) periods, radio and sound film were added to the mix. The human voice, furthermore, assumed a new materiality and cultural role as it came to be more widely recorded and transmitted. Chapter 4 describes the first decade or so of radio broadcasting in Japan, with an emphasis on the political and ideological uses of the new medium and on the meetings of disembodied voices and actual bodies. I look specifically at the new narrative art of sports broadcasting, which codified group identification in novel ways and gained special importance with NHK broadcasts from the 1932 Olympic Games in Los Angeles and the 1936 games in Berlin. I also explore the public ritual of *rajio taisō* (radio exercise), which inaugurated a nationwide regime of bodies moving in sync with the directions of an acousmatic voice, consolidating a mechanism of command and control that reached its apotheosis with Emperor Hirohito's declaration of surrender in the Pacific War.

Chapter 5 is an extended consideration of an entirely new literary genre made possible by a new medium: radio drama. Not long after the first radio broadcasts began in Japan in 1925, a group of writers, actors, and broadcasting professionals came together to form the Rajio Dorama Kenkyūkai (Radio Drama Research Association) to introduce and develop this novel genre of dramatic art. The members of the group included prominent literary figures of the time, such as Nagata Mikihiko, Kume Masao, Osanai Kaoru, Kikuchi Kan, Kubota Mantarō, and Satomi Ton. The group put out five volumes of radio plays in 1925, the *Rajio dorama sōsho* (The radio drama library, published by Shunyōdō), which became the founding documents of radio drama practice in Japan. I discuss the circumstances around the formation of the Radio Drama Research Association, the plays published in the series, and the earliest radio drama broadcasts in Japan. The chapter's theoretical focus is on the possibilities of radio drama as a narrative genre, one that has long been neglected by scholars in the English-speaking world but that enjoyed worldwide popularity until the advent of television (and even beyond, in countries like Germany and Japan). As alluded to earlier, I also describe radio drama's role in the genesis of two creative professions that became increasingly important to cinema, television, and anime during the twentieth century: sound effects and voice acting.

Chapter 6 centers on early theoretical discussions of sound film in Japan. Based on the work of Japanese critics such as Nakane Hiroshi and Yasuda Kiyoo, as well as on the critical writings of the director Mizoguchi Kenji, I explore emerging debates about the uses and functions of film dialogue and soundtrack music. I pay special attention to the writings of Nakane, who has been relatively neglected. Nakane's 1932 *Tōkī ongakuron* (*Theory of Music for the Talkies*, a book-length collection of essays and analyses) was one of the first extended engagements with film music theory in Japanese. He had previously been a musician and member of the *Ongaku to bungaku* (Music and literature) coterie magazine. Although writing from a musician's perspective, he had an acute sense of the need for music especially composed to accompany the moving image.

I also devote a portion of this chapter to the development of dialogue for *jidaigeki* (period dramas), which in a real sense had to be invented for the genre by drawing on actual historical usage, traditional theater, and the affiliated genre of period fiction. As with the creation of a written vernacular, new forms of technologized cultural production demanded the invention of a new language, except this time one that was retrospective of an imagined past.

VOICE AS COMMODITY, VOICE AS AURA

The development and introduction of these technologies of sound reproduction and transmission had a number of varied and often countervailing effects, in every instance a dialectical relationship at work. On the one hand, by extending the reach of the voice across time and space, they conferred on it a new textual and historical weight. The voice could now become a historical record in its own right, as well as a commodifiable entity.

At the same time, however, these technologies stripped the human voice of its aura (a notion articulated in Walter Benjamin's 1936 essay "The Work of Art in the Age of Mechanical Reproduction") by abstracting from the voice only what could be reduced to sound. The voice was relieved of its "presence," its ontological weight, which, if we follow the Benjaminian logic, was rooted precisely in its nonreproducibility and, in the case of the voice and other sonic phenomena, in its ephemerality. This is surely one reason why the emperor's voice was not allowed to be recorded until the declaration of surrender, as doing so would have stripped it of its numinous power. Even though most of the listeners to the emperor's broadcast could barely make out the specific words he was saying, both because of the poor quality of the recording and transmission and because of the emperor's opaque idiolect, that didn't matter: The simple fact that his voice had been recorded and broadcast at all signified the end of his deification, an event that could have been occasioned only by a catastrophic compromise of the integrity of the nation-space and its semiotic universe—that is, unambiguous defeat in war and the impending occupation promised by that defeat.

Yet as in every truly dialectical relationship, a countervailing phenomenon existed alongside this one: The reproduction of the voice made it more spectral and imbued it with an aura of a different cast. An early user of the telephone who blurted out that the voice on the other end sounded "just like a ghost" was not alone in his reaction to the eerie nature of the disembodied voice. As Michel Chion suggests, such a voice, the voice whose source is never seen, the *acousmêtre*, exercises the following four powers in the subject's psychic economy: "the ability to be everywhere, to see all, to know all, and to have complete power. In other words: ubiquity, panopticism, omniscience, and omnipotence."[21]

> Why all these powers in a voice? Maybe because this *voice without a place* that belongs to the acousmêtre takes us back to an archaic, original stage: of the first months of life or even before birth, during which the voice

was everything and it was everywhere (but bear in mind that this "everywhere" quality is nameable only retrospectively—the concept can arise for the subject who no longer occupies the undifferentiated everywhere).[22]

This acousmatic orality, made possible by technology, was a novelty in the Japanese context as well; the traditional oral narratives had always involved a *visible* speaker or narrator. The power of the disembodied voice was put to work in modern Japan in the project of state formation and social control soon after the technology became available and long before the Shōwa emperor made his historic broadcast. The broadcast of his voice triggered two turns of the dialectical screw: the first demoted him from god to human being, stripping him of his aura, and the second made him the phantom emperor of a phantom realm.

In terms of literary discourse, the (re)turn to a phonocentric conception of language in both Japan and the West coincided with another parallel movement toward "faithful transcription," literary naturalism itself. Although literary naturalism in the Japanese context paradoxically had a cast of extreme, almost hermetic, subjectivity, the late nineteenth-century discourses of naturalism in Europe and America promoted a stripping away of subjectivity for objective and photographic description and heralded an even further stripped-down praxis of existence that Friedrich Kittler termed "psychophysics."

> In 1900 speaking and hearing, writing and reading were put to the test as isolated functions, without any subject or thought as their shadowy supports. "Between finitude and infinity the word has ample room to be able to do without any help from thought." Rather than the long genetic path of the word from its beginning in nature to its end in culture, what counts is the signifier's mechanism and how it runs under either normal or pathological circumstances.... The victory of psychophysics is a paradigm shift. Instead of the classical question of what people would be capable of if they were adequately and affectionately "cultivated," one asks what people have always been capable of when autonomic functions are singly and thoroughly tested.... There is no universal norm (inwardness, creative imagination, high idiom, Poetry) transcending the particular functions. Each has a standard only in relation to defined experimental subjects and conditions.[23]

This dissolution of the subject in favor of the isolated functions of speaking and hearing, writing and reading, in time became manifest in Japanese literary practice, although not under the banner of naturalism (*shizenshugi*) but rather under the auspices of the New Perception school (*shinkankakuha*).

In the meantime, however, *shizenshugi* and the *shishōsetsu* (I-novel) in Japan remained faithful to the idea of another sort of transcription: that of interiority, of the inner voice. As Karatani's work suggests, there are intimate relationships among phonocentrism, the voice, and narrative interiority. The phonocentric turn inaugurated the twin movements that literary historians have long considered the foundations of the imagined entity of "modern Japanese literature": writing in the vernacular and writing interiority. At the same time, this phonocentric turn ensured the eventual demise of "modern Japanese literature" by displacing writing from its position of centrality in cultural discourse and thereby setting the stage for writing to be replaced by other media (first film, then television) as the primary loci of narrative energy.

As the title of this introduction is meant to suggest, the experience of sound and the experience of modernity are analogous in both concrete and poetically suggestive ways. Japanese modernity, heard from a distance, resonates with the babble of voices performed, transcribed, recorded, broadcast, and amplified: the voices of young Meiji exchange students traveling across a primitive phone wire in Bell's lab; the voice of a Meiji ambassador emerging from a tinfoil cylinder thousands of miles away from the place where it was recorded; and, most momentously, the voice of the Shōwa emperor telling his subjects, although not in so many words, that modernity could not be overcome.

1

VOCAL CORDS AND TELEPHONE WIRES

Orality in Japan, Old and New

Technologies of communication and sound reproduction in the Meiji period (1868–1912) helped create new forms of discourse and new emphases of perception. They also contributed to the creation of the *kokutai*, or national body politic, which took the form, to borrow Louis Althusser's classification, of both Repressive State Apparatuses (government, army, police, etc.) and Ideological State Apparatuses (education, communication, culture, etc.).[1] Given the nature of this study, I will concentrate on the latter category, particularly discursive and cultural practice, remembering that repressive and ideological mechanisms are fundamentally interdependent and impossible to fully untangle from one another. The creation of a standardized written language based (even if only loosely) on the conventions of the vernacular was a key ingredient in the creation of the *kokutai* and of a national identity in the modern sense.

The problem of the vernacular leads ineluctably to the matter of the spoken word, to the human voice and the vast universe of discourse that takes place between human beings in the form of sound waves and not inscribed symbols. This realm of discourse, while not completely ignored, has been somewhat neglected in literary and cultural studies, perhaps because its residual traces remain only in the memories of mortal bodies and because only a few of these traces have been, or even can be, translated into a written form. (The transformation from thought or speech to writing is, in every case, a form of translation in which something is lost while at the same time unexpected, even random, patterns of meaning may emerge on the receiving side.) Technologies of communication and sound reproduction allowed this discourse, which in sheer volume dwarfs the entire corpus of written thought by many orders of magnitude, to be extended in space and time in forms that retained more of its materiality and phenomenological aspect.[2] It took a very long time before this happened with any regularity, and many of the earliest recordings have long since been destroyed, but the idea itself began to exert power even before it became a widespread reality.

The voice—its phenomenology, its reproduction, and its transmission—was intimately bound up with the movement to create a written vernacular and a new literary praxis, and also with the larger project of creating a national, and ultimately imperial, state. The human voice was put to work imagining the national community that would confer upon that state its supposed legitimacy.

In the Japanese literary and cultural traditions, a concern with spoken language and orality has long been enshrined in the form of *kotodama shinkō* (lit., "belief in the spiritual power of spoken language"). Although many societies around the world have entertained similar beliefs about the incantatory power of particular words and phrases, few other societies (the example of India's "sonic theology" of mantra is a notable exception)[3] have incorporated such beliefs so integrally into their conceptions of discourse and kept them active for so long.

The concept of *kotodama* was most thoroughly and coherently articulated by the *kokugaku* (national learning) scholars of the eighteenth and nineteenth centuries. In works such as *Goikō* (1769) and *Kokuikō* (1765), Kamo no Mabuchi (1697–1769) suggested an essential dichotomy between *ji* 字 (written language) and *go* 語 (the spoken word), identifying China as "the nation rich in script" (*moji no saiwau kuni*) and Japan as "the nation rich in the magic of speech" (*kotodama no saiwau kuni*). As Kawamura Minato argues, "For Mabuchi, the 'fifty voices' (fifty morae) were the fundamental principle of 'Japan' itself, nothing less than a symbol of the cosmological order that sustained the land of the gods, the 'land of the rising sun.'"[4] Mabuchi's thinking on the matter was later championed by Motoori Norinaga (1730–1801), most forcefully in his debate with

Ueda Akinari (1734–1809) over the purity of the Japanese syllabary as it existed in the archaic period.[5]

As far as I'm aware, Mabuchi and Norinaga never called explicitly for the written language of Japan to model itself on any particular spoken form of Japanese, but they were evidently eager to strip Japanese civilization of what they saw as the ritual defilement of the "Japanese spirit" (which presumably included its writing) by contact with Chinese civilization and to return to a prelapsarian purity very closely identified with orality and with the spiritual efficacy of spoken language.

As Kawamura points out, the valorization of the spoken word in Japan only became possible retroactively with the importation of writing from continental Asia. He writes, "The fact that belief in *kotodama* was born in the Man'yō period is not unrelated to the self-awareness of the 'Japanese' language referred to as *yamato kotoba* that arose from contact with literate civilization, and for the search for psycho-spiritual grounding that arose from consciousness of differences between self and other."[6]

Kawamura then contends that the resurgence of *kotodama* ideology among *kokugaku* scholars was similarly a reaction against a more recent influx of cultural influence from the mainland (as well as a theoretical weapon against their Neo-Confucian intellectual rivals). Seen in this context, Maejima Hisoka's (1835–1919)[7] embrace of phonocentrism, although it didn't take the form of *kotodama* ideology per se, seems less like a unique and novel response occasioned by the singular event of looming Western cultural influence and technological superiority (although, of course, it was that as well) than like a gesture rooted in a very old and often repeated process of confrontation with otherness.

Orality and the construction of identity and community are intimately linked. Written texts are usually of uncertain provenance, but the words that emanate from a person's mouth are (with the exception of certain rare acts of ventriloquism) patently theirs. Beyond the obvious differences among major language groups, there is an infinite number of gradations and distinctions within languages we (through a habit conditioned by modern nationalism) consider as unified entities, such as "English" or "Japanese." Members of linguistic communities, differentiated by factors that include geographic region, education, class, gender, and age, can identify one another and, just as important, can identify outsiders through verbal markers as overt as shibboleths and as subtle as the intonation of a given word. A speaker of Tokyo dialect can quickly identify a speaker of Kansai dialect by the simple presence of the voiced "u" vowel in a word like *futari*, which in Tokyo dialect is unvoiced. Likewise, a middle-aged speaker of Tokyo dialect can immediately identify a teenaged speaker of Tokyo dialect not only through word choice but also through habits of intonation particular to that age group. I include this digression simply to emphasize the degree to which spoken language and the voice itself are so deeply imbricated in issues of both identity and identification. But unless the writing of written texts has been witnessed first hand, they are infinitely falsifiable. Even handwritten texts may simply be transcriptions of another person's words.[8]

The embodiments of residual orality in the Japanese tradition are almost too numerous to mention: *heikyoku* (the bardic tradition of reciting *The Tale of the Heike*), *kōdan* (storytelling about historical themes), *rakugo* (comical storytelling), *naniwabushi* (narrative singing), *benshi* (film narrators), *manzai* (stand-up comedy duos), and the theatrical arts in general, which tend to emphasize narration. Even with the relative expansion of literacy in the Tokugawa period (1603–1868) and the concomitant introduction of texts for popular consumption, orality remained central. As Eiko Ikegami states:

> The rise of commercial publishing in Japan cannot be understood simply as the colonization of oral culture by written culture; rather[,] Tokugawa commercial publishing formed a new bridge between the two worlds, invigorating and transforming both of them.... In this sense, Tokugawa reading was a mental as well as a physical experience mediated by the voice; hence, it resembled participation in the performing arts.[9]

I should add that these Tokugawa texts were not only read aloud, they were often accompanied by illustrations. The abstraction of a written "text" from its sensory context (the calligraphy, the illustrations, the act of reading aloud, even the quality of the paper) would have been alien to most Japanese readers before the Meiji period.

Moreover, vocalized and communal reading persisted well into the Meiji period, as Maeda Ai's essay on the rise of solitary readership makes clear. There were two distinct types of vocalized reading: *rōdoku*, or straightforward reading for transmission and comprehension, and *rōshō*, the practice of students educated in the Chinese classics who read these works for the sonorous and rhythmic qualities of the recitation itself, without necessarily understanding the meaning of the text recited.[10] This "sound-reading," or *sodoku*, is a perfect example of an appreciation for the materiality of the voice that borders on the fetishistic. It also transcends the so-called *wakan* (Japanese-Chinese) dialectic by introducing a sinicized version of *kotodama* spiritualism. According to Maeda,

> The sound-reading of the Chinese classics—wherein repetition of the rhythms and the vibrations of the voiced words creates a kind of "spiritual language" [*seishin no kotoba*] that is radically different from everyday Japanese—represents a form of instruction that imprints the very form of Chinese language [*kango no keshiki*] on the souls of these youth. Even if comprehension of meaning remains beyond reach, the material qualities of the words, their resonance and rhythm, are fully mastered, and the understanding that is attained through reading, explication, and reading groups [*rindoku*] when the students have matured adequately supplements their grasp of these texts.[11]

What is especially salient for me about this phenomenon is that these students did not actually appreciate "the material qualities" or the "resonance and rhythm" of Chinese at all; they appreciated the material qualities of domesticated *onyomi* (Chinese-derived) readings of Chinese characters shorn of everything that gives actual Chinese its sonorous qualities: its tones, most of its rhymes, and even its metrical qualities (*onyomi* often have different mora values than their Chinese equivalents). This suggests to me that what they appreciated was not the "resonance and rhythm" of the Chinese so much as *the materiality of their own voices.*

A brief consideration of the different oral traditions that have been formally codified and professionalized (which still leaves the vast uncharted territory of less formalized forms of oral storytelling and discourse) should offer some idea of how pervasive and thoroughly interwoven in cultural practice residual orality actually is.

Four major categories of popular traditional narrative arts are generally recognized: *hanashimono* (storytelling), which includes *manzai* and *rakugo*; *utaimono* (lyric or epic recitals), with *nagauta* as the representative genre; *katarimono* (ballad recitation), represented mainly by *heikyoku* (recitation of the *Tale of the Heike* accompanied by a *biwa*), but also by *jōruri* and *gidayū* recitations accompanied by a shamisen, as well as by *naniwabushi* (or *rōkyoku*, as it is often called today), which I will discuss in greater detail in chapters 3 and 4; and finally, *yomimono*, of which the *kōdan* lecture–style narratives are the central example.

Most of these genres are taught and preserved through exclusively oral means. *Heikyoku* is the best example and perhaps the template from which similar genres were drawn (unless an even older template exists, which it may well). *Rakugo* is also taught from master to disciple without any recourse to written texts even to this day, although students now use audio and video recordings to aid in the memorization of stories and in the internalization of certain performance points, a perfect example of the confluence of technology and orality that forms the central argument of this chapter.[12]

Western students of orality have taken a particular interest in *heikyoku*, largely because the tradition provides a still-living (although just barely) example of a type of oral recitation similar to that of the Homeric epics. Their main point of entry to the field has been the work of Eric Rutledge, who did fieldwork in Japan as an apprentice to Inokawa Koji, a blind *heikyoku* master.[13]

Although chanters in the *heikyoku* tradition often worked with texts that were written down and reworked, it was still a primarily oral tradition because most of its practitioners were blind and illiterate. Rutledge based his research on the mnemonic devices used by *heikyoku* practitioners and the ways in which these devices lead to characteristic errors in recitation. In so doing, he formulated a typology of performance error that can serve as a useful rubric for understanding how oral texts change over time in their retelling.

Throughout its history, Japan has had a tradition of adding a narrative accompaniment to its dramatic arts: *utai* in Noh, the *tayū* chanters in bunraku (puppet) theater, and narration in kabuki. As Donald Richie explains, "All premodern Japanese theater is a pictorial expansion of verbal storytelling.... Rather than being presented as an occurrence, drama is presented as a recounted occurrence."[14]

John Scott Miller tells us that oral storytelling in the form of *kōdan* and *rakugo* reached its peak of popularity during the Meiji period, owing to a number of factors.[15] Large numbers of migrants were arriving in Tokyo from rural communities, thus creating new audiences for a form of entertainment that was inexpensive and made no special demands in terms of education. Every aspect of life—social, technological, cultural—was undergoing rapid transformation and reconfiguration, creating tensions and perplexities that common people sought to address (as people throughout history have done) through narrative means. Oral storytellers wasted no time in incorporating contemporary events and references into their narratives, while at the same time performances of famous practitioners (most notably San'yūtei Encho [1839–1900]) were being set down in *sokki* shorthand, transcribed, and then widely disseminated.[16]

Naniwabushi narrative ballads were also extremely popular *yose* entertainments during the mid- to late Meiji period. Their popularity exploded during the early years of the twentieth century when performances began to be recorded and sold commercially on SP discs. Their popularity waned during the Taishō period (1912–1926) as cinema rose to a position of dominance in popular entertainment, but *naniwabushi* were resurrected in the 1930s as a vehicle for nationalist sentiment. As Hyōdō Hiromi points out, *naniwabushi* provided the oral narrative glue by which the modern Japanese state was made to cohere into a conceptual entity. Although Hyōdō doesn't explicitly reference Benedict Anderson's notion of "imagined communities," it is clear that *naniwabushi* served a role analogous to mass media such as newspaper journalism in the formation of nationalist ideology.[17]

Even with the advent of silent cinema, narrative orality remained vital, even into the period of the talkie, in the form of the institution of the *katsudō benshi*. By the 1920s the *benshi* had become so powerful that one writer asserted that three main creative intelligences were at work in a motion picture: the director's, the screenwriter's, and the *benshi*'s. As Jeffrey Dym writes, "Some *benshi* wielded so much power that they could turn comedy into drama and drama into comedy, at will. A second-rate *benshi* could destroy a good movie; a first-rate *benshi* could turn a lesser movie into a highly entertaining production."[18] Although different genres of oral narrative took turns at assuming preeminence as the media ecology changed over time, the pulse of oral narrative remained vital throughout the prewar period.

Enka singing is another, if somewhat further removed, example. *Enka* has its roots in a number of premodern oral traditions. News in the late

Tokugawa period was disseminated through the well-known *kawaraban* commercial broadsheets as well as by *kudoki* singers who would travel through town singing the news in *yanrebushi* or *hitotsu tose bushi* melody and meter. This practice continued after the *kawaraban* no longer existed. Even after modern-style newspapers were introduced in the Meiji period, the number of literate subscribers was only a small fraction of any given community, and those readers (often with the aid of *furigana* to aid in reading kanji (Chinese characters) would read the newspaper aloud to those in their immediate circles, once again in poetic forms of *yanrebushi* and *hitotsutose bushi*. *Enka* proper came into being in the late 1880s during the waning days of the Jiyū minken undō (Freedom and People's Rights Movement) as a vehicle by which to promote the ideals of the movement among the general populace.[19]

Many discussions of orality focus primarily on the rhetorical features that distinguish oral from written discourse. Theorists of orality such as Walter J. Ong have studied these rhetorical features and drawn from them speculations about the nature of preliterate thought and conceptual organization. According to Ong, thought and expression in primary oral cultures tend to be (1) "additive rather than subordinative" (thought is presented by the process of addition rather than in hierarchies of organization), (2) "aggregative rather than analytic" (that is, with reliance on stock formulaic epithets), (3) "redundant or 'copious,'" (4) "conservative or traditionalist," (5) "close to the human lifeworld" (that is, reluctant to embrace abstraction and analytic categories), (6) "agonistically toned" (filled with bragging and name-calling), (7) "empathetic and participatory rather than objectively distanced," (8) "homeostatic" ("oral societies live very much in a present which keeps itself in equilibrium or homeostasis by sloughing off memories which no longer have present relevance"), and (9) "situational rather than abstract."[20] Although these rhetorical patterns are indeed prevalent in the remaining primary oral cultures that have been studied, a number of scholars have taken issue with some of Ong's conclusions, specifically regarding preliterate subjects' capacity for analytic thought. The debate has been contentious, with critics of orality theory wary of what they consider to be insidious political ramifications of such speculation. Other scholars, such as Jonathan Sterne, have criticized Ong for the diametrically opposed sin of embracing a reactionary attachment to the world of face-to-face oral discourse.[21] My own interest in orality leans toward the less controversial, but in many ways less tangible, issues of vocal materiality and performance. That is, I am interested in the use of the voice as a medium per se.

Each human being's voice is as unique as a fingerprint: indeed, "voiceprint" technology has been used by the United States military since the late 1940s and has been used as a forensic tool by police departments since the late 1960s. The voice is generated by the interaction of vocal cords, vocal resonators (throat, nasal and oral cavities), and vocal articulators (lips, teeth, tongue, soft palate, and jaw muscles). The length and tension of the vocal cords differ from person to person, as do the sizes and shapes of the various vocal resonators. People also manipulate their vocal articulators in many different ways. The process of learning how to speak is not an exact science; it is acquired by mimicry and trial and error at a very early age, often in very idiosyncratic ways. Different languages demand different forms of vocal articulation in order to produce their distinctive phonemes. Any learner who has had trouble pronouncing the voiced dental fricative "th" in the word "the" in English or the trill of the "r" in Spanish knows that we cannot simply make our vocal articulators perform a certain way at will, that early learning and practice are essential.

The uniqueness of each individual voice is probably one reason why the word "voice" has become, in the English language at least, synonymous with the idea of identity. Writing courses exhort students to find their own "voice." Interestingly, this use of the term "voice" seems to straddle the boundary between metonym (the voice is an aspect of the person) and metaphor (one's voice is as unique as one's identity, but one can still have an identity without having a functioning physical voice), just as the voice itself straddles the boundary, as Michel Chion has noted, between materiality and immateriality.

Despite the limits dictated by the physical characteristics of an individual's voice, it still has tremendous range and plasticity. Voices can be trained to perform in unusual or extreme ways (as they are by singers, vocal artists, and radio and television personalities); they can be mimicked (as they are by comics and other impersonators); and voices are also altered over time by the effects of age, overuse, smoking, drinking, and so on. As

Nakano Jun and Suzuki Matsumi have argued independently of one another, culturally conditioned habits of vocalization can also change over time and have changed drastically in Japan over the past few decades.[22]

Michel Chion, Kaja Silverman, and Slavoj Žižek theorize the voice from a psychoanalytic, specifically Lacanian, standpoint. Lacan conceived of the voice as an *objet petit a* (a group composed of the gaze, the voice, the phallus, feces, "nothingness"), objects of desire that can never actually be obtained and that thus, in their very lack, sustain the perpetual rotational energy of the psychic drives. *Objets petit a* thus also play an important role in the formation of fetishes and are themselves often fetishized.

Chion maintains that with Lacan it becomes possible to conceive of the voice, in all its immaterial materiality, as an object in its own right rather than merely as a medium for speech. Because the voice plays such a central role in human desire through its role as an *objet petit a*, it also creates an acoustical hierarchy whenever it is present. Chion quotes Christiane Sacco: "'The presence of a body structures the space that contains it' (meaning of course the human body). Let us paraphrase this to say that *the presence of a human voice structures the sonic space that contains it.*"[23] Far from being a purely theoretical speculation confined to Lacanian esoterica, this relative predominance of the human voice in relation to other sonic phenomena is verified by the findings of a host of different disciplines: psychoacoustics (which tells us that human hearing is most sensitive in the frequency ranges occupied by the human voice), musicology, cognitive psychology, evolutionary theory, and phenomenology. Sensitivity and attentiveness to the human voice serve a myriad of vital functions that are self-preservational, social, and aesthetic. It is no accident that our ears have evolved, above all, to hear one another.

It thus makes sense that the voice occupies a central position in both the aesthetic valuations and the libidinal economies of the human subject. Yet many questions remain: Why has it taken so long, relative to other objects of inquiry, for the voice to become a serious subject of scholarly study? Why do some cultures appear to be more attentive to vocal performance and others less, or with different emphases?

As we have seen, it's difficult to find a cultural community outside the Japanese archipelago that has maintained such a diversity of oral traditions throughout the period of modernization, technological transformation, and beyond. There are no doubt a host of historical, sociological, and cultural reasons for this. I speculate that the Japanese tradition was especially sensitive to the medium of the voice *as material and as an object in its own right*, whereas (and these are, of course, rough generalizations teeming with exceptions) the Western tradition has a slight bias toward considering the voice a kind of "transparent" medium for speech, that is, for language itself. The exceptions I have in mind involve the theater and various vocal arts of singing, recitative, and so on. In Japan, however, vocal performance and keen attention to the texture and modulation of the voice are considerably more widespread. Mine is a subjective comparison and purely anecdotal, but few visitors to present-day Japan fail to notice the artificiality (or, less pejoratively, the *artfulness*) of the vocal transformations assumed by department store guides, subway and train conductors, elevator operators, and so on. In sushi restaurants, over the telephone, in the subcultures of the yakuza (gangsters), salarymen, and teenaged girls—the air pulsates with the textures of assumed voices: stratospheric falsettos, gruff rumbles, and everything in between. Much time and energy could be devoted to recording, describing, and cataloging the styles of vocal performance of the various segments and microsegments of Japanese society. The richness of the vocabulary of vocality in Japanese can hardly be a coincidence.[24]

The performance-oriented and material aspects of the voice in Japan are rooted in several different factors. One is that Japanese is representative of "pitch-accent" languages, in which differences in pitch serve the same function that stress does in the English language. Japanese also resembles a true tonal language in that differences in pitch can signify different meanings for words that are otherwise pronounced the same. The systematic study of tonal variation in Japanese dates back to the very end of the ninth century, when *shōten* accent marks were imported from China. In the eleventh century, this system of notation came to be applied to words written in kana as well, and has been in continuous use ever since, particularly in texts meant to be performed aloud. *Shōtenbon*, accent manuals, exist for the *Kokinshū* and other anthologies of poetry. Research shows that speakers of tonal languages such as Chinese and Vietnamese and, to a lesser extent, speakers of quasi-tonal languages such as Japanese, tend to possess perfect pitch at levels significantly higher than those of speakers of non-tonal languages.[25] This heightened aural facility may also be instrumental in a heightened consciousness of the performance-oriented elements of oral discourse. Moreover, certain features of oral narrative genres may have percolated over time into everyday speech. Mimicry is a key element of oral performance, and who better to mimic (even if only in a more subdued fashion) than professional performers?

Whereas vision in the European traditions has sometimes been dubbed the "noblest" of the senses, occupying a privileged place at the top of a vertical hierarchy in which the tactile and olfactory senses tend to come out on the bottom because of their associations with animal corporeality, thinkers and artists in the Japanese tradition have been less inclined to parcel the sensorium into distinct, hierarchically graded channels. In almost every case, traditional Japanese performing arts are prototypical *Gesamtkunstwerke*, incorporating visual design at every level, dance (or, at the least, stylized movement), poetic utterance, and vocal performance (sometimes overtly musical, but always stylized). Courtship in the Heian period (794–1185) was a multidimensional performance involving a complex dynamic of vision willfully obstructed and then eventually granted, of voices heard behind a screen, of incense, and of poetry and calligraphy. The tea ceremony is an opera of visual presentation, formalized uses of space, stylized movements, rhythm, aroma, and taste. This multidimensional interplay of the senses reaches a kind of spiritualized apex in the synaesthesized spaces of *haikai* poetics, in the faintly white call of Matsuo Bashō's duck.

This being the case, the conspicuousness of and attendance to the particulars of vocality are due not to some pronounced preoccupation at the expense of other senses or other regions of lived experience, but rather to a leveling and democratization of the senses.

If we are to understand the ways in which information passes (or fails to pass) from one human being to another, our inquiry must be marked by a similar willingness to embrace the entire spectrum of human sensory interaction. Psychological research over the last five decades has shown that most face-to-face human communication is, in fact, nonverbal. Although it is probably impossible to make blanket statements that extend across all times, cultures, and individual utterances, psychologists have estimated that anywhere from 40 to 90 percent of human communication occurs through nonverbal channels. For our purposes, the exact quantification (which in any event is probably impossible) is not as important as the rough proportion, which is substantial by any reckoning. Much of the total message (not to be confused with the more limited domain of semantic content) is conveyed through what linguists call "paralanguage." This includes facial expressions, gestures, eye movements, posture, and so on, as well as vocal cues such as tone of voice, rate or speed of speech, pitch variations, volume, vocal coloring (changes in vocal timbre, of which assumed voices are an extreme example), the use of vocal fillers or interjections, rhythm, resonance, articulation, and the like. Emotional cues, in particular, are usually perceived first through nonverbal channels when they are articulated in words at all. The skilled and artful use of paralanguage is an integral part of the work of the *rakugoka*, the *benshi*, and other narrative performers, but codified conventions of paralanguage in Japan were not just limited to the performing arts. They regulated spoken interactions in every sector of society, from the residence of the daimyo (feudal lord) to the home of the most humble peasant.

The introduction of technologies of sound transmission and reproduction first made it possible for the rich communicative potential of paralanguage to become operative across space and time, to take place in situations other than face-to-face meetings or live performances. The extraverbal communicative functions of the voice could be recorded, archived, transmitted, slowed down, sped up, and replayed over and over again. It is little surprise, then, that the societies exposed to these technologies would turn again to the phenomenon of the spoken word and consider it anew. In fact, it was only after the invention of the technologies of audiovisual reproduction that students of human communication even began to fathom the extent to which communication depends on nonverbal factors. With the introduction of film and other audiovisual media, physical nonverbal signals (for example, kinesthesics and microexpressions) could also be recorded and reproduced. As these new media were introduced into the media ecology, the relative strengths and shortcomings of the media already present in that ecology became more conspicuous. As discourses migrated to different media depending on what they were trying to accomplish, these relative strengths and weaknesses became even more pronounced owing to the reinforcement and the burgeoning mastery of each medium's intrinsic possibilities.

The resurgence of phonocentrism in Europe and America can probably best be traced through developments in the study of linguistics in the nineteenth century. Although phonetics had been studied in Europe since the Renaissance, until the late nineteenth century the dominant strain of linguistic study was philological, not phonological. The study of phonetics enjoyed a resurgence with the publication of Alexander Melville Bell's *Visible Speech* (1867), Eduard Sievers's *Principles of Phonetics* (1876), and Henry Sweet's *Handbook of Phonetics* (1877), all part of the groundwork that helped pave the way for Ferdinand de Saussure's (1857–1913) work in the early twentieth century.[26] It may be mere coincidence that this hitherto relatively neglected branch of linguistics enjoyed a renaissance at around the same time that technologies of aural recording and transmission were being invented and put to use. It is also possible, as some have argued,[27] that the causal relationship was actually reversed, that a newfound interest in breaking down, inscribing, and analyzing transient sonic phenomena (whether they were spoken languages or other aspects of the sound world) was the impetus for the inventors and industrial concerns that created these new technologies. The phenomenon is complex enough that a clear and decisive answer will remain elusive. There can be no question, however, that emerging audio technologies served to encourage even further the phonological or even phonocentric turn that linguistics had begun to take. Saussure himself cited the phonograph as a device that could record instances of *parole* and thereby give linguists and other students of language documentary access to *langue*.[28] The twentieth-century study of phonetics is impossible to imagine without some means of audio recording and reproduction.

TECHNOLOGIZED ORALITY AND LANGUAGE REFORM

On one level, to argue that the development of a standardized vernacular is fundamentally tied to the development of media technology is to argue the self-evident: Languages are the currency of self-defining and self-delimiting communities. As Benedict Anderson observed, for a nation-state to define or imagine itself as a "community," there must exist some shared means of discourse among the members of that community.[29] It is not enough, however, for the members of such a community to be able to communicate among themselves; they must also have a steady stream of information about the exterior of the community (in this case, the nation-state) in order to define themselves contextually (and, in many or most cases, oppositionally).

Anderson's seminal study of how the national imaginary is constituted centers largely on print media, and he was certainly right to insist that print media plays a definitive role in such processes, especially given that the rise of national consciousness took place before electric media had been invented. One benefit of such an approach is that the evidence is textual and, in most cases, archived and open to examination. It thus becomes possible to paint a very clear and full picture of the process at a high level of resolution.

It is obvious, however, that print media are not the only mass media. Our understanding of the formation of both modern Japanese society and discourse cannot begin to pretend to comprehensiveness until all the "discourse networks," to borrow Friedrich Kittler's term, have been adequately accounted for. According to Yoshimi Shun'ya,

> It goes without saying that the nation-state, as a field of simultaneous and homogenized communication, was even more perfectly actualized when the printed reproduction of writing could in turn be electrically transmitted by telegraph. We have already considered the ways in which telegraphy gave birth to a chain of aural media, and the strength of the influence it exerted over those media. What this suggests is that the telephone, in the early stages as a kind of "telegraph of the voice," as well as other post-nineteenth-century electronic media, actually served, contrary to McLuhan's expectations, to make even more thorough the simultaneity and homogenization of the nation-space that print capitalism had first initiated.[30]

This "simultaneity and homogenization" of the nation-space, this creation of a new communal imaginary centered on the nation-state and the person of the emperor, would have staggering consequences for Japan's subsequent history.

The mass media and nationalism have a close relationship; that between the voice and nationalism is less obvious. With this in mind, I would like to turn to the history of the technologies of communication and sound reproduction that entered Japan during the Meiji period and that played pivotal roles both in the "phonocentric turn" that Karatani Kōjin described, as well as in the creation of the national imaginary.

"THE VICTORIAN INTERNET"

The history of the idea of electric telegraphy dates, surprisingly, to February 17, 1753, when an anonymous writer known only by the initials "C. M." wrote a letter to the *Scots' Magazine* in which he suggested a simple signaling system using one wire assigned to each letter of the alphabet and a frictional generator that sent shocks down each of the wires. There is no evidence that this "C. M." or anybody else built such a device, but for the next few decades, numerous attempts were made to send electrical signals over long lengths of wire. These attempts always ended in failure, however, because it seemed impossible to generate a current strong enough to travel far enough to make such a device useful.

In the meantime, French and British inventors developed various means of optical telegraphy; that is, they devised large visual signaling devices that sent coded signals from one watchtower to another. Similar (though less complex) code-and-signal systems had been used even by the ancient Greeks.

In 1825 the British inventor William Sturgeon (1783–1850) invented the electromagnet, a device without which any form of electronic communication would have been impossible. In 1830 an American, Joseph Henry (1797–1878), discovered that using the right type of battery and using a chain of smaller batteries instead of one larger battery was enough to send a signal over a length of wire more than a mile long. In 1835, Samuel Morse (1791–1872), a professor of art and design at New York University, sent pulses of current along a wire that in turn deflected an electromagnet. The following year, he modified the device so that these movements of the electromagnet embossed a series of dots and dashes on a strip of paper. He assigned each letter in the alphabet its own series of dots and dashes, creating the coding system that took his name and remained in use well into the twentieth century.

It seems self-evident that any practicable coding system for a device of this type would necessarily be phonetic or alphabetic in nature. It is conceivable, however, that a system could be designed in which each *word* would be assigned its own code—in other words, a system rather similar to kanji themselves. In principle, such a system could be even more *efficient* (in the time required for transmission) than an alphabet-based coding system. By assigning either a unique code or a number to each individual word, one can ultimately reduce the number of dots and dashes necessary to convey a particular string of words. The problem, however, is that the burden of memorization in such a case is practically impossible, and thus the time required for human operators to look up and "translate" these codes into intelligible language (and vice versa) expands exponentially.

This is precisely what happened in China. When telegraphy was introduced there in 1880,[31] there was as yet no standardized system of phoneticization or romanization, and so each character was assigned a numerical code. When a message was sent, it had to be converted into this numerical code, then into Morse code, and then converted back at the receiving station. The result was that telegraphy was slower and more expensive in China than elsewhere. In Japan, however, the situation was mitigated by the preexistence of the two kana syllabaries, *hiragana* and *katakana*, and *katakana* was the medium in which telegrams were encoded. No radical linguistic reforms were necessary to make telegraphy as cheap and as practical in Japan as in other nations (in fact, the kana syllabary may have been even more efficient than the alphabet, requiring fewer characters per word).[32]

Although the first functional telegraph line (between Tokyo and Yokohama) didn't go into operation until late 1869, telegraphy had been known to the Japanese at least from 1853, when early telegraph machines were brought to Japan by Commodore Matthew Perry's (1794–1858) fleet. Even earlier, in 1849, Sakuma Shōzan (1811–1864) built a prototype telegraph on the basis of information found in a Western text or texts, most likely a Dutch translation of Noel Chomel's *Encyclopedia*.[33] Shōzan was a largely self-educated polymath who, acutely aware of China's weakness vis-à-vis the Western colonial powers (he wrote a treatise in 1842 entitled *Kaibō hassaku* [Eight strategies of coastal defense]), and devoted his life to the study of technologies that he believed could spare Japan from a similar fate (albeit with a few inexplicable excursions into subjects like viticulture).

Commodore Perry's fleet brought a telegraph along when they landed in 1854 and demonstrated the device to officials of the shogunate, who were apparently very taken with it, seeing it as an icon of civilization.[34] While studying in the Netherlands, Enomoto Takeaki (1836–1908) became the first Japanese to become proficient in the use of the telegraph.[35]

Not until 1866 and the publication of Fukuzawa Yukichi's (1835–1901) *Seiyō jijō* (Conditions in the West) did the larger public become aware of the telegraph's existence and its manifold uses.[36] Indeed, the cover of the first edition of Fukuzawa's epochal work features a drawing of the globe crisscrossed by telegraph wires.

Seiyō jijō was also the first work published in a style that, although not exactly a close approximation of the vernacular, was greatly simplified for the purposes of wide intelligibility. This work, as well as follow-up books like *Seiyō tabi annai* (Guide to travels in the West, 1867) and *Seiyō ishokujū* (Food, clothing, and shelter in the West, 1867) were written on the basis of notes taken during travels in 1860 and 1862.

Seiyō jijō was an immediate best seller. The first edition sold 150,000 copies, with the total number of copies of all editions sold reaching as high as 250,000. As Matsuda Hiroyuki notes, in a society in which the literacy rate was only about 30 percent, sales figures like these suggest that nearly every literate adult in Japan had access to the book.[37]

An obvious contributing factor to *Seiyō jijō*'s success was no doubt its simplified style. Although Fukuzawa retained the *nari-beshi* verb termination of *wabun* literary style, he made a determined effort to strip his prose of the deliberate ostentation common to the scholarly writing of the time. His desire to be clearly understood was so great that he reportedly asked his maid to read the book, and then he rewrote any passage whose meaning was not immediately clear to her.[38]

In December 1866, Maejima Hisoka submitted his "Kanji on-haishi no gi" (Proposal for the Abolition of Chinese Characters) to the shogun, Tokugawa Yoshinobu (1837–1913). Although Maejima made no mention of the telegraph in this document, he was no doubt familiar with Fukuzawa's work, and it is an open question whether he was not already then thinking about the forms that telegraphy might take in Japan. Maejima went on to found the Japanese postal service in 1871.

The Meiji Restoration saw work begin in earnest on a nationwide telegraph network. A Tokyo–Yokohama line was completed in 1869, Osaka–Kobe in 1870, Tokyo–Nagasaki in 1873, Tokyo–Aomori in 1874, and Aomori–Hakodate in 1875. With lines now extending from Hokkaido to Kyushu, work began on subsidiary lines to less critical locations such as Sendai and Yamagata.[39]

Denmark's Great Northern Telegraph Company had already laid underwater telegraph lines from Europe to Shanghai when work on the Japanese telegraph network began in the late 1860s. In 1871 the same company laid down cables between Shanghai and Nagasaki, and Vladivostok and Nagasaki, thus placing Japan within a day's telegraph reach of London. Unfortunately, the fact that the line between Nagasaki and Tokyo was not yet complete meant that it would take an additional seven to eight days for a message to reach Tokyo using the new postal service that had just been established that year.

In these early days, the telegraph was limited to military, police, and governmental uses. Indeed, as Yoshimi Shun'ya points out, the new telegraph lines were constructed, not accidentally, in precisely those geographic regions where the Meiji emperor was about to visit. Military telegraphy played a significant role in putting down the Saga Rebellion of 1874, as well as in the Taiwan Expedition of the same year. To put it simply, from nearly the moment of its operational functionality, the telegraph was put to work in the consolidation of the nation-state and the projection of Japanese imperial power.

Even after it became widely available to private citizens, the cost of the telegraph was often prohibitive. In 1885, the revised Telegraphy Law established a flat nationwide rate for telegraphy: 7 sen per message of fewer than twenty kana characters, with an additional 2 to 5 sen added by each way station along the transmission route. Private citizens other than businessmen tended to use the telegraph only in case of emergency.

Although telegraphy was thus not a technology that many ordinary people in early Meiji society used on a regular basis, the impact that it had on the public imagination in Japan was similar to that of the Western nations. The introduction of the telegraph stimulated a turn toward phonocentrism as well as a greater emphasis on colloquial usage in two ways, one practical and one sociological.

First, the telegraph placed a premium on clarity, brevity, and efficiency. The medium of telegraphy commodifies language by turning it metaphorically into a precious and limited resource that cannot be "wasted." Although an emphasis on quick and clear communication had been a hallmark of warfare, commerce, and trade for the length of human history, the telegraph was able to quantify the economic benefits of concision in a very unambiguous way, down to a price per word. Kana syllabaries were clearly a far more efficient medium of telegraphic transmission (at least, in the early stages of telegraphy before computerized telegraphy in the twentieth century changed this) than a laborious process of encoding and decoding Chinese characters.

Second, the telegraph became the materialization of the imaginary of national community, on the one hand, and the very real workings of consolidated state power, on the other. It became the first medium by which a person in Tokyo could communicate with a person in Osaka in a matter of minutes, and at the same time, of course, it was the first medium by which a centralized state government could wire orders immediately to military forces in Saga to put down a rebellion. The modern nation-state requires a unified, standardized language, but for the modern nation-state to exist at all, it requires organs of communication (and thence control) that can reach into every corner of that state and can do so quickly enough to render unambiguous the state's monopoly on power. In *The Culture of Time and Space, 1880–1918*, Stephen Kern explains how railways and the telegraphic wires that ran alongside them became the impetus for the adoption of standard time and the establishment of time zones around the world.[40] The synchronization of time and the standardization of language went a long way toward realizing the "simultaneity and homogenization of the nation-space" identified by Yoshimi.

One major work of Japanese literature in which we see this synchronized and homogenized nation-space most clearly is Natsume Sōseki's (1867–1916) *Kokoro*. By the time of the book's publication in 1914, the process of national consolidation had long been complete, and the telegraph had become a common feature of everyday life. The book begins with the arrival of a telegram. The narrator is at the beach in Kamakura with a friend when his friend receives a telegram informing him that his mother is ill and demanding that he return home immediately (by train, of course). This is the first of several telegrams that are sent and received in the course of this book: a telegram from Sensei asking the narrator to come visit him in Tokyo, the narrator's reply that he cannot come because of his father's condition and General Nogi Maresuke's (1849–1912) recent death, along with Sensei's terse reply that the narrator is no longer needed. The final telegram of the book, although the earliest in the chronology of the diegesis, is the one that Sensei sends to K's family to inform them that he has committed suicide. Although the postal service is the mode of communication of first resort for nonurgent messages, the telegraph becomes the medium by which matters of greatest import, matters of life and death and historical moment, are conveyed from one part of the archipelago to another, from one corner of the imagined community of Japan to another.

The telegraph established the idea of a network of wires spanning the nation that would make its dispersed inhabitants known and intelligible to one another even across great distances. It would also make them "seen" and "heard" by the organs of centralized state authority and subject to the immediate wishes of that authority. It would make the figures of that authority, such as General Nogi, vivid personalities and members of that "community" (soon to become, in the imperialist rhetoric, a "family") whose actions would be immediately relayed to that public in terms of the urgency reserved for family emergencies. This network, brought to life by an incessant stream of audible dots and dashes, in time transformed into a network of the voice.

TELEPHONE TIMES

Even though Japanese exchange students were among the first ever to use the telephone, the new invention was slow to take hold in the Japanese archipelago. The first domestically produced device was manufactured in 1878 and was set up in the offices of the Kōbushō (Ministry of Industry). The first user of the device exclaimed, "Ohh, it's just like hearing the voice of a ghost!"[41]

A proper phone line, between Tokyo and Atsumi, was not constructed for twelve more years, until 1890. Japan began building a telephone network quite late, later even than unlikely candidates such as Chile, Thailand, and Romania.[42] Matsuda lists several reasons for this delay. First, the telephone arrived at a time when the nationwide telegraph network had only recently been completed. In a sense, the previous technology had not yet had enough time to "settle" into the fabric of life, not to mention the enormous cost of creating a new telecommunications network so soon on the heels of having just completed one.

Another delaying factor was the sound quality of early telephones, which, as may be imagined, was abysmally low. Indeed, it was not uncommon for the connection to be so bad that hardly anything could be understood on either end. These explanations seem less convincing, however, when we consider that governmental authorities, particularly the police, wasted no time in putting the telephone to work.

In 1890 the government began accepting subscribers to the service, of which there were only seventy-four. The government then launched a campaign to attract more users and invited more than eight hundred celebrities, financiers, journalists, and the like to try out the device for themselves. The results of this effort were even more dismal: only twenty-three people signed up. There were mitigating circumstances, however: Tokyo was then in the middle of a cholera epidemic, and the rumor had spread that the disease could be transmitted over the phone lines.[43] Another fear was that the telephone was a fire hazard.

In time, however, the service began to attract more customers and expand to other cities. In 1893, telephone service began in Osaka and Kobe, and by 1896, the demand had increased so much that there was a long waiting list to sign up. Between 1896 and 1902, forty-two additional telephone exchanges and 32,115 new subscribers were added to the network.[44]

Although having a telephone in one's home remained prohibitively expensive for most people, the use of the first public phones was relatively affordable. Intracity calls at any of the fifteen public telephone offices in Tokyo cost 5 sen, and a call between Tokyo and Yokohama cost 15 sen. At this time, 5 sen had the same purchasing power as 500 yen did in 1991.[45] In 1893 Osaka and Kobe opened telephone offices, and by 1898 a line was opened connecting Tokyo and Osaka. For the first time, the human voice could be carried from one of Japan's commercial and power centers to the other.

The introduction of the telephone to Japan created various anxieties and perplexities. The anecdotes regarding these early encounters suggest that the Japanese at first approached the machine almost as if it were an organic entity. Kaneko Kentarō's surprise at the fact that "it works in Japanese too" makes the telephone out to be some kind of monolingual "language relay" that hears the message and then repeats to it the person on the other end, instead of a neutral device that simply transforms sound waves into electrical signals abstracted from any possible semantic or semiotic content.

Kaneko's initial conceptualization of how the device should work was perhaps the more intuitive of the two. Indeed, the earliest attempts at sound creation and reproduction involved the creation of "automata" that imitated the action of the human diaphragm and vocal organs. Inventors could conceive of sound only in terms of the material objects that produced it, rather than focusing on the nature and characteristics of sound itself, much like the inventors who tried to build flying machines by devising flapping birdlike wings instead of exploiting the principle of lift through differential pressure, the basis of the modern airplane wing. In due course, attention shifted to the process of hearing and thus, by extension, to the human ear itself. Yet the approach remained firmly rooted in somehow trying to rebuild or reverse-engineer actual human organs: In 1874, Alexander Graham Bell and Clarence Blake constructed the ear phonoautograph, a machine that traced sound waves on a sheet of smoked glass with a small stylus. The stylus was attached to the excised middle ear of a human cadaver, which in turn vibrated when a person spoke at it through an amplifying mouthpiece.

SŌSEKI'S PHONE

Telephones first began to appear in literary works around the turn of the century. One of the earliest documented appearances of a telephone in a literary work is found in Saitō Ryokuu's (1868–1904) *Ararezake* (1898). At the time there were still only around 3,370 subscribers to Tokyo's phone service.[46] As the twentieth century progressed, however, and the number of subscribers (as well as the number of public phones) increased, the new technology became more conspicuous in contemporary fiction.

The first writer to own a telephone was probably Kunikida Doppo (1871–1908), who had a phone installed in his home in 1904.[47] But the first writer to make extensive use of the telephone was, in all likelihood, Natsume Sōseki. As an employee of the *Asahi shinbun*, Sōseki had the use of a phone in his company lodgings, and his diaries are filled with records of phone calls made and received.

One flurry of telephonic activity occurred in September and October 1909 with his friend and at the time chairman of the South Manchurian Railway Company, Nakamura Yoshikoto (or Zekō, 1867–1927) in preparation for Sōseki's trip to China and Korea that formed the basis of the travel memoir *Mankan tokorodokoro* (Here and there in Manchuria and Korea). A sampling of the entries:

> 9/7: Nakamura called, asking to see if I can make it to the ball tonight.
> 9/8: Nakamura called, asking me to come speak with him. Went a little past eight, listening to him blow hot air about this and that.
> 9/9: Received a call from the civil government office, asking when my itinerary will arrive.[48]

We see from the frequency of the calls and the relative triviality of their content that by this time the telephone was familiar to a man of Sōseki's station, although members of less privileged classes were not completely unfamiliar with the device either. Public phones began appearing in telegraph offices as soon as the line between Tokyo and Yokohama was completed 1890, and public telephone kiosks began appearing on street corners in the autumn of 1900.

Narratives of modernization often associate the introduction of new technologies with increasing regimentation and systematization. Historical studies of temporality have often focused on the ways in which industrialization and capitalist modes of production concretized time and made it convertible with money: time as "currency." In contrast, technology's potential to generate temporal disorder and disarray is addressed only infrequently.

The primary users of the telephone were large commercial interests, which until then had largely relied on messenger boys to deliver urgent messages to clients and business partners. The users who probably received the greatest benefit from the new device, however, were the newspapers, which had to compete with one another to be the first to report breaking stories. As expensive as telephones were to own and use, they were evidently a worthwhile investment for newspapers and allowed them to carry out their mission with greater efficiency.

For most people, however, the telephone was valuable more as a curiosity than as an efficient means of communication. Given the fact that most urban dwellers didn't own telephones, it was difficult—though not impossible—for them to make use of the devices. Although the relative scarcity and expense of telephones persisted all the way into the early postwar period, during this same period the popularity of telephony grew dramatically. How did this happen?

STEPPING OUT TO TAKE A CALL

People could telephone each other even when neither party owned a phone. The practice, called *yobidashi denwa* (telephone summons), was instituted by the Teishinshō (Ministry of Communications) in 1900. A caller without a phone line would go to the telephone office to request a call. The telephone clerk would call the exchange operator, who would connect to the telephone office nearest the recipient of the call. The receiving office would issue a *yobidashi tsūwaken* (telephone summons ticket), which would be delivered to the recipient's home, like a telegram. The ticket would be valid for seven days and sometimes included an appointment time for the call to take place, although the caller often would wait at the telephone office until the recipient could be brought to the receiving telephone office to accept the call.

The process was very time-consuming—indeed, it was a waste of time and money in comparison with other widespread and cheaper forms of communication—but that didn't stop people from using it. In its first year, 6,600 *yobidashi denwa* were carried out. Ten years later, in the single year of 1910, 580,000 such calls were placed. In 1935, 2,260,000 *yobidashi* calls were connected. It was clearly a popular service, even though it took much more time, and cost more, than a telegram.[49]

Given the inefficiency of the *yobidashi* system, we are left to wonder why it was embraced and used so enthusiastically. Most *yobidashi* calls were long distance, which leads Matsuda to speculate that they were used mainly for merchants to communicate with far-flung producers and growers about prices, crop yields, and so on. He also surmises that journalists used the system to file reports with their newspaper editorial offices. This might have been true in the early days of telephone service, but these explanations can't account for the explosive growth of the practice well into the 1930s. Companies and suppliers that did regular business could have scheduled periodic phone calls without the need for the added intermediary of the *yobidashi* ticket. Similarly, newspaper offices had phones installed so their journalists could have called the newspaper directly from a public phone or telephone office without having to add the extra step of issuing a *yobidashi* ticket.

Many of these *yobidashi* calls were placed to family and friends living in the provinces. Callers could have communicated by letter, and in more urgent situations by telegram, but above and beyond mere communication, they wanted to participate in the ritual of modernity that the telephone represented. They also wanted, simply, to hear one another's voices even when one or both parties didn't have a phone installed. In other words, technologically mediated listening over long distances offered users *pleasure* derived fetishistically from both from technological magic and from the sensual medium of the human voice.

The inconvenience of telephony wasn't limited only to those who didn't have phones in their homes. As Sōseki said of the device, "I bought a phone because I needed it (to make calls), but I have no use for the calls that are made to me."[50] His disciple Uchida Hyakken (1889–1971) wrote,

> The telephone in Sensei's house had some kind of gauze or bandage wrapped around the bell so it wouldn't make a sound when a call came. When he was feeling depressed he found the telephone extremely annoying. When he first got it, he just left the receiver off the hook, but the people at the telephone exchange made a big stink about that, so he simply rigged the phone not to ring even when somebody called.[51]

Sōseki had a well-documented aversion to noise, which no doubt contributed to his dislike of receiving telephone calls, but it's safe to assume that he also objected to the telephone's ability to pull him from whatever he was working on, to take his time and disrupt his concentration. In that way, the telephone *did* in fact participate in the temporal tyranny of modernity; just as clock time orders human activity according to an abstract template divorced from the needs and demands of a particular activity and thereby limits the subject's self-determination, the telephone partitions and disorders time for the convenience of another.

The limited number of telephones also meant that those who didn't own them would ask their neighbors from time to time to borrow theirs. In addition to the potential annoyance of incoming phone calls, telephone owners had to contend with the distraction and disruption of neighbors asking to use their phones.

The practice of borrowing a neighbor's phone was quite widespread and, on the surface at least, was considered socially acceptable until the widespread deployment of public telephones beginning in 1901. These public telephones were known in Japanese as *jidō denwa* (automatic phones), not because they could make calls directly (they couldn't—they still needed to rely on an operator), but because one didn't have to pay an attendant—one could just place one's coins in the chute. The operator could tell how much money the caller had put in by the sound of the coin landing in the coin box; a 5-sen coin apparently made a "*chin*" sound, and a 10-sen coin made a "*bon*" sound.[52]

Although the telephone did present a time-efficient means of communication when both parties possessed one, it also had serious and more economical competition in the form of telegrams and regular mail. During the late Meiji and Taishō periods, mail was delivered in Tokyo approximately ten times a day. A letter could be sent from Azabu to Asakusa within three and a half hours, which meant that in Tokyo at least, a telegram did not offer much of a time advantage over regular mail delivery. Moreover, with the establishment of special delivery in February 1911, deliveries could be made even more quickly.[53]

There were also significant bottlenecks in urban telephone systems during the first decades of telephone service. The number of telephone exchanges could not keep pace with the number of new subscribers and the operators, who tended to be young women between the ages of fourteen and twenty-five, were often pushed to the breaking point.[54] The typical operator had to master an exchange board with hundreds of plugs and usually had to stand and stretch to reach the extremities of the board. The work was thus both psychologically and physically taxing. In addition, the lines were often busy, leaving both caller and operator frustrated. Various attempts were made to reform and improve the system, but the crush of new subscribers always left the network one step behind demand. As one newspaper editorial explained in 1918, "Recently, telephone exchange service has become particularly unacceptable. A call that, as a general rule, should take eight seconds to go through can take ten minutes, even twenty, from the time one rings the operator. A call that only takes twenty to thirty seconds to go through is on the fast side."[55] According to Nishimoto Ikuko,

FIGURE 1.1 Postcard of Fukui Post Office Telephone Exchange. Photo courtesy of the Duits Collection.

the operators were swamped. During peak usage times, an operator might be expected to handle between 270 and 280 calls an hour, with that figure occasionally rising as high as 350 calls an hour for experienced operators. The system was designed on the assumption that the average operator would handle 185 calls an hour. Tanizaki Jun'ichirō (1886–1965) recounted that "calling from Yokohama to Tokyo took half a day, long enough to go to Tokyo and come back. Actually, it really was faster just to go to Tokyo and come back."[56]

Away from the commercial centers of Tokyo and Osaka, telephone transactions were susceptible to all kinds of playful mischief. One particularly amusing example comes from Yamagata City, where telephone service was instituted in 1907. The telephone operators were taught to answer with the by-now standard opening of "*Moshi moshi*," to which the caller would often respond, "*Kame yo, kame yo.*" The operator would repeat, "*Moshi moshi*," to which the caller would again repeat, "*Kame yo, kame yo.*" Then both operator and caller would sing together, "*Moshi moshi kame yo*," the opening lyrics of the popular children's song "Usagi to kame" (Rabbit and Turtle).[57]

FIGURE 1.2 Telephone switchboard, Kosaka Mining, Smelting, and Refining Works. Photo courtesy of the Duits Collection.

The rhetoric of efficiency and time-saving that often surrounds new technologies is just as often contradicted by the actual consequences that a given technology has for temporal order and time management. Today, for example, we see how the internet accelerates the movement of information while at the same time offering forms of distraction that grind actual productivity to a halt. The preceding examples paint a more complex picture of how the telephone allowed—or did not allow—its earliest users in Japan to save time and communicate with one another more efficiently. A host of social, economic, and material factors prevented the device from living up to its billing as a means of near-instantaneous communication. And yet telephone owners and nonowners alike often went to great trouble and expense to talk on the phone with each other. Clearly the ability to engage in immediate back-and-forth communication once the call was connected, which was not possible with other forms of communication, contributed to this phenomenon, but early telephone use in Japan also suggests that technologies are often embraced even when they are relatively expensive and inefficient. The telephone was a crucial nexus where the social, the cultural, the economic, the material, and the phenomenological intersected. Even at its most disruptive and inconvenient, it was an object of desire and compulsion.

2

SOUND AND SENTIMENT

Modernization has erased the sound of the geta from Japan.
—NAGAI KAFŪ

AN ARCHEOLOGY OF SOUND

There is a remarkable chapter in Kurosawa Akira's (1910–1998) memoir *Gama no abura* (translated into English as *Something Like an Autobiography*) in which he recalls the sounds of his childhood in the Taishō period (1912–1926). The list is so rich and evocative that I quote it here at length:

> The sounds I used to listen to as a boy are completely different from those of today. First of all, there was no such thing as electric sound in those days. Even phonographs were not electric phonographs. Everything was natural sounds. Among those natural sounds were many that are lost forever. I will try to recall some of them.
> The resounding "boom" of midday. This was the sound of the cannon at the Kudan Ushi-ga-fuchi army barracks, which fired a blank each day, precisely at noon.
> The fire-alarm bell. The sound of the fire-watchman's wooden clappers. The sound of his voice and the drumbeats when he informed the neighborhood of the location of a fire.

The tōfu seller's bugle. The whistle of the tobacco-pipe repairman. The sound of the lock on the hard-candy vendor's chest of drawers. The tinkle of the wind-chime seller's wares. The drumbeats of the man who repaired the thongs of wooden clogs. The bells of itinerant monks chanting sutras. The candy seller's drum. The fire-truck bell. The big drum for the lion dance. The monkey trainer's drum. The drum for temple services. The freshwater-clam vendor. The nattō fermented-bean seller. The hot-red-pepper vendor. The goldfish vendor. The man who sold bamboo clothesline poles. The seedling vendor. The night-time noodle vendor. The oden [dumpings-and-broth] vendor. The baked sweet-potato vendor. The scissors grinder. The tinker. The morning-glory seller. The fishmonger. The sardine vendor. The boiled-beans seller. The insect vendor: "Magotarō's bugs!" The humming of kite strings. The click of battledore and shuttlecock. Songs you sing while bouncing a ball. Children's songs.[1]

A recurring theme in this list is the sound of vendors: their cries, their bells and whistles, their drums. This is the primordial form of advertising, a gesture as old as humanity itself: a man or woman making noise in order to be noticed. Noise makes demands on our attention that visual phenomena do not. We can ignore the seen and make it unseen; we can look away or have something "drop from our sight" (*miotosu*, "overlook, fail to notice"). But we cannot turn away from the heard. We can only try to block our ears (an often unacceptable alternative, because then everything—what we do not want to hear and what we want or even *need* to hear—is lost) or simply remove ourselves from the scene (which is usually an even more unacceptable cure than the first). Sound exerts a subtle tyranny.

This is a paradox because sound is so ephemeral and so often ignored in the narratives through which we attempt to understand our world. Instead, sight has generally been the privileged sense throughout history. There are potential explanations for this. Of all the senses, vision in the healthy and unimpaired person is the most acute, the sense with the broadest spectrum of perceptibility and the greatest ability to make fine distinctions. Although our vision is neither as acute at large distances as that of, say, a hawk, or as efficient at low light levels as that of a dog, for all-around performance—acuity, light sensitivity, color discrimination, and the like—a human being's sense of sight is extraordinarily adaptable to different conditions. Our hearing is generally not as sensitive as that of four-legged mammals, and of course our olfactory sensitivity is only a tiny fraction of a dog's.

The predominance of sight is reflected in various words and figures of speech, especially in Western languages: "visionary," "enlightenment," "I see what you mean," and so on. Our vision is the interface by which we navigate the world and is the most pervasive metaphor for how we understand it.

Nobody, though, would deny the importance of hearing. All too often, however, that importance does not register except in the context of speech and music. The word "soundscape"—a term coined by Canadian composer R. Murray Schafer to designate the sounds comprising the auditory environment—did not come into existence until the early 1970s. It is curious that for thousands of years of human civilization, we had no single word to describe such a ubiquitous facet of embodied life.[2]

That ubiquity is perhaps part of the problem. The soundscape is taken for granted in ways that visual phenomena are not—it is just "there." We notice it only when it changes in some particularly annoying, frightening, or perhaps pleasing way.

One of the most acute descriptions of the sound world comes not from Schafer or another musician or theorist of sound, but from Walter Ong:

> All sensation takes place in time, but sound has a special relationship to time unlike that of the other fields that register in human sensation. Sound exists only when it is going out of existence. It is not simply perishable but essentially evanescent, and it is sensed as evanescent. When I pronounce the word "permanence," by the time I get to the "-pence," [sic] the "perma-" is gone, and has to be gone.
>
> There is no way to stop sound and have sound. I can stop a moving picture camera and hold one frame fixed on the screen. If I stop the movement of sound, I have nothing—only silence, no sound at all. All sensation takes place in time, but no other sensory field totally resists a holding action, stabilization, in quite this way. Vision can register motion, but it can also register immobility. Indeed, it favors immobility, for to examine something closely by vision, we prefer to have it quiet. We often reduce motion to a series of still shots the better to see what motion is.

There is no equivalent of a still shot for sound. An oscillogram is silent. It lies outside the sound world.[3]

As we will see in the next chapter, the technology of the phonograph provided a way to detain this evanescence. Sound *qua* sound remained as rooted in motion and as ephemeral as ever, but at least it could be stored and mechanically reproduced. Sound could not be stopped and held, but it could be replayed over and over again.

Schafer was working in a North American tradition of attentiveness to sonic environments that originated with the work of the experimental composer John Cage (1912–1992), especially his work for piano, *4′33″*, which features a pianist sitting silently at a piano for the length of the piece's title. The work is at once conceptual and profoundly sensual, forcing the audience to attend closely to the ambient sound world by framing it in a formal recital context. Cage, in turn, was inspired by his understanding of Zen Buddhism, particularly the interpretation of Japanese Zen that had slowly filtered into American consciousness through the work of D. T. Suzuki (1870–1966). In 1950 Cage took a course with Suzuki at Columbia University, an event that had a profound impact on his later thinking.[4] Although the history of the Japanese-Western cultural encounter, particularly in the nineteenth century, often seems unidirectional in terms of the predominant flows of exchange, this is one case in which a Western artist openly and wholeheartedly took his cue from a Japanese thinker.

PREMODERN SOUNDSCAPES

Kurosawa's inventory gives us some sense of the sounds of Taishō Japan, many of which were holdovers from the early modern period. It goes without saying, however, that the soundscapes of Japan have continually changed throughout history. But because most of this history predates recording technology, we have little direct physical evidence for any of it. This is a history that must be imagined by reading the testimony of "ear-witnesses" as well as by listening to the physical objects (the geta, the bush warbler, the temple bell) that generate the sounds mentioned or described in those testimonies.

The best sources of information in this regard are those forms of discourse that attend carefully to the particulars of everyday life: literary forms such as diaries, poetry, and novels. The sound world often becomes submerged in the stream of daily consciousness, and consciousness is usually an activity of reification, one that finds very little to reify in the ephemerality of sound. Only the heightened attentiveness and receptivity of the literary imagination has time for such seeming trifles: the discourses of history (and, later, the social sciences) until relatively recently took no interest in such minutiae, preferring to concentrate on social, political, and economic history.

I will not attempt here anything like a comprehensive catalog of the sounds of premodern Japan, but I will mention a few of the more notable ones, and speak broadly about the nature of these soundscapes that were eventually replaced by the sounds of modernity.

Schafer distinguishes between what he calls "lo-fi" and "hi-fi" soundscapes. A "hi-fi" soundscape has a high ratio of "signal" to "noise"; that is, individual sounds may be heard without crowding or masking. In Schafer's schema, premodern, and particularly rural, soundscapes tend to be "hi-fi" because sounds can be heard, identified, and appreciated. In contrast, industrial urban soundscapes are "lo-fi" because of the density of sounds, particularly loud, noisy sounds.[5]

Japanese literati have shown a particular attentiveness to sound since at least the archaic age and the period of the *Man'yōshū* (Collection of ten thousand leaves, ca. 785). Not surprisingly, the objects of this early acoustic sensitivity were aspects of the natural world: the sounds of wind and water and especially the sounds of living things, usually birds and insects, although the sounds of mammals that had elegant associations (most notably deer, whose sound is referenced in several *Man'yōshū* verses) also found their way into poetic representation.[6]

By the Heian period (794–1185), this culture of auditory attentiveness was firmly in place. Canonical works from that era and later are rich in references to features of the auditory world.[7] For example, a number of the chapters in the *Genji monogatari* (*Tale of Genji*) are structured around practice of listening. Chapter 38, "Suzumushi" (The Bell Cricket),[8] is a signal example. An aging, retired Genji arranges a "concert" of singing crickets to entertain Her Cloistered Highness, Onna san no Miya. The middle of this chapter describes an extremely rich acoustical scene:

At dusk on the fifteenth night, Her Highness sat before her altar, near the veranda, abstractedly calling the Name. Two or three young nuns were offering flowers. The holy-water vessel rang, there were water sounds, and all this bustle over such unfamiliar tasks put her in a very melancholy mood. Just then, as so often, Genji entered. "The crickets are singing everywhere this evening!" he remarked and quietly joined her, in low but inspiring tones, to chant the great *darani* of the Buddha Amida. There were indeed many crickets singing, and among them the bell crickets' voices rose bravely and beautifully above the rest. "All the autumn crickets' songs are lovely," he said, "but Her Majesty especially preferred pine crickets, and those are the ones she gathered from distant moors to release in her garden. I hear very few went on singing there, though. Pine crickets probably do not live long, despite what their name suggests. They really and truly sing only in the mountains, where no one can hear them, or among the pine forests below, which suggests that they prefer solitude. The bell cricket's gentle freshness is what makes it so appealing."[9]

Genji then calls for his *kin* and begins to play almost as if in accompaniment to the crickets.

This brief passage evokes several different sounds, all brought together and considered to be part of a continuum: the water vessel, the water itself, the chanting of a Buddhist sutra, the singing of numerous species of cricket, and Genji's playing of the *kin*. The man-made, ordered, and musical sounds of the chanting and the instrument are not foregrounded at the expense of the ambient sounds of the environment; rather, the sonic environment is taken as a whole.

Haikai (linked verses) inherited the soundscapes and sonic associations of earlier periods and reworked them in novel and powerful ways. The relative brevity of *haikai* meant that an entire verse could often be structured around a single evoked sound, and making such use of sound became a favorite technique of Matsuo Bashō (1644–1694) and other poets. Indeed, some of Bashō's most famous verses are perfect examples of the centrality of sound to his poetic universe:

furuike ya	The old pond
kawazu tobikomu	the frog jumps in
mizu no oto	the sound of water

umi kurete	The sea darkens
kamo no koe	the voice of the wild duck
honoka ni shiroshi	faintly white
kame waruru	The water jar cracks
yoru no kōri	on this icy night
mezame ka na	I lie awake

This attentiveness to isolated and often quiet sonic phenomena points to a rural auditory environment relatively free of noise and rich in what Schafer would call "hi-fi" sounds. Lest we imagine that early modern Japan was solely a place of meditative quiet, however, we should remember that the sounds of urban Edo presented a very different auditory scene. Even conservative estimates reckon the city's population to have been approximately half a million throughout most of the Tokugawa period (1603–1868), with other estimates doubling or even tripling that figure as Edo entered the late eighteenth and early nineteenth centuries. Even before the teahouses, pleasure quarters, fireworks, and various forms of raucous popular entertainment such as kabuki are taken into account, the sheer density of the population suggests a considerable amount of noise and bustle.[10] After Edo was transformed into Tokyo and its population increased even more dramatically, the levels of noise could logically only increase. Moreover, with the importation of machines, the ambient noise changed in quantity as well as quality.

AUDITORS ABROAD

The encounter with sonic alterity, mediated by an organ that cannot *look* but can only *move* away, an organ that cannot close itself but can only be covered, is fraught with possibilities and anxieties. Sound is not visible, and when it is heard, it almost seems to take place in some internal dimension of the listening subject. The sounds we hear mix with, and sometimes interfere with, the running monologue of our thoughts, surely one reason why unwelcome sounds can be so unnerving. Whereas many of the Westerners who visited Japan in the decades after its opening to the outside world exhibited a ready willingness to take in and appreciate visual artifacts such as textiles and ukiyo-e prints, the number who could tolerate, much less embrace, the auditory culture of nineteenth-century Japan was much smaller.

The sites where different cultures come into contact with one another, where difference becomes contiguous with difference, present historians and theorists of culture with zones of conflict, exchange, and hybridity (all of which are processes that can readily be mapped and narrated) as well as with emergent and often transient properties in the realms of perception, epistemology, and subjectivity. These emergent properties, as the term implies, are not intrinsic to the cultures involved, nor are they some form of hybrid, mixture, or syncretion of the cultures in contact. Rather, they emerge in the "in-between," the result of relationships, of temporary and contingent configurations of subjects and objects that are unique and unrepeatable. As transient and contingent transformations of subjectivity, they are harder to narrate than the more obvious allegories of coherent, reified "cultures" scuffling with one another, either on the worldly plane of war and economics or the abstract plane of ideas and values. Sound—in its invisibility and transience, its play of shifting, formless energies—has a similarity to and affinity for thought and especially affect, which renders it a powerful inducer of transformed subjectivity and relationship. Literary and personal narratives provide the platform for recording these fleeting changes of subjectivity. Furthermore, the writing of sonic alterity yields illuminating glimpses of this relationality in motion.

The reactions of Westerners to the sounds of Meiji-era Japan (1868–1912) are well documented in the extensive library of travel diaries, descriptive guides, and fictional works produced by these early voyagers. Most of them arrived with a predictable set of orientalist and colonialist assumptions about the culture that greeted them, and while some of those assumptions were confounded by a civilization whose standards of comportment were in many ways more refined than their own, the exotic and incomprehensible *sounds* of Japan offered many of them an easy target for derision and cultural chauvinism. At the same time, these travelers demonstrated an attentiveness to sound *as such* that is largely missing from the writings by the Japanese of the time.

Nineteenth-century Western visitors to Japan took an almost universal dislike to the music they heard there. The American writer and lecturer John Lawson Stoddard (1850–1931), who held a generally positive view of Japan and quite accurately prophesied in 1897 that "the most important dramas of the coming century will probably be enacted on the shores of the Pacific," wrote:

> One cannot, however, praise the music which is here produced. It would be highly amusing, if one were deaf; but when one's hearing is acute, a little of such music goes a long way. None of the most enthusiastic admirers of the Japanese has dared as yet, to praise their music. To Occidental ears the twanging of their banjo strings and, above all, their caterwaulings are positive torture.[11]

British Army officer Henry Knollys (1840–1930) went a step further, writing in 1887 that Japanese ensemble music produced "a clamour which is not merely discordant and harsh, but which is almost as evil as the Chinese music I have described in a former work, and which, without any sort of affection, brings on the European a sensation of bodily pain. Indeed, Japanese music betrays the hoof of their comparatively recent barbarism."[12]

This musical incomprehension, however, was often mutual, at least during the first decades following Japan's opening. As British Japanologist Basil Hall Chamberlain (1850–1935) wrote about an Italian opera troupe that he saw perform in Yokohama some time around the year 1900,

> But oh! The effect upon the Japanese audience! When once they had recovered from the first shock of surprise, they were seized with a wild fit of hilarity at the high notes of the *prima donna*, who really was not at all bad. The people laughed at the absurdities of European singing till their sides shook, and the tears rolled down their cheeks; and they stuffed their sleeves into their mouths, as we might our pocket-handkerchiefs, in the vain endeavour to contain themselves.[13]

The sheer intensity and nonnegotiability of these reactions to musical and auditory alterity, which were as or even more drastic than similar reactions to culinary alterity, show that contrary to the received wisdom that music is a "universal" language, it is in fact one of the forms of human expression *least* capable of crossing cultural borders. This remains true even today: Although it is easy to laugh at these quotations as examples of a benighted nineteenth-century attitude toward difference, it's just as easy to demonstrate that the number of Westerners today who actually listen to traditional East Asian music is far smaller than the number who eat East Asian food, watch East Asian cinema, appreciate East Asian visual art and display it in their homes, or read East Asian literature in translation. Many of us are just as guilty, even if in a more polite form, of the same inability to cross musical boundaries as the writers I've just quoted.

The reaction of the baffled opera audience in Yokohama notwithstanding, that so many Japanese intellectuals cultivated an appreciation for Western classical music neatly illustrates the asymmetries of economic, military, technological, and cultural power that existed between Japan and the West at the time. These asymmetries gave Western travelers to Japan license to dismiss Japanese music *as music*, but they did not allow them to ignore Japanese sounds *as noise*. Despite their best efforts to assert their dominance over that noise through the strategy of colonial historiography—that is, the containment of alterity through the medium of writing—sound, music, and noise managed to retain a surplus or residuum of difference and, even more important, autonomy, an uncanny and infuriating ability to tear through the ordering frames of the travelers' discursive strategies.

The subject positions of Western listeners in late nineteenth-century Japan were more complex than that of the stereotypically naive and belligerent imperialist. For the auditor abroad, listening is defamiliarized, which triggers a paradoxical shift in listening strategies. On the one hand, auditory events (including spoken language) are stripped of their semiotic functions, placing the listener in a situation of hermeneutical blindness or, in this case, "deafness." On the other hand, this properly hermeneutic displacement is accompanied by heightened attentiveness, and perhaps even sensitivity, to the ambient *materiality* of sound. Language and music are no longer language or music but are bare sound, and depending on the listener's capacity to tolerate the interpretive uncertainty of sound *as* sound (rather than as a linguistic or expressive signifier), this sound is then often perceived as noise.

Enhanced awareness as a function of novelty yields useful results for the sonic archeologist of the Japan of this period. Some of the best accounts of early Meiji Japanese soundscapes come from the journals and other writings of foreigners resident in Japan. This is not surprising because, as I mentioned previously, ambient sounds tend to fall into the category of everyday minutiae, the texture of lived experience that the native often takes for granted (and hence fails to notice) but that the outsider perceives acutely—so much so, in fact, that he or she is sometimes overwhelmed by it. In his study *Meiji no oto: Seiyōjin ga kiita kindai Nihon* (The sounds of the Meiji Period: Post-restoration Japan as heard by Westerners), literary scholar Naitō Takashi catalogs the observations and reactions of Western visitors to the sounds of a modernizing Japan.[14]

Descriptions of sounds heard in Japan by early Western visitors like Lafcadio Hearn (1850–1904) and Edward S. Morse (1838–1925) naturally focus on sounds not heard outside Japan: the various grades of clickety-clack made by geta, the distinctive cries and grunts made by vendors and boatmen and rickshaw men, the sounds of wooden clappers and fulling blocks.

Morse was an American zoologist hired by the Japanese government as the first professor of zoology at the Tokyo Imperial University. His residence there lasted from 1877 to 1880, but he subsequently returned to Japan for shorter visits. His *Japan Day by Day* is so chock-full of sonic impressions that it is practically an encyclopedia of the soundscapes of early Meiji Japan. Although it would be impossible to list them all here, a few are worth noting. Morse's chronicle begins with his first landing in Yokohama, where he immediately encountered the sounds of Japan in the form of the rhythmic chants of the scullers rowing him from his boat to the shore: "And such a peculiar series of grunts they made, keeping time with each with sounds like *hei hei cha*, *hei hei cha*, and then varying the chanty, if it were one, putting quite as much energy into the grunts as they did into the sculling."[15] This is the first introduction of a recurring motif throughout the journals, the way in which vocal utterance serves as a guide and accompaniment to work, particularly group work and work requiring great physical exertion. A few pages later, Morse mentions a pile driver lifted and lowered by eight men:

> An odd, monotonous chant was sung, and at the end of the stanza all pulled together, and then suddenly letting go, the weight dropped with a thud. It seemed a ridiculous waste of time to sing the chanty, for such

it was, without exerting the slightest effort to raise the weight. Nine tenths of the time was devoted to singing!¹⁶

Morse also very quickly noticed the "curious, resonant clattering" of geta, which was also one of the first sounds that Lafcadio Hearn noticed. These were not the only clacking sounds, however:

> At night you occasionally hear a curious clacking sound beaten in regular rhythmic raps. You find that these sounds are made by private watchmen who at intervals go about the grounds to inform the owners that some one is on guard.
>
> At times, night and day, you hear a plaintive sort of shrill whistle. This sound is made by blind men and women who go about the streets to advertise their calling, which is that of masseurs.¹⁷

Most of the sounds that Morse records in the journal of his visit are those that he would not have heard back home. In fact, when he does hear something familiar, such as the clicking of an American sewing machine, it strikes him as out of place.

Morse's observations extended to common paralinguistic vocalizations:

> A curious feature of conversation among these people is the constant ejaculation of "Ha" or "Hei." For example, one is talking to another and at every slight pause the other says, "Hei," and the first one says "Ha." It is an indication that he is listening and understands and is a sign of respect. Also, in talking to each other they make a noise with the mouth as if they had burned the tongue with hot tea and were cooling it by drawing in air, or a sound similar to that made by a hungry boy when he sees something very good to eat. This sound is one of self-depreciation or respect.¹⁸

Not all Western visitors were as open-minded about or appreciative of the Japanese soundscape as Morse. The famed travel writer Isabella Bird (1831–1904) found tortuous nearly everything she heard in Japan, music and ambient sounds alike. In *Unbeaten Tracks in Japan*, she wrote:

On one side a man recited Buddhist prayers in a high key; on the other a girl was twanging a *samisen*, a species of guitar; the house was full of talking and splashing, drums and tomtoms were beaten outside; there were street cries innumerable, and the whistling of the blind shampooers, and the resonant clap of the fire watchman who perambulates all Japanese villages, and beats two pieces of wood together in token of his vigilance, were intolerable. It was a life of which I knew nothing, and the mystery was more alarming than attractive.[19]

Many Western travelers to Japan were, probably understandably, unhappy with the Japanese custom of drinking and singing until the late hours of the night. Bird described a night she spent at an inn in the town of Tochigi:

I lay down on my precarious stretcher before eight, but as the night advanced, the din of the house increased till it became truly diabolical, and never ceased till after one. Drums, tom-toms, and cymbals were beaten; *kotos* and *samisens* screeched and twanged; geishas (professional women with the accomplishments of dancing, singing, and playing) danced, accompanied by songs whose jerking discords were most laughable; storytellers recited tales in a high key, and the running about and splashing close to my room never ceased. Late at night my precarious *shōji* were accidentally thrown down, revealing a scene of great hilarity, in which a number of people were bathing and throwing water over each other.

The noise of the departures began at daylight, and I was glad to leave at seven.[20]

Bird, the representative of a stronger, quasi-colonial power, finds herself helpless, victimized even, by the sounds of the native. The assault is not deliberate, since the Japanese guests at the inn are simply doing what they normally do, but their music, their "joyful noise," is itself a kind of violence. Jacques Attali says of this in *Noise*:

First, . . . *noise is violence*: it disturbs. To make noise is to interrupt a transmission, to disconnect, to kill. It is a simulacrum of murder.

Second, ... *music is a channelization of noise*, and therefore a simulacrum of the sacrifice. It is thus a sublimation, an exacerbation of the imaginary, at the same time as the creation of social order and political integration.[21]

As Attali tries to demonstrate, the relationship between noise and music is fundamentally a political one. If music as a channeling of noise is a simulacrum of the channeling of violence into sacrifice and political order, then the dismissal of the Other's music as "noise" is a political as much as an aesthetic declaration, a decomposition of the Other's social order into chaos, violence, barbarism.

As with music, however, there is a reciprocity in these sonic encounters that complicates a simple paradigm of a colonial gaze or "ear." During his studies in England, Natsume Sōseki changed boarding houses five times in London, where peace and quiet seemed especially hard to find.[22] Sōseki shared this longing for quiet with one of his literary heroes, Thomas Carlyle (1795–1881). In an essay entitled "The Carlyle Museum," Sōseki recounts his visit to the writer's former home, to which Carlyle had added an attic study for the sole purpose of keeping out the noises of the outside world. Here Sōseki meditates on noise:

Noise. The noises that tormented Carlyle in England were the same as those that tormented Schopenhauer in Germany. Schopenhauer wrote, "Kant has published a treatise on dynamics. I, however, write in order to toll the knell of energy. The noise made by something which one strikes, the noise of something rolling along everything comes from a misuse of the vital force. As for me, I simply feel torments day after day. My reasoning will make most people laugh, since when they hear noise they feel nothing. But if there are those in this world who are insensible to logic, indifferent to thought, to poetry and even to art, they are thus incapable of forgetting themselves, and there is no doubt that the failure of their mental system is the cause of the slowness of their comprehension." Carlyle and Schopenhauer are in truth two kindred nineteenth-century souls.[23]

Sōseki, no doubt, felt himself to be a part of that kinship. The "misuse of the vital force" that resulted in the noises of the preindustrial would not only remain as they were but would also be multiplied in some of the most drastic ways imaginable.

Indeed, if we had to choose one word to characterize the soundscape of modernity, that word would have to be "noise." While we have no recordings or readings of ambient noise levels in the preindustrial era, it is probably safe to say that ambient noise levels did not approach those of the early decades of industrialization and electrification. This does not mean that preindustrial communities, particularly urban ones, were necessarily *quiet*: they were filled with the sounds of hawkers selling their wares, of horses' hooves on city stones, and so on. Emily Thompson refers to Buddhist scriptures dating from 500 BCE that listed the ten noises in a great city, including "elephants, horses, chariots, drums, tabors, lutes, song, cymbals, gongs, and people crying 'Eat ye, and drink!'" But, as Thompson states,

> The sounds that so bothered Carlyle and Goethe were almost identical to those that had been identified by the Buddha centuries earlier: organic sounds created by humans and animals at work and at play. These sounds constitute the constant sonic background that has always accompanied human civilization. With urbanization they were certainly concentrated; with industrialization, however, new kinds of noises began to offend.[24]

Sound structures our perception of both time (in the form of rhythm, for example) and space. The most important and most easily recognizable example of this is the phenomenon of reverberation, which is made up of the multiple reflections or echoes produced when sound is generated in an enclosed space. Reverberation is influenced by multiple factors, including the size and shape of the space as well as the materials against which the sounds reflect (a tiled bathroom, for example, is more reverberant than a wooden barn). People can often intuit important information, especially that concerning size, about a space just by hearing a sound recorded in that space and its attendant reverberations. Modern-day sound engineers often add artificially synthesized forms of reverberation to musical recordings to give them a greater sense of fullness as well as to mask minor imperfections in sound or performance. These artificially induced reverberations thus can *create* spaces in the listener's imagination that didn't exist during the recording process.

Particularly loud or harsh sounds also structure space by creating zones that would be painful or distressing to enter without some form of hearing protection. A number of metaphors common in the English language—"wall of sound," for example—reinforce this notion of sound as an architect of space. Some noises that are so overpowering or deafening as to push us away can create acute discomfort and even a sense of claustrophobia or of being trapped. As I noted earlier, we cannot *selectively* escape certain sounds in the environment: Either we endure them or try to escape them altogether by leaving the scene or blocking our ears. This sense of relative powerlessness in the face of sonic assault is probably one of the reasons why noise pollution has been shown to have serious implications for people's overall health:

> There is a vast literature linking noise pollution to all manner of psychological and even physical disturbance. In addition to the most obvious problem of hearing loss, noise has been suggestively linked to anxiety, depression, impaired mental performance and learning, immune suppression, gastrointestinal illness including ulcer, cardiovascular disease and hypertension, insomnia, and greater susceptibility to both chronic and acute illnesses.[25]

The power of noise to disrupt one's life and even one's health was perhaps perceived more acutely by those who were alive to hear the sonic transition from a preindustrial to an industrial soundscape. Thompson describes at length the various noise abatement movements and projects in the United States dating as far back as the turn of the twentieth century. Despite these efforts, the problem only got worse as various machines became ubiquitous, and it peaked with the introduction of electric amplification in the late 1920s.

Even though Japan's urban environments were a few years behind those of the United States in terms of the sheer density of sound, the net effect may have been rendered the same by differences in building construction and population density. Sound, space, and architecture have integral relationships, as the preceding discussion of reverberation makes clear. The techniques and building materials employed in the creation of most Japanese homes during the Meiji, Taishō, and early Shōwa (1926–1989) periods resulted in interior spaces that were less reverberant (wood, tatami, and paper all tend to absorb sound instead of reflecting it) but, at the same time, more sonically porous. That is, because the typical Japanese home contained less sonic insulation sounds could travel easily from the outside to the inside of the home (and vice versa) and from room to room. The often-noted differences in notions of "privacy" in Western and Japanese cultural contexts are illustrated by the relative absence of acoustic privacy afforded by the typical Japanese home. This sense of porous borders extended to the public realm of sound as well and, to some extent, still does. To this day, both mainstream politicians and right-wing nationalist agitators try to reach the public by driving through neighborhoods in trucks equipped with massive loudspeakers. Nuisances of that sort are far less likely to be tolerated in European and American communities, even in urban settings.

HARMONY AND NOISE: THE CULTURAL LOGIC OF WESTERN MUSIC IN JAPANESE MODERNITY

The first incursions of Westernized modernity into the Japanese soundscape came not in the form of Western machines but in the form of Western *music*. The significance of this event should not be underestimated, and it isn't in Japan, where the history of the importation of Western music has received intensive scholarly scrutiny.[26] Much of this attention is due to the explosive success that Western classical music has enjoyed in Japan, where over the past century and a half it has become completely domesticated. Japan has the largest market for recorded Western classical music in the world, followed by the United States (another nation for whom this particular musical idiom was in fact an import of sorts). Tokyo alone has nine major symphony orchestras (more than any city in the world), and none of the major orchestras of the world would exclude Tokyo and other major Japanese cities from their international touring schedules.

Jacques Attali contends that music serves a vital representative function, one more abstract than the significations of language. In his view, music mirrors the vectors of power in society at large, transmitting to the listener a nonsemantic aural reflection of the social body and the historically situated codes by which it operates.

[Music] is a mirror, because as a mode of immaterial production it relates to the structuring of theoretical paradigms, far ahead of concrete production. It is thus an immaterial recording surface for human works, the mark of something missing, a shred of utopia to decipher, information in negative, a collective *memory* allowing those who hear it to record their own personalized, specified, modeled meanings, affirmed in time with the beat—a collective memory of order and genealogies, the repository of the word and the social score.

But it reflects a fluid reality. The only thing that primitive polyphony, classical counterpoint, tonal harmony, twelve-tone serial music, and electronic music have in common is the principle of giving form to noise in accordance with changing syntactic structures. The history of music is the "Odyssey of a wandering, the adventure of its absences."[27]

Music's very immateriality is what makes it the most sensitive, most nimble precursor of both the symbolic and the material future. "Music is prophecy," Attali writes.

Its styles and economic organization are ahead of the rest of society because it explores, much faster than material reality can, the entire range of possibilities in a given code. It makes audible the new world that will gradually become visible, that will impose itself and regulate the order of things; it is not only the image of things, but the transcending of the everyday, the herald of the future.[28]

Attali seems to have in mind the more-or-less "organic" development of music within a given cultural and historical horizon. What happens, however, when an entire musical tradition, and a highly developed one at that, is rapidly imported into a cultural milieu that has had limited prior exposure to it?

These two scenarios (indigenous versus imported music) are, of course, simply points on a continuum: There is no such thing as a purely indigenous, organically developed music. As a medium of expression freed from the local moorings of language, music can readily cross borders. Nonetheless, as we've seen, musical tastes are often extremely conservative in a way that tastes in visual art, for example, may not be. According to Naitō Takashi,

The cultural conservatism of sound is far stronger than that of seeing. Prejudices are readily apparent.

Even the fervent *Japonist* and writer Edmond de Goncourt (1822–96) demonstrated nothing but strong aversion to the music of East Asia. Many Westerners who heard the music of noh theater couldn't hide their distaste, referring to it as "cacophonous" and "discordant."[29]

As we discussed, Meiji-era Japanese had similar reactions to Western music. Although Western music, including Western classical music, has been absorbed over time in many parts of the world where it arrived as a foreign, and indeed strikingly alien, import, in some parts of the world to this day Western music has only a tenuous hold at best. A conspicuous example is India, where the mainstream musical culture has shown relatively little interest in adopting Western musical elements and idioms. What interest it has shown has been limited mainly to using selected Western instruments (such as the violin) and selected technologies (recording technologies, of course, as well as audio effects and processing) to perform and present indigenous musical idioms in novel ways.

Japan could have similarly rejected Western music, and in fact, Japan's first exposure to that music, in the form of the liturgical music brought to Japan by Francis Xavier (1506–1552) and subsequent missionaries in the mid- to late sixteenth century, was abortive. It is open to speculation whether Western music could have taken hold in Japan had the feudal authorities not suppressed it. With most of its towering achievements still ahead of it, the European musical tradition also had less to offer in the late sixteenth century than it did three centuries later in the Meiji period.

Extensive knowledge of Western music began entering Japan as early as 1800 through the work of scholars of Western learning (*rangaku*, lit., "Dutch studies") such as Katsuragawa Hoshū (1751–1809) and Ōtsuki Gentaku (1757–1827), first in the form of dictionary entries describing Western musical instruments and music-related terms. The first Japanese book devoted specifically to European music was *Daiseigakuritsukō* (Treatise on Western music) by Udagawa Yōan (1798–1846). Much of this knowledge was purely academic, although it is evident that the Dutch settlers in Nagasaki performed Western music regularly and that the Japanese around them were exposed to it.[30]

Though the feudal authorities of Tokugawa Japan strove to keep out the Jesuits' liturgical music, Meiji bureaucrats were more than happy to adopt Western music as a tool for education and state formation. The first point of entry was the military band, which was seen by the Japanese of the time as a key component of a modern fighting force. The Satsuma clan formed a military band in 1869, and national army and navy bands were formed in 1871. Western music then moved into the school curriculum. Ury Eppstein has written of the early history of Western music education in Meiji schools, which was introduced into the curriculum by Isawa Shūji and Megata Tanetarō (1853–1926).[31]

I first mentioned Isawa Shūji in the introduction, one of the Japanese exchange students who found their way to Alexander Graham Bell's lab and who became the first Japanese ever to speak across a phone line. After returning to Japan in 1878, Isawa began laying the groundwork for Western musical education there, a foundation that remains intact to this day. Along with Megata, he submitted a proposal to the minister of education to establish a music research study group, a proposal that was accepted in 1879. Isawa became the group's chair, and that same year he became principal of the Tokyo Normal School and invited Luther Whiting Mason (1818–1896), his former teacher and, at the time, probably the most prominent music educator in the United States, to Japan. He helped Mason secure a post at Tokyo Imperial University. In addition, Isawa championed the use of a modified version of Melville Bell's Visible Speech to teach the deaf and the mute how to speak, to cure stuttering, to aid in music education, and, perhaps most ambitiously, to standardize Japanese dialects nationwide. He was not very successful in this last ambition—broadcasting did far more to standardize spoken language than Visible Speech ever would—but he was remarkably successful at treating stuttering, apparently curing more than five thousand stutterers in his lifetime.

In 1895 Isawa moved to Taiwan, which Japan had acquired in the Treaty of Shimonoseki that same year. There he founded a Japanese-language school outside Taipei at Zhishanyan (芝山巖), the first Japanese-language school outside Japan.[32] The list of Isawa's contributions to multiple fields of knowledge is long. He was the author of dozens of short- to medium-length tracts on subjects ranging from music education to school administration to gymnastics to comparative phonetics. By any standard, he was a cultural conservative and a true believer in the Japanese imperial project, but he was also a pragmatist. For example, after arriving in Taiwan, he wanted to replace Chinese characters with *katakana* for the Taiwanese to use with Chinese. As Faye Yuan Kleeman notes, however, he soon changed his mind after working with the Taiwanese students and even criticized the National Language Research Council's insistence on teaching only kana. The curriculum that he settled on—a judicious and holistic balance of kanji, kana, *kokugo* (national language), *kanbun* (classical Chinese as used by the Japanese), and calligraphy—was ahead of its time. It was very similar to the *kokugo* curriculum adopted nationally in the home islands with the revision of the Shogakkōrei (Elementary School Order) in 1900.

Luther Whiting Mason helped Isawa formulate his approach to musical pedagogy and later helped with the founding of the Tokyo School of Music (now the Tokyo University of Fine Arts and Music), of which Isawa became the first head in 1888.

Isawa's original rationale in the late 1870s was utilitarian, as he intended to use Western music as a means to "improve health" and aid in pronunciation. In the late 1880s and early 1890s, however, his rhetoric became more explicitly moralistic and nationalistic. Teachers and students were encouraged to "cultivate the spirit of reverence for the emperor and patriotism and not to lose it."[33] Western music offered the perfect medium with which to forge the soundtrack of national indoctrination: More accessible than traditional *gagaku* court music, more stolid than traditional Japanese popular music, it was the substrate in which the national subject identity could grow.

A significant number of Japanese writers came to embrace Western music as it slowly filtered into the Japanese cultural milieu. Indeed, a few of them, such as Mori Ōgai (1862–1922), served as the earliest intermediaries in that process of importation. The list of Meiji-era literati who took a keen interest in Western music is impressive: Ōgai attended dozens of opera performances during his time in Germany; Shimazaki Tōson (1872–1943) spent a year at the Tokyo School of Music (founded by Isawa, as noted earlier); Ueda Bin (1874–1916) grew up in a cosmopolitan home where he was exposed to Western music from a young age and was well read in the history and theory of classical music; Nagai Kafū (1879–1959) attended numerous opera and concert performances in the United States and France, and was one of the most acoustically sensitive of twentieth-century Japanese writers; Ishikawa Takuboku (1886–1912), perhaps more acoustically inclined even than Kafū, was deeply influenced by Western music, particularly that of Wagner. Both Ōgai and Kafū even tried writing opera libretti.

Kafū was infatuated with Western music for a time, particularly during his travels in the United States and France. In New York he went on a frenzy of opera-going during late 1905 and early 1906:

Dec. 6: Heard *Hansel and Gretel* at the Metropolitan Opera.
Dec. 18: Saw *Carmen* at the Herald Square Theater.
Jan. 4: Read the libretto for *Rigoletto*.
Jan. 5: Heard *Tristan und Isolde*.
Jan. 6: Heard *Don Pasquale*.
Jan. 8: Heard *Tosca*.
Jan. 22: Heard *Tannhäuser*.
Feb. 3: Heard *Aïda*.
Feb. 16: Heard *Lohengrin*.
Feb. 22: *Parsifal*.
March 3: Saw Caruso in *Lucia di Lammermoor*.
March 6: Heard *Die Walkürie*.
March 10: Heard *Die Götterdammerung*.
March 18: Heard a Russian orchestra at Carnegie Hall.[34]

This infatuation rose to a hyperbolic frenzy as he sailed back home to Japan from France in 1908 and tried to find the means with which to express his sadness. As he looked out at the clouds over the Mediterranean Sea, he thought to himself, "I'd like to try to sing a beautiful song in the most beautiful voice I can muster." He then began singing a Western-style tune, "La, la, la . . . ," but soon realized that he couldn't. Then he considered singing something in Japanese:

> Ah, but if trying to sing a difficult Western tune is discouraging, how much deeper the discouragement would be if I tried to sing a Japanese song! People often sing "Oshirō Takashima," which they praise as a fine, melancholy melody. But a packhorse driver's song like that bears scant relevance to a voyage such as this, and seems so out of place while

watching the sun set over the Mediterranean and recalling the Greek myths. *Takemoto, Tokiwazu* and other *jōruri* [puppet plays] ballad forms do an excellent job of conveying complex emotions, but those are not so much songs as accompanied recitatives, too cool and objective to resort to when emotion suddenly erupts. There are *Utazawa* melodies, but those are nothing more than thin laments from the distant past of the pleasure quarters. The noh recitative is antique and elegant and possessed of Buddhist pathos, but it's completely out of place on a state-of-the-art steamship in the twentieth century. It should be heard on a rush-floored boat, accompanied by the sound of an oar as one gazes on the pine trees on the distant shore, like a scene out of a *sumi-e* ink painting. Then there are *Satsuma biwa* ballads and the rhythmic recitation of Chinese poems, but those, too, belong among the exceedingly simple colors characteristic of the Japanese landscape, where their primitive monotony can at least effect a kind of naive, melancholy beauty.

I realized that no matter how much agony I felt because of my raging and overflowing emotions, I belonged to a people that didn't possess the music that could express those emotions or evoke them. Was there any other such people [*kokumin*], any other such race [*jinshu*], in the world?[35]

Here Kafū seems to have internalized a triumphalist vision of Western music as *real* music, *universal* music; he has internalized the Eurocentrism of the Western visitors to Japan mentioned earlier. He eventually and at least partially overcame this fit of cultural self-hatred after his return to Japan. In the novel *Reishō* (*Sneers*, 1909), he observes:

Today along the resplendent thoroughfares of Asia, the bells of new gospel ring forth. But in the back streets, along the muddy waters of the canals, the inextinguishable whispers of the shamisen remain, wandering in the dark night, chirping like insects nestled in an embankment above which the locomotive, voice of civilization, thunders past. Listen for a moment: In the music of our ancestors, in Takemoto, Tomimoto, Bungo, and Kiyomoto, the melodies produced by three frail strings are enough to summon the emotions of the moment of death, even without the complex structures found in Western symphonic music such as harmony and polyphony, counterpoint and canon. Kōu felt an unbearable sense of loneliness and sadness at the simplicity and monotony, at the dullness, of Japanese music.[36]

In this revised conception, the very characteristics of Japanese music that Kafū had felt rendered it inadequate to express his surging emotions now allow that same music to embody an existential pathos that is somehow impersonal ("the emotions of the moment of death"—the very moment when personality slips away) and is therefore more vast and all-encompassing than the merely personal. In the juxtaposition of these two passages, the dichotomies of Western European and East Asian aesthetics are brought into stark relief. We should note, too, that Kafū stages a confrontation between the "voice of civilization"—the locomotive, symbol of Western technology and its brute power—and the singing of the insects, which becomes, all at once, a trope for nature, "Asia," and the frail and plaintive music of Japan.

Kafū was not the only Japanese to embrace a kind of musical *Nihon kaiki*, or "return to Japan," but over the following decades such figures came to represent a smaller and smaller share of the populace as Western or Westernized music continued its long but inexorable march toward transforming Japan's auditory culture into one dominated by European and American musical idioms.

The Meiji and Taishō writers who embraced Western music were not simply adding yet another lifestyle accoutrement to their experience of the modern. Instead, they were exposing themselves to radically different sonic articulations of affect and subjectivity. To the extent that they opened themselves or submitted to the influence of those articulations, their own affect and subjectivity were subtly altered. The rhythms and gestural qualities of Western music, so different from anything in the traditional Japanese musical repertoire, arguably left traces in the memories and writings of these cultural figures.

No fully satisfactory theory of the relationship between music and mind exists, but certain aspects of a theory articulated by Laird Addis, based on Susanne Langer's partially developed theory, are useful here:

> Passages of music are *isomorphic* with certain possible states of consciousness. While music may also be, almost surely is, isomorphic with other actual and possible events and states of affairs, because consciousness and sound have a profound ontological affinity with respect to time and because human nature is what it is, music is a quasi-natural *representation* of possible states of consciousness to human beings such that, at some level of awareness that is not ordinarily that of what one is

attending to, we are presented with those possible states of consciousness by music, that is, music *brings them to mind*, if not always to the conscious mind. Finally, certain subtle differences in both the intentions and especially the modes of states of consciousness that are *ineffable*, that is, cannot be captured in language, can be represented to us by music; where language fails, music can sometimes succeed in symbolizing to us the nuances of mood and other aspects of consciousness.[37]

Addis's theory is also, to my mind, incomplete in a number of respects: It is resolutely formal and philosophical, taking no account of music's physiological aspects (the changes it occasions in heartbeat, respiration, the subconscious tension in the vocal cords that arises "sympathetically" to changes in pitch, as well as the profoundly spatial and kinesthetic qualities of music that tie it to physical movement, that is, to gesture and dance) or its sociological and anthropological dimensions (the cultural learning that conditions our understanding of and emotional affinity to certain musical idioms over others, as well as the performance and listening contexts—ritual, commercial, and other—that determine the social meanings of music). I nonetheless agree with his contention that passages of music are isomorphic with states of consciousness. Addis suggests that this is so because sound and consciousness have an affinity because of a singular shared characteristic: both require *time* but not *change* in order to exist. This, however, I disagree with. The isomorphism of sound and consciousness, in my view, exists not because neither requires change in order to exist but because both actually *cannot* remain static and fixed. Both are in a constant state of evanescence. As Walter Ong pointed out, "There is no way to stop sound and have sound." In the same way, it is impossible to "stop consciousness" and "have consciousness." Forms of consciousness can be locked into various forms of representation (as can music), but those representations do not have the same nature as consciousness itself. Both sound and consciousness are arguably spatiotemporal[38] patternings of quanta (volume, emphasis, intensity) and qualia (color, timbre, emotion), patternings that, precisely because of their very *spatiotemporal* essence, cannot attain temporal fixity. This isomorphism or affinity is what allows sound (and especially music) to exert such singularly powerful effects on consciousness.[39]

So, to return to the triggering occasion of these speculations, what exactly did Western music contribute to the Meiji soundscape?

The major distinguishing feature of so-called Western classical music (which is generally understood as encompassing art music of the Baroque up to twentieth-century serialism) is its use of harmony. To the "horizontal" elements of melody and rhythm, which are almost universal, European art music added the systematic exploitation of harmony, which operates in both the vertical and horizontal dimensions. This did not happen overnight, or even really as a result of deliberate effort. Harmonic practice as it became formalized in the classical style of the eighteenth century became possible only because of the adoption of twelve-tone equal temperament tuning, which, by dividing the octave into twelve steps of equal frequency ratios (as opposed to "just intonation" tuning, in which notes are related by ratios of whole numbers),[40] allowed musical instruments of fixed tuning (such as the piano or harpsichord, as opposed to the violin or human voice) to modulate easily from one key to another. Harmony is vertical in that it involves the simultaneous sounding of multiple notes, but it also works horizontally through its rhythmic (micro) and structural (macro) functions. Although many other musical traditions incorporate sounds of different pitches sounded together contrapuntally or as a kind of protoharmony, only the European art tradition assigns to harmony the multitude of functions and uses that it does. This has had several consequences: Western art music is melodically a good deal less complex than the various musical idioms of Asia, which, free of the moorings of harmonic practice, have developed highly sophisticated modal and microtonal approaches to melody; it is also rhythmically less complex than many of the musical traditions of Africa and Asia. Furthermore, tonal harmony has tended to restrict the practice of musical improvisation in favor of through-composed "pieces" that are subject to differences of interpretation but that otherwise remain relatively static and fixed. Jazz music, which is arguably a hybrid tradition, is a major exception.

These limitations to melodic and rhythmic complexity were the price paid to erect a musical system in which harmony became the central organizing principle, one that created a bridge between the immediate pleasures of melody and rhythm and the larger structural organization of a movement or longer work. It also, for lack of a better term, afforded

European art music (and its folk and popular offshoots) a "fullness" and three-dimensionality rich with expressive possibilities. Those possibilities were exhaustively, and sometimes radically, explored by composers of the Romantic period, creating a harmonic syntax of affect and expressivity that, in addition to the political and economic forces involved, has arguably contributed to the worldwide penetration of music in the Western tonal idiom, especially popular forms such as rock, pop, and dance music.

Words will not suffice to describe the types of expressive effects made possible by this harmonic language; I must refer the reader to the music itself. But we can at least generalize that harmony renders its effects through the creation and subsequent resolution of tension. This is accomplished through chord progressions that wander away from a starting tonality and that eventually return after having explored a range of consonant and dissonant relationships. These effects occur over brief durations as the chords progress and, in long-form works, over longer intervals as the tonality modulates from one key to another. To those habituated to the harmonic conventions employed (that is, to anybody who grew up hearing such music and who isn't tone deaf), the tensions and resolutions created by chord progressions are felt quite viscerally and are often evocative of heightened states of emotional and often physical arousal. The *structural* functions of harmony in art music are generally more intellectual in nature and require more formal training to appreciate fully. In the hands of a skilled composer, melody, rhythm, harmony, and structure work together synergistically to generate the aesthetic effect of the composition, but harmony is the structural linchpin that holds these elements together.

There is no exact literary equivalent of harmony, but there are some approximate analogues. One possibility is the aesthetic ideal of *waka* poetics, *yojō* (余情, sometimes pronounced *yosei*), often translated somewhat fancifully as "overtones," the oblique or unstated implications of a verse, or the traces of affect that linger even after the verse has been read. Although there is a certain conceptual overlap (certainly in the translation "overtones," which, in the musical sense, are the acoustical basis of harmony), the analogy is tenuous, as *yojō* is most often based on allusion and cultural/historical context. The reverberations are generated between the words and the cultural knowledge that is brought to the work by the reader, whereas musical harmony is present in the composition itself, and quite obviously at that.[41] That said, since language can be only linear (words cannot, in any real sense, be blended or stacked on one another) such allusive and contextual resonance may be one of the few types available at the level of language.

Literary "harmony" (if we accept that such an analogy is even tenable) most likely operates at two levels: that of language and that of narrative. These may be likened to chord progressions and to structural harmony, respectively. The outlines of the latter are more immediately apparent. Narratological features such as those identified by Gérard Genette (order, frequency, duration, voice, and mood)[42] can be manipulated to create forms of tension and release, as well as structural patterning, similar to structural harmony. "Harmony" at the level of linguistic texture is more subtle and harder to analyze, but in addition to the type of allusive and contextual resonances just cited, we might invoke the notions of heteroglossia and dialogism articulated by Mikhail Bakhtin.

The literary genre that can best accommodate the sensibility inculcated by this type of music is, of course, the novel. The novel is commodious enough to support such architectonic structural ambitions and such a multiplicity of voices. We might conjecture that the literary artists who had most thoroughly internalized the conventions of Western classical music also wrote the fictions that were the most complex or articulated in regard to narrative structure and linguistic texture.

We can tentatively propose that this was often the case. The novelists who had actively embraced Western classical music—Ōgai, Kafū, Rohan—*tended* to operate outside or around the conventions of Japanese I-novel naturalism. The poets and critics such as Takuboku and Ueda Bin who embraced Western music were firmly modernist in their approach. The one proponent of naturalism in the group, Shimazaki Tōson, was—in his sociological ambitions, historical scope, and pose of objectivity—a good deal closer to European naturalism in spirit than were I-novelists like Tayama Katai.

Stephen Snyder has contended that despite Kafū's self-styled reputation as a nostalgic elegist for the lost traditions of Edo, he was in fact a literary modernist who was acutely conscious of narratological strategies and who produced texts that were playfully referential to their own fictionality and linguistic textures. His model in this endeavor was Mori Ōgai, who in his last major work in the novel genre, *Gan* (*The Wild Geese*, 1911–1913), plays an elaborate game of shifting narrative focalization and deliberate thwarting of readerly expectations. Snyder writes:

> The "clumsiness" of *Gan* is a purposeful attack on the machinery of narrative illusion, machinery Ōgai himself had been partially responsible for creating in modern Japanese fiction. But in creating this machinery, Ōgai never satisfies himself that its end result is a worthwhile one....
>
> Although its conclusion is essentially a negation, *Gan* is, in the context of the role Ōgai played in Kafū's development, a work of central significance. It points to the crucial linkage in Kafū's fiction between the topic of sexual desire and the techniques for manipulating readerly desire.[43]

The creation of readerly desire, as well as its thwarting, extension, and satisfaction, are understandably couched here in the terms of sexuality, but they could just as easily have been couched in the terms of tension and release, consonance (the satisfaction of expectations) and dissonance (the thwarting of expectations)—that is, in the language of harmony.

I am not suggesting that only those authors who openly embraced Western musical idioms created works that seemed to reflect the kinds of linguistic and narrative features that one might associate with a kind of literary "harmony." One need only think of Tanizaki Jun'ichirō, whose works were as intricately plotted and as richly textured in language as those of any other modern Japanese writer and yet whose flirtations with Western music were youthful, brief, and shallow. Nonetheless, Western music was still "in the air," an essential component of an array of Western cultural cargo that was entering the streams of discourse and experience in Japan at the time.

The cultural implications of Western tonal practice extend beyond the realm of literary-aesthetic practices, however. As Attali illustrates through one example after another, music prefigures political and economic formations and also represents the ways in which society channels sacrificial violence. He argues that harmony was originally understood, in both Greece and China, in its relation with nature:

> The scale is the incarnation of the harmony between heaven and earth, the isomorphism of all representations: the bridge between the order of the Gods (ritual) and earthly order (the simulacrum).... This explains

the fundamental political importance of music as a demonstration that an ideal order, the true image offered by elemental religion, is possible.[44]

This naturalistic conception of harmony began to be replaced in the late eighteenth century by a rationalist and quasi-scientific conception. The representation of order imposed on noise through the application of rationalized principles became the linchpin of a similar ideology in the social sphere, yet another "isomorphism of all representations":

> Thus in the eighteenth century, reason replaced natural order and appropriated harmony as a tool for power, as proof of the link between well-being and science. To those who availed themselves of it, music made harmony audible. It made people believe in the legitimacy of the existing order: how could an order that brought such wonderful music into the world not be the one desired by God and required by science? ... An ideology of scientific harmony thus imposes itself, the mask of a hierarchical organization from which dissonances (conflicts and struggles) are forbidden, unless they are merely marginal and highlight the quality of the channelizing order.[45]

Attali points out that the practice of music legitimated the prevailing order in countless other ways: the visible power relations of conductor, soloist, and orchestra, for example, as well as the ways in which music became commodified as an abstract representation. "This idea of the exchangeability of music is disruptive, because it places music in the context of abstract, generalized exchange, and consequently of money."[46]

The political and economic power of music is thus deployed across multiple vectors: the organized sounds themselves, the aesthetic and social rhetorics that attend to the sounds, the social formations that come into being around the performance and reception of those sounds, as well as the rights apportioned by law to composers, performers, publishing companies, and the like.

The acceptance and absorption of Western music in Japan was temporarily slowed in the 1930s and 1940s as domestic society fell more firmly in the grip of militarism and nationalism and as Japan grew more geopolitically isolated. The backlash against foreign music came from both the government and the public. In 1934, foreigners other than Germans and

Italians were banned from performing in Japan, and in 1937, all foreign music other than German and Italian music was banned.[47] Most of the more zealous patriots wanted nothing to do with music from *any* foreign country. To an age like ours that has been conditioned to believe that art and culture are next to powerless, these may seem like excessive measures. But given what the nationalists hoped to achieve, the banning of foreign music was remarkably astute.

The bureaucratically mandated adoption of Western music in the Meiji period had served as an expedient. In order to recreate Western political and economic structures, it proved useful to embrace Western music, to channelize noise and political violence in the same ways. The harmonic conventions of the Western tradition were put in the service of ideological ends very similar to those they had served in early modern and Enlightenment Europe. But in the long run, the wholesale displacement of Japanese music by Western music in the national educational curriculum proved to be a form of cultural suicide, one from which Japanese musical culture never fully recovered. Japanese music retreated into the closed world of the *iemoto* system (a monopolized lineage of licensed teachers) and the slightly more open world of hobbyists and enthusiasts. While vestiges of it remained in popular song, it ceased to be a shared musical idiom. By the time the authorities tried to reverse that trend as Japan descended into war, it was already, in a sense, too late. Even though live performances of certain kinds of music were banned, by the late 1930s a vast number of recordings of every type of foreign music had already been imported into and disseminated throughout Japan. And even if it hadn't been too late, the defeat in war and subsequent American occupation completed the process of rendering Japanese musical idioms alien on their native soil. Japanese music had become an Other within, noise from an irretrievable past.

3

THE GRAIN IN THE GROOVE

Inscribed Voices, Echoed Temporalities

ARCHIVED SOUND

Thomas Edison (1847–1931) submitted the patent for his phonograph, or "Speaking Machine," on December 24, 1877, and the patent was granted on February 19, 1878. Edison's device, coming two years after Alexander Graham Bell's successful transmission of the human voice, was not the first attempt at creating a mechanism to reproduce sound. Neither was it the first device to operate on the principle of "writing" sound waves on a surface. In 1857 Édouard-Léon Scott de Martinville (1817–1879), a French amateur inventor, had invented a device called the phonoautograph that inscribed sound vibrations onto lamp-blacked paper. The device served the limited use of measuring and analyzing sound, but it could not *reproduce* it, whereas Edison's tinfoil cylindrical phonograph could.

Although the phonograph later came to be used primarily as a medium for musical entertainment, Edison's initial conception (belied clearly enough by the "Speaking Machine" name he gave it in his patent application) was that it would serve as a tool for business dictation and perhaps also be used in various forms of speech and language training.[1]

According to Kurata Yoshihiro, word of the device first reached Japan in the form of an article published on February 28, 1877, in the *Yomiuri shinbun*'s biweekly science magazine, *Manabi no akatsuki* (*Dawn of Learning*). Another article appeared a year and a half later, in the July 16, 1878, edition of *Bungaku zasshi,* published by Dōjinsha, this time a paraphrase by Kōzu Senzaburō of a notice in *Harper's Weekly*.[2] More thorough descriptions of the device's exact manner of operation were soon forthcoming. The October 1878 issue of *Gakugei shirin,* published by Tokyo University, devoted an eighteen-page spread with diagrams explaining how it worked. This was followed in 1880 by a ninety-two-page book, *Kinsei ni daihatsumei: Denwaki-sogenki* (Two major modern inventions: The telephone and phonograph).[3]

The first public display of the phonograph in Japan occurred on March 28, 1879, at the Tōkyō Shōhō Kaigijō in Kobiki-chō. That particular device had been built by the Scottish physicist and engineer James Alfred Ewing (1855–1935). He had arrived in Japan the previous September and built his prototype on the basis of descriptions of Edison's device. Ewing was working at the time as a professor of mechanical engineering in the newly established science and engineering faculty (*rigakubu*) of Tokyo Imperial University, where he also, significantly, built Japan's first seismograph. Ewing gave the presentation in English with interpretation provided by the *yōgaku* (Western studies) scholar Yano Jirō (1845–1906) and the agriculturalist Tsuda Sen (1837–1908). Ewing recorded a song in English while one of the Japanese recorded a *hitotsutose-bushi* folk song, and both were played back successfully. Fukuchi Gen'ichirō (1841–1906, also known as Fukuchi Ōchi), president of the *Tōkyō nichinichi shinbun,* stepped up and shouted into the horn: "If this device is perfected, newspapermen are in trouble" (*Konna kikai ga dekiru to shinbunya wa komaru*), which was met with laughter by the large number of assembled newspapermen.[4]

In a write-up of the demonstration, the *Asahi shinbun* described it as "a device that stores away words" (*kotoba o shimatte oku kikai*). The *Tōkyō nichinichi shinbun,* in far more breathless terms, called it a device that "can store away people's words and then emit them 10 million *ri* away or a thousand years later."[5]

As these notices make clear, the first Japanese to experience the phonograph conceived of it, as Edison himself had, as a device intended primarily to store and reproduce spoken language. History and the market would later demonstrate that recorded music would be the far more popular and profitable use of the phonograph, but that was still many years in the offing.[6] The rhetoric of the *Tōkyō nichinichi* article in particular—redolent as it is with the numerical hyperbole of classical Chinese—makes clear that the first Japanese to encounter the device understood well that the new technology had erased all temporal and spatial barriers to the propagation of the spoken word.[7] Just as important to a culture whose ideas of legitimacy had largely been conditioned by the textual and historical fetishes of the Confucian cultural sphere, the spoken word had now become materialized, textualized, and *archivable*. Thus, following these notions to their logical conclusion, recorded speech was worthy of study as a historical text and/or artifact. As Lewis Mumford noted, the photograph, moving picture, and phonograph

> gave modern civilization a direct sense of the past and a more accurate perception of its memorials than any other civilization had, in all probability, had. Not alone did they make the past more immediate: they made the present more historic by narrowing the lapse of time between the actual events themselves and their concrete record.[8]

At the same time, the phonograph was a propitious medium for the recording and dissemination of Japan's numerous traditions of oral narrative. It was thus a medium through which the tension between orality and literacy could in one sense be reconciled even as it created new tensions among the "real," the auratic, and the mechanically reproduced.

Over the next decade, Edison's design was significantly improved, although most of the improvements were made not by Edison himself—he was immersed simultaneously in a host of other projects—but by Alexander Graham Bell who, along with his apprentice Charles Sumner Tainter (1854–1940), hit on the idea of replacing Edison's tinfoil cylinder with a wax cylinder, resulting in a new device they dubbed the "graphophone," and by the German American inventor Emile Berliner (1851–1929), who in 1888 developed a method of recording using the now-familiar disc, albeit one made out of hard rubber. In 1895 these were replaced by a shellac compound, which remained the standard material for disc recordings until early experiments with vinyl (originally intended only for radio play) in the 1930s.[9]

In January 1889, ten years after its first unveiling in Japan, a formal demonstration of the principles and functioning of Bell and Tainter's graphophone was arranged by Inoue Kaoru (1836–1915) at the Rokumeikan, to an audience of more than two hundred notables, including Itō Hirobumi (1841–1909), Moriari Arinori (1847–1889), Enomoto Takeaki (1836–1908), and, significantly, Maejima Hisoka, who at the time was deputy minister of communications.

The demonstration consisted of the playback of a recording made in Washington, D.C., by Japan's ambassador to the United States, Mutsu Munemitsu (1844–1897). In the recording he is reported to have said, "I hereby introduce this machine. I believe this machine promises to be extremely useful and so request that every effort be made to make it known throughout Japan."[10] The assembled dignitaries were shocked; those who knew Ambassador Mutsu attested that the voice was in fact his.

On February 4, 1889, the device was introduced to the Meiji emperor and the imperial family. In 1890, Edison presented the latest electric motor–driven model of his Edison Phonograph Company's phonograph, which sold for $100 at the time (approximately $2,600 in 2017 dollars). Edison sent another new model in 1903, and the following year the Meiji emperor composed the following verses:

ima koko ni	Is there a person
hito no iru ka to	here in front of me now?
omou made	I think
kometaru koe no	the voice inside the box
sayaka naru kana	is that clear.
sue made mo	How endless
kikamahoshiki o	my desire to listen.
takuwaeshi	The stored voices
koe no tayuru ga	fade away.
oshiku mo aru kana	I long to hear them again.

It's reported the Meiji emperor liked to listen to *Satsuma biwa* recordings at night before going to sleep.[11]

Sound-recording devices were given a number of different names in Japanese by the competing newspapers, including *soonki* (蘇音機, "sound-reviving machine"), *sogenki* (蘇言機, "speech-reviving machine"), *shagenki* (写言機, "speech-tracing machine"), and *satsuonki* (撮音機, "sound-capturing machine"). As these names suggest, the Japanese originally conceived of the devices as the aural equivalent of photography, which had been introduced to Japan at the end of the Tokugawa shogunate (1603–1868). The *Tokyo nichinichi shinbun*, once again even more enthusiastic than its competitors in its reception of the new technology, wrote: "The day before yesterday was truly an auspicious day. Two of the essentials of civilization, shorthand and the graphone [sic], were tested and demonstrated their great effectiveness, much to the astonishment of all assembled."[12] The technology was conceived, along the lines that Edison had imagined, as being used for practical tasks, including dictation, and thus was seen as an advance on shorthand. The idea that the phonograph is a machine that "writes" sound is of course explicit in the etymology of the device's English name. As James Lastra has elucidated, inscription and simulation were the two master tropes by which emerging technologies in the late nineteenth century came to be understood.[13]

Although the phonograph left a considerable impression on the dignitaries assembled for this demonstration, another year passed before members of the general public had an opportunity to see and hear one. The first semipublic demonstration took place in Osaka at the Imamiya Commerce Club in January 1890. This first open public demonstration was a recording of brief performances by famous kabuki actors, including Ichikawa Danjūrō IX (1874–1903), probably the most esteemed entertainer in all of Japan at the time. Prior notice of the demonstration—including the vital fact that attendees would be able to hear Danjūrō's voice (a rare opportunity given that he never performed in the Kansai region)—was carried for several days in the local newspapers and ensured a very sizable turnout. A similar demonstration took place in Kyoto the following month. The third city in Japan where a public demonstration of the phonograph was held was Shizuoka, in March.

Finally, in June 1890, Tokyo became the fourth Japanese city to hold a public demonstration of the new device. The event took place at the Ōzan Pavilion, situated in Asakusa's Kannon-dō compound. A notice advertising the demonstration described the phonograph as a "device that speaks by himself" (the oddness of my translation may be clarified by reference to the original Japanese: *hitori de mono o iu kikai*). The advertisement used as one of its selling points the machine's ability to reproduce a speaker's *kowairo*, a word that has no exact English equivalent but broadly refers to vocal quality, timbre, texture, and tone. This all-important quality of *kowairo* was echoed in the description of the event recorded by the writer Ōtei Kinshō:

> How very interesting it was. You press your ear against a tube and next thing you know you hear the exact voices [*kowairo*] of Danjūrō and Kikugorō. Your heart is lifted and your ears are pleased by the strains of "Sumōjinku," "Katsubore," and "Harusame." With your eyes you look at the flowers in the garden, but in your ears you find yourself at the theater or banquet hall.[14]

We see here an early listener's response to the recording medium's capacity to both reproduce the materiality of sound, particularly the human voice, and "transport" listeners to another, imagined, space. This is a phenomenon that we take so much for granted today as to barely notice it, but recorded sound made it possible for the first time to experience such a disjunction between one's visual and auditory environments.

Another report, from the *Jiji shinbun*, explains that the device was installed in order to revive flagging visitor interest:

> When the Ōzan Pavilion first opened, there was no end to the customers who were drawn in wanting to see the rare and unusual. It had a good reputation, but once most of the people in the capital had visited, nobody felt like going again. It became quite desolate inside the pavilion, but not surprisingly, the park director—who doesn't miss a thing when it comes to driving foot traffic—has placed Edison's invention, the phonograph, in the pavilion, and the number of visitors has increased. Since recordings of the voices of ordinary people would lack impact, he called on the actors, who fortunately happened to be touring at the nearby Ichimuraza, to record themselves with the same voices they would use on stage [*butai no koe sonomama ni fukikomaseta*] some of the most famous parts of *Ehon Taikōki—Amagasaki*, with Kikugorō as Jūjirō, Sadanji as Mitsuhide, and Jusaburō as Satsuki. The ramblings of a supremely crafty man, the admonitions of a kindhearted mother, the remonstrations of a chaste woman . . . they all create the impression that if you close your eyes and listen as they reverberate throughout the pavilion, you might believe that the actors were dressed up in costume right in front of you. How delightful![15]

The rhetoric of fidelity evident in this and the previous quotation should be taken with a grain of salt. When listening to these phonograph and "graphophone" recordings today, with their low volume, overwhelming noise, and narrow band of reproduced frequencies, we have trouble even making out what the people are saying, much less being fooled into thinking that they're right in front of us.[16] The criteria for what counts as high-fidelity reproduction have changed dramatically in pace with technological advances, but judging from these descriptions, the recordings of the time were at least good enough to help identify the speaker.

The use of the term *kowairo* (which is also the word used for vocal impersonation and mimicry) and the description *hitori de mono o iu kikai* seem in a strange way to anthropomorphize the device. They create the impression, however subtle, that the device is less an impersonal medium than a kind of impersonator, one that somehow hears, remembers, and mimics rather than records and reproduces. As we saw in chapter 1, when the telephone was first introduced to Tokyo in 1890, one of the barriers to its widespread adoption, in addition to the prohibitive cost, was the rumor that cholera, which was epidemic at that time, could be transmitted through the telephone.[17] What seems to be at work in these early imaginings around 1890 is that auditory media were like organic entities, almost alive.

What I wish to emphasize here, however, is the degree to which the phonograph's earliest public demonstrations relied on the kabuki performance tradition, and especially the recognizability of its stars' voices, in order to validate the claims being made for it. In the prerecording age, kabuki stars' voices were among, or perhaps even the *only* voices that one could expect to be widely recognized. The only possible competition came from *yose* entertainers, but it is difficult to think of many who combined the recognizability and ability to draw an audience of kabuki stars like Danjūrō, Kikugorō, or Sadanji. In a very real sense, then, kabuki helped establish the phonograph in the public imagination.

RECORDING IN JAPAN

In 1891, the first domestically produced phonograph was claimed to have been built in Okazaki, Aichi Prefecture, by Chūjō Yūjirō, a maker of timepieces and medical devices. He was followed a year later by the publisher Hasegawa Takejirō (1853–1938), who was well known for his *chirimen*, or crepe-paper books on Japanese subjects written in European languages, which were intended for expatriates in Japan as well as for export. Hasegawa had been importing phonographs into Japan since 1889 in partnership with an American entrepreneur, but with the help of an engineer named Obana Sen'ichi, he began producing his own (unaware that Chūjō had already succeeded in doing so) and selling them for 70 yen each.[18]

The first dedicated phonograph dealership, Sankōdō, was opened in Asakusa in 1899 by the brothers Matsumoto Takeichirō and Matsumoto Saburō, along with Katayama Sen (1859–1933), a prominent socialist who in 1922 cofounded the Japan Communist Party, and Yokoyama Shin'ichirō, both of whom helped the Matsumoto brothers import foreign-made records. Katayama and Yokoyama left the partnership when the Matsumotos joined forces with the F. W. Horn Trading Company[19] based in Yokohama. In addition to selling imported cylinders, Sankōdō recorded Japanese traditional music onto wax cylinders and sold those as well.

The U.S.-based Columbia Phonograph Company began selling gramophone discs in 1902, which the watch and jewelry purveyor Tenshōdō began importing and retailing in 1903. The new, improved device that played these discs was given a new name, *shaseiki* 写声機, accompanied by a *rubi* reading of *grahofuon* グラホフォン, or graphophone. The new discs were called *heienban* 平円盤, or simply just *jisuku* ジスク.

Sankōdō began importing discs soon after Tenshōdō, and the competition between the two importer/retailers accelerated the diffusion of the medium. Gramophones and discs were still extremely expensive, with the latter retailing for anywhere between 1 yen, 75 sen, to 5 yen each (at a time when an *ekiben* [station lunchbox] sold for 15 sen).

The expansion of the market for recordings in Japan continued unabated until the Russo-Japanese War, which, despite being a military victory for Japan, had grim consequences for Japan's economy. Unlike the Treaty of Shimonoseki, which ended the first Sino-Japanese War, the Treaty of Portsmouth precluded any demands of indemnity. The war had been financed with debt incurred to lenders in the United States and United Kingdom, and taxes had to be maintained at wartime levels in order to service that debt. Because recordings were still expensive enough to count as luxury items, the business bottomed out until the only dealers left in Tokyo were Tenshōdō and Jūjiya, a bible store in

Ginza that had branched out into Western musical instruments and then recordings.

The market for recordings gradually recovered. In 1907 F. W. Horn and Matsumoto Takeichirō (there is little mention of his brother Saburō beyond the original founding of the firm) decided to establish their own record company, Nichibei Chikuonki Kabushiki Kaisha (Japan-America Gramophone, Inc.). Matsumoto, however, died before the corporation was registered on October 31, 1907. The board of directors was composed of F. W. Horn, five of his employees (four of whom were American and only one of whom was Japanese), and an American vice president of Tokyo Electric. The firm was financed at first by the American directors, with an initial capitalization of 100,000 yen and a stock price of 100 yen.[20] It took another two years before the company could complete its factory and begin sending records to market. In 1910 Nichibei Chikuonki merged with Beikoku Chikuonki Shōkai (America Gramophone Trading), which had been in existence for a number of years and of which Horn was the sole proprietor, in order to form Nihon Chikuonki Shōkai (Japan Gramophone Trading, hereafter referred to as Nicchiku[21]).

Sound recordings were quickly becoming valuable commodities, and the recording business grew more lucrative with time, even though under the 1899 Copyright Act the copyright status of sound recordings was still vague.[22] This encouraged the proliferation of producers that simply made pirated copies of other companies' recordings and sold them at lower prices. Because this practice was technically not illegal at the time, it forced record companies to try to differentiate their products from those products' pirated copies. Accordingly, two-sided records produced in Germany by Lyrophone had been imported into Japan since 1912. Tōkyō Chikuonki (Tokyo Gramophone) began producing two-sided records in 1914, and Horn's Nicchiku followed suit shortly thereafter. The pirate record companies responded by lowering the prices by a third on their already cheaper, single-sided records.[23]

TŌCHŪKEN KUMOEMON

Tōchūken Kumoemon (1873–1916; his real name was either Okamoto Minekichi or Yamamoto Kōzō) was the most popular *naniwabushi* recitalist of the late Meiji (1868–1912) and early Taishō (1912–1926) periods, a time when *naniwabushi* was the most popular form of mass entertainment in Japan. This was not a coincidence, because Kumoemon helped transform *naniwabushi* into a cultural craze and, even more important, into a commodity. He did not do this single-handedly, however. Another powerful force driving *naniwabushi*'s rise was its promotion by Miyazaki Tōten (1871–1922) and the nationalist Gen'yōsha secret society, which saw in it a powerful vehicle to foster a rebirth of *bushidō* values and garner public support for the Russo-Japanese War of 1904–1905. Before this, in 1902, Miyazaki had become Kumoemon's apprentice, taking the artistic name Tōchūken Ushiemon and working professionally for six or seven years.[24]

Naniwabushi performances feature a single chanter (called a *rōkyokushi*) performing a mixture of improvised melodies (*fushi*) and spoken narrative (*kotoba* or *tanka* 啖呵, lit., "caustic words") accompanied by a shamisen player (*kyokushi*), who also provides periodic verbal interjections (*kakegoe*) to help keep time and offer encouragement.

As this indicates, *naniwabushi* as a form lent itself readily to the creation of a star culture. Because so much of the melodic content is improvised, the differences among performers go beyond vocal characteristics, singing skill, and personal presence, and a *rōkyokushi* is also an improvisational composer whose melodic imagination is an integral component of his identity.

Kumoemon possessed all the qualities necessary for superstardom in the *naniwabushi* world: a distinctive voice, exquisite performance skill, melodic imagination, striking appearance, and a personal biography that gave his star persona depth and resonance. Even though *naniwabushi* narratives tended to be ideologically conservative stories of loyalty and duty, stories that were enlisted to encourage and sustain the climate of militarism that eventually plunged Japan into colonial adventure and war across East Asia and the Pacific, the affective tone of *naniwabushi* was plaintive and its audience was working class, leading some to dub it the "Japanese blues."

During the Meiji period, *naniwabushi* evolved from street performance to one of the arts performed in the *yose*, small variety performance halls that generally seated about a hundred people.[25] Kumoemon was the first to perform in larger, much more prestigious venues: His first breakthrough success was a run at the Hongō-za in 1907, but his popularity arguably reached its pinnacle in July 1912, when he first performed at the Kabuki-za, the crown jewel of theaters, where only one other non-kabuki actor had ever performed before.[26]

AN OUTLINE OF COPYRIGHT HISTORY IN MODERN JAPAN

During the middle of the seventeenth century, the bookstore guilds (*hon'ya nakama*) in Kyoto and Osaka were given authority by the Tokugawa shogunate to control printing and publishing within their respective domains. The earliest recorded incidences of printing piracy occurred in the late seventeenth century, with bunraku puppet plays being the source texts most often targeted. The bookstore guild in Edo was officially recognized later, in 1721, and provided with a *nakama ginmi* (guild examiner) by the Edo government *bugyō* (magistrate). The *nakama ginmi* prosecuted pirate editions.[27]

The arrival of Commodore Perry's fleet in 1853 and subsequent threats of armed intervention forced the shogunate to sign a series of unequal "treaties of amity" with the United States and then with Great Britain, the Netherlands, and Russia, which in turn led to unequal commercial treaties with all four nations in 1858 and 1859. These treaties included trade terms that were profoundly disadvantageous to Japan and conferred "consular jurisdiction" (or extraterritoriality) to all citizens of those nations on Japanese soil. In subsequent years, the shogunate, and then the Meiji government, signed similar treaties with eleven more European countries.[28]

Fukuzawa Yukichi is credited with introducing the Western concept of copyright to Japan in 1868 in his *Seiyō jijō gaihen* (Conditions in the West, supplementary volume) with the word "copyright" translated as *zōhan no menkyo* (license to print).[29] Fukuzawa embraced the concept with such enthusiasm that after the first copyright law was passed, he pressed lawsuits against unauthorized reproductions of his own works with such tireless zeal that the statute was later amended to deter excessive use (indeed, abuse) of the law. In addition to these lawsuits, he took out newspaper advertisements censuring the offending publishers.[30]

Fukuzawa was influenced by the Anglo-American notion of copyright, which dates back to the eighteenth century and the efforts of the printing guild known as the Stationers' Company. This tradition differed somewhat from what had developed in France and Belgium, which, as the name *droit d'auteur* (right of the author) suggests, was oriented toward the proprietary and moral rights of authors, rather than "copyright" per se, which emphasized the proprietary rights of publishers.

The first approximation of a copyright law, the Shuppan jōrei (Publishing Statute), appeared in 1869 and included protections against reproduction as well as provisions for government censorship. Masuda Satoshi points out, however, that *hanken* (copyright or, literally, "printing rights") were not explicitly identified until the revision of the law in 1875.[31] Both the original law and the revision recognized the "moral right" of authors in addition to the economic interests of publishers, while the 1875 revision included musical works (that is, printed sheet music) under the terms of protection. In 1876 the Shashin hanken jōrei (Photo Copyright Statute) extended copyright protection to photographs for a term of five years. In 1887, the Hanken jōrei (Copyright Statute) for printed works, the Kyakuhon gakufu jōrei (Script and Music Statute) for dramatic scripts and printed music, and the Shashin jōrei (Photograph Statute) for photographs replaced these laws. These three statutes were combined without major alteration into the single Hankenhō (Copyright Law), in 1893.

Before this, in 1882, the Meiji government began negotiating with its treaty partners to eliminate some of the more egregious conditions of the unequal treaties, beginning with extraterritoriality. In 1885 Kurokawa Seiichirō (1849–1909), a councillor with the Japanese legation in Italy, was sent to Bern, Switzerland, to attend the Berne Conference on copyright. The Berne Convention for the Protection of Literary and Artistic Works was signed by the original signatories in 1886 and made effective in 1887. Kurokawa sent a detailed report on the agreement in late 1886 to Inoue Kaoru, minister for home affairs. Japan did not immediately accede to the convention but undoubtedly made the 1887 revisions just cited under the convention's influence.

In July 1894 the Treaty of Commerce and Navigation Between Great Britain and Japan was signed, with terms significantly more favorable to Japan than previous treaties had been, except for the following proviso: "3. The Japanese Government undertakes, before the cessation of British Consular jurisdiction in Japan, to join the International Conventions for the Protection of Industrial Property and Copyright."[32]

Acceding to the Berne Convention seemed like a small price to pay for eliminating the far more humiliating concession of extraterritoriality. Mizuno Rentarō (1868–1949) was dispatched to Europe to study its copyright systems. He wrote: "[N]ow in Europe all the countries which are considered civilized acceded to the convention. With those countries Japan will associate herself next year. While it will be disadvantageous, it will be an honor for us."[33]

The most disadvantageous elements to Japan were: provision 5, which conferred translation copyright protection for ten years; provision 7, which allowed writers and publishers to prohibit translations of their press articles; and provision 9, which granted the same protection to authors of dramatic and musical works. The Columbia- and Yale-educated legislator and legal scholar Hatoyama Kazuo (1856–1911) expressed his profound misgivings about the convention, which, he argued, would unfairly impede the flow of the signatory nations' much-needed knowledge to Japan. He bolstered this argument by holding up the example of the United States (which was not a signatory to the convention), where publishers reprinted British books without permission, sold them for much cheaper than the originals, and even exported them back to Great Britain, where they undercut the original editions.[34]

Mizuno's draft of the Copyright Act was most heavily influenced by the German Literary Copyright Act and the Belgian Droit d'auteur.[35] The law was enacted in 1899 and Japan acceded to the Berne Convention that same year. The 1899 Copyright Act was the statute of reference during the Kumoemon case.

This brief history alerts us to the fact that the copyright system adopted by Japan in the late nineteenth century was largely the product of a transnational (specifically, European) consensus that didn't take local conditions into account. The limitations on translation rights were an especially bitter pill for Japan to swallow. That said, the basic notion of unauthorized reproduction (that is, piracy) had been familiar to Japanese publishers and authorities since at least the late seventeenth century.

THE KUMOEMON CASE

In his book *Noise: The Political Economy of Music*, Jacques Attali notes,

> Actually, the definitive birth of the star took place when popular music entered the field of the commodity. The evolution of the star is what really developed the economy of representation and necessitated a guarantee of remuneration, an exchange-value, for popular production, which had been overlooked by the creators of the copyright.[36]

It was in this context of intense competition among record companies and rampant piracy that the Kumoemon record case (Kumoemon onpu jiken)[37] unfolded. In December 1911 a German trading merchant named Richard Werdermann bet heavily on Kumoemon's ability to sell records, and he paid Kumoemon 15,000 yen (at a time when the average skilled worker's daily wage was around 1.5 yen) for the exclusive right to sell a series of five records of Kumoemon's performances.[38] This was a remarkable sum, but its extravagance was mitigated by the fact that Werdermann had 72,000 copies of the records pressed under the Lyrophone Record label, which returned a royalty of about 21 sen per record, or only 5.5 percent of the retail price of 3 yen, 80 sen, per record charged by Werdermann's partner in the enterprise, Sankōdō. A recording team came to Tokyo from Germany to make the recording in Sankōdō's studio. They then took the master discs back to Germany, where copies were pressed and then reimported to Japan.[39] The records were released in May 1912.

Werdermann was surprised to learn, however, that his ideas of copyright were at odds with both his performer's and those of the pirate record companies that had sprung up in Japan in the absence of any clear copyright laws. First, Tōkyō Onpu Kaisha, one of the pirate record companies, released 1,800 copies of these recordings in late June at the cut-rate price of 1 yen per record. Second, Kumoemon turned right around and in July made a series of recordings for Nicchiku, thereby violating what

Werdermann considered the exclusivity of their agreement. Nicchiku paid Kumoemon 10,000 yen for that performance and sold the resulting records for 1 yen, 50 sen each, thereby also undercutting the more expensive Lyrophone releases. Werdermann promptly sued both Tōkyō Onpu Kaisha and Nicchiku. The suit against Nicchiku was settled out of court.[40]

Werdermann claimed copyright infringement and asked Tōkyō Onpu Kaisha for 13,996 yen in damages. Nomi Yoshihisa, a legal scholar, makes a number of important points about this case: First, the copyright law was ambiguous regarding the protected status of performances. The relevant clause (Copyright Act, Article 1, Clause 1.2) reads as follows: "The right to reproduce writings, lectures, drawings, engravings/sculptures, models, photographs, and other literary, scholarly, or artistic works resides with their author." Because musical performances were not explicitly protected, Werdermann decided to sue on the basis of a copyright infringement of the sourcebooks (*tanehon*) of the reproduced pieces. This was immediately problematic because the reproductions were not printed sourcebooks but *recordings* of the performances of those sourcebooks.

Second, Werdermann filed the lawsuit as a private action, in other words, solely on behalf of himself and not on behalf of himself and Sankōdō and/or Kumoemon. This made it difficult to determine the exact scope of the damages incurred.

Despite these technical issues, Werdermann won the case in the Tokyo District Court on November 11, 1912. The court justified its decision as follows:

> The Copyright Act identifies which finished works are protected by copyright; Article 1, Clause 1 of the act makes clear that it applies broadly to "mental/spiritual creations" [*seishinteki sōzōbutsu*] of a literary, scholarly, or artistic nature. Moreover, it goes without saying that as civilization advances and knowledge grows day by day and month by month, providing us ineluctably with new ideas and materials, the applicable scope of the law must expand along with it. Works of an "artistic nature" are those in which we detect an artistic conception that then arises within our own senses. This interpretation applies especially to musical works, which express a musical intention—in other words, original artistic products that are constituted by melodies or tunes. It makes no difference whether the composition is an arrangement of sounds produced by a

musical instrument or a human voice. It thus follows that the presence of the expression of a unique musical intent is constitutive of a musical work. In addition, recent developments in the production of mechanical musical instruments have resulted in the material continuity of one-time musical lectures, and the right of reproduction of such must be protected as a matter of course. . . . Thus we cannot avoid the conclusion that mechanical reproduction of such musical lectures without the consent of the author constitutes an infringement of copyright.[41]

"Mechanical musical instruments" here is a reference to the gramophone. Although the district court ruled in Werdermann's favor, the monetary award was only 2,000 yen, or around one-seventh of what he had asked for.

Legal opinion on the decision was sharply divided. One of the most vociferous dissents came from the patent lawyer Araki Toratarō (1865–?), who argued in the January 20, 1913, issue (no. 837) of the *Hōritsu shinbun* (Legal news) that although written musical compositions were protected by the copyright laws, performances were not. But even if they were, Kumoemon's performance, as an iteration of a canonical work in a performance *tradition*, could not count as original, even if Kumoemon's voice and melodic improvisations were different from those of other *naniwa-bushi* performers.

Araki begins his attack by claiming that the district court's decision had overstepped its bounds because it issued a ruling on Kumoemon's claim to copyright when in fact the suit was filed by Richard Werdermann. This was a valid point, and the ambiguity regarding whose interests were actually at stake persisted all through the case and its appeals.

Beyond this, the German-trained Araki uses philosophical questions of aesthetics to assail the decision. His argument is both complex and very much at odds with our contemporary normative conceptions of what constitutes art and intellectual property:

Kunst—that is, "arts and crafts" [*gigei*], the fruits that arise from human beings' effort and skill, take two forms: the plastic arts (the arts of painting, sculpture, cuisine, swimming [*sic*], etc.) and the acoustic arts (singing, music). When we translate *Kunst* or "art" as *bijutsu*, we include music in that definition, but we don't stop to consider that our superficial inquiry into the subject has not yet decided that question. In every country, musicians and fine artists make a distinction between the two, and in our country as well, they are recognized as distinct and independent; that there are separate academies for fine arts and music exemplifies this.

Art [*bijutsu*] refers to concrete, tangible objects that are beautified by human effort and skill, not to intangible forms that convey to us aesthetic concepts. Thus, even though we add the character *bi* [beautiful] to numerous items like *bion* [beautiful sound] and *bishoku* [delicious food], that doesn't mean it's possible to call everything that gives rise to aesthetic concepts "art." In the present case, calling Kumoemon's voice "art" because it is beautiful would be laughably foolish. In particular, crafts and fine arts are products of artifice [*jin'iteki*] and thus the complete opposite of something that occurs naturally [*tennenteki na mono*]. Mount Fuji may possess surpassing beauty, but that doesn't make it art. The exquisiteness of Kumoemon's voice is a natural endowment, not a product of human agency.

...

It is only when you have an authored work—that is, original thought and its products—that you can establish copyright. Has Kumoemon engaged in musical authorship, written a score, or composed anything? No, his authorship of original music is recognized only in the imaginations of the presiding judges.[42]

Araki's argument is rooted in two sets of assumptions, one clearly articulated and the other unspoken. The first, relating to *Kunst* as tangible result of aesthetic skill and labor, is a product of Western aesthetic and philosophical assumptions rooted in nineteenth-century Romanticism and still very much operative at this time in both Japan and the West. Araki's unwillingness to include Kumoemon's artistry in this sanctified realm is, however, a product of the second set of assumptions, based on an understanding of Japanese performing arts as traditions on which individual performers can lay no claims of ownership.

Masuda Satoshi contends that issues of translation were at work as well. The original French text of the Berne Convention, which provided the basis for much of the final version of the 1899 Copyright Act, refers to "production du domaine littéraire, scientifique ou artistique," with this last word rendered as *bijutsu* in the Japanese statute. According to Sasaki Ken'ichi, the term *bijutsu* carried the same meaning in 1899 (when the act was ratified) as the Japanese term *geijutsu* carries today—in other words, it applied to all the arts, including music. According to Masuda and Sasaki, the meaning of *bijutsu* had already begun to narrow by the Taishō period, thus creating legal confusion.[43] Araki argues, however, that his contemporaries (in 1913) included music in the domain of *bijutsu* and that they were mistaken in doing so. Given the timing of the appearance of his article at the beginning of the Taishō period, we might speculate that he even contributed to the word's semantic shift.

The defendants appealed, lost again in appellate court on December 9, 1913, appealed again, and the case went to the Supreme Court of Judicature (Daishin'in), where the lower courts' decision was ultimately reversed on July 16, 1914. This became a landmark (and much-criticized) case in the annals of Japanese copyright law, with the Supreme Court ruling that improvised material—as a *naniwabushi* recital was—lacks any creative intention on the part of the performer and is expressed in a way that prevents its repeated perception.

Nomi breaks down the Supreme Court's decision into three parts. The first part was an attempt to define exactly which kinds of works fell under copyright protection and which did not. The decision acknowledges that making phonographic recordings of a musical work counts as an infringement of copyright because the reproduced work allows one to "perceive the original" (*gensaku o kankaku seshimu beki shudan hōhō to shite*). The decision reads:

> Recording [*shachō*] another's musical performance to a gramophone counts as a forgery under Article 29 of the Copyright Act, and thus performed music should also be protected under copyright law as a musical "work," provided that the musical work includes new melodies that have not appeared in prior works.[44]

Thus, recording a live performance without permission is forgery, but making and selling copies of another's recordings are not so clear. Note, too, that this emphasis on melody is very much in line with our contemporary understanding of musical copyright, which (somewhat arbitrarily) recognizes melodies, but not rhythms or chord progressions, as copyrightable "works." Furthermore, the Supreme Court's interpretation of the law calls for those new melodies to assume a *fixed* and *definite* (*teikeiteki*) form. Although Kumoemon's melodies were new, they were improvised during the performance, and this, according to the Supreme Court, rendered them unfixed (even though the sound recording is precisely what "fixes" them by any other standard), and the recordings were thus not protected.[45]

With regard to the argument that Kumoemon's performance fell under the category of lecture (*enjutsu*), the court ruled that what is protected by the Copyright Act in lectures are their ideas and details, not their vocal delivery, the tone of voice, or any other characteristics of performance. Since the lyrics that Kumoemon sang expressed the reality of the "people of old" (*kojin*), his performance was nothing more than the superimposition of his melodies and unique vocal characteristics. What was missing was a "symbolic encoding" (*kigō*) of the melody that would have allowed another person to repeat it, and that absence, according to the decision, ruled out copyright protection.

It's difficult to escape the conclusion that the Supreme Court's decision was also based on elitist disdain for *naniwabushi* as an art form. That is, it repeatedly refers to *naniwabushi* as "low-grade music" (*teikyū ongaku*), a judgment surely based not on the judges' musicological expertise but on their association of the art with the lower classes. The level of creativity and skill necessary to improvise the long melodic arc of a *naniwabushi* narrative is arguably greater than that demanded of a composer who has days or even weeks to write down a short melody, but this is lost on them. By associating copyrightability with symbolic inscription rather than reproduction, however, the judges throw out much of the traditional Japanese music baby with the *naniwabushi* bathwater. They seem to realize this in their almost plaintive tone when they compare Japanese music with the codified and inscribed edifice of Western music. The term *wagakuni* (our country), with its loaded affective shading, appears four times in the decision, and three of them are in reference to Japanese music: one is the denigrating reference to *naniwabushi* just mentioned, and the other two compare Japanese music unfavorably to Western music because of its relative dearth of notation.[46]

AFTERMATH

The 1914 Supreme Court decision was a blow to the record companies, especially Nicchiku, which, as a domestic firm, could not offset the resulting losses with profits from other markets. Although the Supreme Court's decision referred to the specific circumstances of the Kumoemon records (that is, the improvised nature of *naniwabushi* melodies), it was widely read as a license to reproduce freely *any* kind of recording, and the record companies gave up trying to stop the pirate record producers through litigation. Instead, they launched a concerted campaign to introduce legislation.

That would not happen overnight, however, and in the meantime they had to try to cut their losses by engaging in a price war with the pirates. Nicchiku lowered its prices by 50 percent (from 1 yen, 50 sen, to 75 sen per record) to be more competitive with the prices of pirates who were selling copies of Nicchiku's own recordings.[47] This bold strategy was a partial success: Sales doubled the first year but not before Nicchiku was forced to furlough and then lay off a significant number of employees. By the following year, however, sales were up 300 percent. Horn had to wait until 1920, however, for the copyright laws to be changed. But he had little opportunity to enjoy the fruits of this long-awaited change in the law, as he left Japan that same year.[48]

Hatoyama Ichirō (1883–1959, son of Hatoyama Kazuo) introduced a bill to the lower house of the Diet with the following argument:

> For a literary, artistic, or musical work to have its copyright recognized, it is not necessary for it to be a completely new work. If an already existing work is reworked in a way that calls for technique or skill, such a work's copyright is recognized. The Copyright Act recognizes that a translator applies a skill distinct from [that of] the original work.[49]

On the face of it, this seems to recognize the contribution of the performing artist, but in its context, it is actually an argument establishing the contribution of the record manufacturer. This is apparent upon inspection of the text of the amendment: "One who uses a device designed for mechanical reproduction to reproduce his own or another's musical work will be considered an author and will be protected under this act.

However, the rights of the original author will not thereby be precluded."[50] The protection of the original author's rights is not neglected, but that protection is added almost as an afterthought and is framed in negative terms: "shall not be precluded" (*samatageru koto nashi*) rather than in affirmative terms that give those rights precedence. Furthermore, the "original author" in this case is the composer of the written score (whose rights were already protected) and not the performing artist.

ANALYSIS

Hosokawa Shūichi[51] draws three conclusions about the copyright law of the era, based on both the Kumoemon case and the next major copyright brouhaha in Japan, the so-called Whirlwind Plage, which was drawn out for much of the 1930s:[52] The first is the largely arbitrary and ad hoc nature of the copyright system, driven as it was by short-term commercial and nationalistic interests. The second, related to the first, is that decisions related to copyright were not limited to the interests of the creators but also to those of the various other actors involved in the process of production and reproduction. Third, the designation of "legitimate" and "illegitimate" subject positions is always the provisional and changeable product of the complex interplay of the interests and expectations of these various actors. Hosokawa's aim in his piece is to critique, from the perspective of historical sociology, teleological descriptions of the development of copyright. His deconstruction of any such teleology is buttressed by contemporary de facto reality. Although sound recordings are still very much protected under copyright, the copyrights' monetary value has diminished dramatically as digital methods of storage and delivery have made recorded music essentially free for consumers and relatively minor sources of revenue for the artists themselves. One can listen to practically any recording in existence for free on YouTube, and even if one wishes to pay for music, one can subscribe to an unlimited music streaming service for a relative pittance and listen to millions of tracks whenever one wants and as much as one wants. The only people who still pay to *own* musical recordings are those who are wedded to antiquated technologies, those who pay expressly in order to support musicians in light of these new economic realities, and those willing to pay a premium for audiophile-grade sound sources. Copyright protections for recorded music, though still on the books, are in fact evaporating before our eyes in the current media ecology. We have, in a sense, come full circle.

The tangled course of the Kumoemon case and its aftermath reveals profound instabilities in the status of musical performances and sound recordings in both the law and contemporary common sense. Masuda Satoshi observes that the chaotic development of copyright law in relation to sound recordings was a function of the fact that foreign concepts of copyright were imported into the Japanese context, beleaguered by problems of translation, and thus followed an incoherent path of development. "In particular, the copyright system in Japan was transplanted [*ishoku sare*] amid frictions with Western cultures and copyright systems, only slightly altered without any compromise with actual cultural practices, and ultimately fixed as a system that reconciles competing culture industry interests."[53]

Mitsui Tōru argues much the same thing in the title of his chapter "Copyright and Music in Japan: A Forced Grafting and Its Consequences." This is a common paradigm employed to make sense of the many changes wrought in Japan during the late nineteenth and early twentieth centuries, that of cultural collision and the "transplanting," "grafting," or otherwise imposing of foreign cultural values onto something conceived of as native soil. These metaphors are evocative (and, indeed, provocative) but tend to overlook both the agency of the "soil" and the mundane reality that many of these ideas of ownership and protection were not really new in the Japanese context. As we saw earlier, pirated editions of printed texts were considered a problem by Tokugawa publishers and authorities alike and were prosecuted accordingly. Although the Berne Convention was, in many respects, foisted upon Japan in exchange for better treaty terms, the only elements of the convention to which Japan seriously objected were those relating to translation rights, and those objections were not based on a cultural (that is, quintessentially "Japanese") misapprehension or denial of the ideas of copyright or the relative value of translation as intellectual labor; they were pragmatic objections based on a developing nation's immediate needs for outside knowledge and the practical difficulties of securing translation rights from thousands of miles away in an age of primitive telecommunications. This was indeed a case of competing interests but not of epistemic rupture.

The development of recording copyright law in Japan was certainly chaotic during the first two decades of the twentieth century. A study of comparative copyright law indicates, however, that this type of chaotic and ad hoc development was nearly universal. The decisive factor in this chaos was not the (foreign) cultural origins of ideas of copyright but rather the new media that destabilized definitions everywhere of what constituted works of art and intellectual property. In a chapter in his 1912 legal textbook *Copyright, Its History and Its Law*, Richard Rogers Bowker surveyed the development of copyright relating to "mechanical music" across Europe and United States, looking at laws dating as far back as the 1793 French copyright law that contained provisions addressing mechanical music, such as that produced by musical snuff boxes (*boîtes à musique*).[54]

The situation in France in the early twentieth century is instructive. A decisive ruling was issued on February 1, 1905, by the civil court in Paris. Attali quotes the decision:

> Finding that disks or cylinders are impressed by a stylus under which they pass; that they receive a graphic notation of spoken words, that the thought of the author is as though materialized in numerous grooves, then reproduced in thousands of copies of each disk or cylinder and distributed on the outside with a special writing, which in the future will undoubtedly be legible to the eyes and is today within everyone's reach as sound; that by virtue of this repetition of imprinted words, the literary work penetrates the mind of the listener as it would by means of sight from a book, or by means of touch with the Braille method; that it is therefore a mode of performance perfected by performance, and that the rules of plagiarism are applicable to it.

He adds:

> An astonishing text: it equates the record with the score. Written reproduction determines the record's exchange-value and justifies the application of copyright legislation. It should also be noted that in this judgment sound reproduction is considered a popular by-product of writing,

anticipating a time when specialists would decipher the recording directly.[55]

Again we see the primacy of writing. Sound recordings may be protected only on the grounds that the inscriptions on them will someday be legible and comprehensible *by the eyes* as a written representation of sound. According to this reasoning, *sound itself* cannot be copyrighted. Seen in this light, Hatoyama's justification for revising the copyright act, which claims that recording is a kind of reworking that adds value, at least allows the value of sound as sound, as reproduction, to be asserted, even if it does not address it directly.

Japan was not the first nation to grant explicit copyright protection to phonograms, but it was also far from the last. The chaos was even more protracted in some other, perhaps surprising, contexts. The United States, a nation that over the last century has been very attentive to the protection of corporate property rights, did not explicitly grant copyright protection to sound recordings until the 1971 amendment to the Copyright Act of 1909. Although the 1909 act stated that "all the writings of an author" were subject to copyright, U.S. courts generally did not regard sound recordings as "writings." The 1971 amendment was largely a reaction (lobbied for by the Recording Industry Association of America) to the advent of 8-track and compact cassette tapes, which music enthusiasts had started using to make unlicensed copies of LP discs.[56]

The legal arguments and counterarguments in Japan and elsewhere show strongly that the medium matters in the social and cultural understanding of what constitutes both art and commodity. The very definition of art is conditioned by the predominant and most prestigious media of the age: The arguments for protecting recordings liken them to writing, while the arguments against it differentiate them from writing. Both take the medium of writing axiomatically as the basis of the definition of a copyrightable work. In this context, the medium of the phonogram made it possible for the first time to "write" sound, that is, to fix it in a repeatable form. When sound could be recorded, it also meant that the ephemeral aspects of artistic practice, such as nuances of performances and even the timbre of the voice, could be fixed and therefore reified and commodified. The ephemeral vagaries of performance and the contingencies of performers' natural endowments had not been recognized by the episteme of writing as work, and the Kumoemon case brought this fact into sharp relief. This is where the real epistemic rupture is to be found, not in the ideas of ownership and piracy. The eventual recognition of the value of these fugitive qualities, however, was not traced to the recognition of their value as such (although the rhetoric addressed that value); it was traced to the recognition of the *commodifiability* of those qualities. We know this because the primary beneficiaries of the change in the copyright law in 1920 were the record companies, not the performing artists.

Noteworthy in this regard is Kumoemon's own decision not to honor his contract with Werdermann. This aspect of the case has received the least attention from Japanese scholars of both law and history, presumably because it is read as a straightforward case of breach of contract and nothing more. Although the contract was the first of its kind in Japanese history,[57] I think it unlikely that Kumoemon unwittingly violated the agreement because he somehow did not understand the concept of exclusivity. The contract was quite clear: "You will not record these works, or any other works that you have previously performed in public, for another company. Furthermore, in the event of an offer to record a new work for another company, you must obtain prior approval from Sankōdō."[58]

The historical record suggests that Kumoemon was not the most principled of people, in either his personal life or his business dealings. Perhaps the most scandalous anecdote concerns his relationship with Ohama, the wife of his one-time teacher Mikawaya Baisha. Kumoemon and Ohama eloped and were forced to leave Tokyo because of the scandal this caused. According to Hyōdō and Smith, the problem was not that Kumoemon had stolen another man's wife, as this was common enough in *naniwabushi* circles—it was that he had also stolen his greatly talented shamisen accompanist.[59] His track record in financial matters was no better. In addition to the gambling habit that Kumoemon shared with many other chanters, a story from the December 16, 1912, issue of the *Yomiuri shinbun*[60] reports that Kumoemon was summoned to the local police station after having been accused by a business associate of fraud to the tune of 6,000 yen.

It would be easy enough, given this reputation, to consider Kumoemon's action to be a simple case of greed, but I read it instead as a conscious or perhaps unconscious challenge to the very possibility of ceding control of one's labor. Kumoemon accepted that distinct performances could be recorded and commodified, but his voice and labor were his to do with as he wished.[61] He seemed to treat the recordings as performances like any other, that is, as labor, for which he received a performance fee. The fact that the royalties were greater with greater sales was no different from making more money if more tickets were sold for a concert. Just as he would not limit his performances to a single venue, he would not limit his recordings to a single record company. Every performance is unique, so while the performances he recorded for Werdermann were Werdermann's "exclusively" to use as he pleased (Kumoemon laid no claim to them, nor was he a coplaintiff in Werdermann's suit against the pirates), the performances he recorded for Nicchiku were different performances on which Werdermann could lay no claim. This might explain why Kumoemon himself was relatively unconcerned about the pirating of his records. He certainly didn't pursue any legal action, as did, for example, Fukuzawa Yukichi.

Kumoemon's great-grandson Okamoto Kazuaki writes that Kumoemon actually had no interest in recordings until his *naniwabushi* rival Yoshida Naramaru II (ca. 1880–1967) released a set of recordings in 1910 with the Nicchiku Nipponophone label and saw a surge in his popularity as a result.[62] Kumoemon decided to record his performances only so his own star wouldn't be eclipsed by Naramaru's.[63] If this is true, Kumoemon's understanding of recordings as a medium is similar to the one that musical artists today have been forced to embrace as a result of the dematerialization and demonetization of recordings—that is, they use recordings more as marketing tools and advertising for live performances than as marketable commodities in their own right. Kumoemon's decision to record with Nicchiku, the firm that released Naramaru's records, also makes sense in light of this rivalry.

That said, calling this the "Kumoemon case" is something of a misnomer. Although Kumoemon and the nature of his performing art were ostensibly the matters under judgment, Kumoemon was not a plaintiff in the case, and both the court's decision and the legislation crafted to counter that decision were applied without discrimination against or differentiation among all types of recordings. What was fundamentally at issue were the economic interests of companies that produced records, and Japan's eventual embrace of copyright laws to protect those interests was neither unusually belated (coming more than half a century before the

United States did the same), nor carried out reluctantly or in a climate of confusion over what copyright meant. In other words, it was not an example of the oft-cited phenomenon of "uneven modernity." Instead, the laws developed in the same manner in which they developed in the rest of the modernized world, that is, as a result of competing interests navigating emergent material realities. As usual, the most economically powerful and politically influential interests triumphed. But in the midst of this very typical might-making-right narrative, a space opened up in which the seeds of the recognition of ephemeral performance as "work," in the sense of both labor and artistic artifact, could be planted. What was "merely improvised and momentary" was now commodifiable and archivable. This recognition ushered in a new kind of star system as well as a new understanding of performance as property.

KABUKI'S COMEBACK

Despite its early relationship with the phonograph, kabuki was not among the performing arts that received the earliest and most intense interest of record companies and listeners. That distinction belonged to *yose* entertainments such as *naniwabushi* and *rakugo*. I cannot say with certainty why this was so, but many possible explanations come to mind: The SP (78 RPM) discs of the time were limited to three minutes per side, not an ideal unit to present anything but short popular songs, but notably unsuited to kabuki. Kabuki performances also presented special recording challenges, ones that could have been skirted by having performers dispense with staging and simply perform into microphones in studios, but this came with attendant losses in the energy and atmosphere of those performances.

An article in the November 15, 1921, issue of the *Yomiuri shinbun* announced Nicchiku's release of what is claimed to be "the first kabuki record," a somewhat ambiguous assertion since the article maintains, "It's not that there haven't been kabuki recordings up to this point, but they have been extremely unsatisfactory."[64] Beginning with this release, kabuki recordings experienced a minor boom. Judging from the purchases of ads in the major daily newspapers, sales of commercial kabuki recordings seem to take off in 1921 and continue until around July 1925. And then suddenly the advertisements stop. Why?

I hypothesize two contributing factors. One was the appearance of radio, which did include occasional broadcasts of portions of kabuki plays. It is difficult to believe, however, that these infrequent broadcasts would have satisfied kabuki aficionados, who until that time had been willing to spend considerable sums of money to purchase SP records of their favorite kabuki stars.

A more convincing explanation for this four-year window of kabuki recording popularity is the fate of the Kabuki-za in Tokyo. In October 1921 a short circuit in the electrical system sparked a fire that destroyed the theater. Then just as the rebuilt Kabuki-za was nearing completion in 1923, the Great Kantō Earthquake and the accompanying firestorm burned it to the ground once again.

After the 1921 fire, the Kabuki-za performers moved to the Ichimura-za, so by no means were Tokyo kabuki fans deprived of live performances during the theater's closure. Furthermore, the record companies' catalogs and surviving recordings make it clear that kabuki recordings continued to be produced in considerable numbers after the advertising in major dailies ended in 1925. In fact, even though there were more kabuki records released in the 1930s than in the 1920s, there were no more advertisements for a kabuki record in a major daily until October 1940, a gap of fifteen years. After that there was another flurry of advertising from around November 1941 to December 1942—in other words, during the first deliriously optimistic months of the Pacific War, when record companies tried to cash in on the patriotic fever with recordings of *Chūshingura*. At this point, it's clear that the stars mattered less than the ideologically timely content.

This pattern demonstrates that record companies spent money on expensive major daily advertising for kabuki recordings only when circumstances helped ensure that the investment would yield a reasonable return, when recordings of kabuki first became feasible and continuing until the Kabuki-za reopened. The next such window of opportunity came just before and after the beginning of the Pacific War.

As we've seen, the relationship between kabuki and sound recordings dates back to the latter's very earliest days. Kabuki stars provided the *nikusei* (the natural, living voices) and the *kowairo* (vocal color) that demonstrated the phonograph's powers of reproduction. Later, during the age of sound recording commodification, kabuki gave the record companies bankable stars who helped push sales. The benefits did not move in just one direction, however. While the Kabuki-za was closed, kabuki recordings brought famous actors' vocal performances into homes and kept them alive in the public imagination, precisely by turning those voices themselves into objects of desire, fetishized commodities that kabuki fans could now "own."

LISTENING COMMUNITIES

What emerges from all of this is the development and economic maturation of a medium that relied, above all, on the human voice, especially the voices of particular human beings, as the source of its validation and commercial appeal. The earliest phonographs in Japan were not demonstrated by showing off their fidelity to the sound of a violin or tuba, the virtuosity of the instrumentalists playing them, or by emphasizing the practical and productive tasks that Edison originally envisioned. Nor were they marketed as commodities in the Taishō and Shōwa (1926–1989) periods by relying primarily on those capabilities. What "sold" records, in both senses of the term, were the specific grains of specific voices, even when the medium was only barely sensitive enough—realistically speaking—to readily distinguish one voice from another. Listeners were apparently willing to meet the medium halfway, to imagine the reproduced voices as closer to their originals than they actually were. We might call this the "audiophile placebo effect."

The recordings offered in return the capacity to materialize and commodify sound and performance in time. While these had always been sold as events, as experiences, they could now be captured and scaled, enabling the emergence of a truly mass auditory culture, one that would make record companies and some recording artists very wealthy while creating cultural reference points shared by entire generations of consuming subjects. While creating a shared body of auditory memories for specific generational cohorts, recorded music also generated a consciousness of musical historicity. As William Howland Kenney writes about the American context, but in terms that also apply to twentieth-century Japan,

Here at the juncture of social repetition and collective memory, the phonograph played a more important cultural role from 1890 to 1945 than the discourses on either recorded sound or on memory have recognized. Although isolated scholarly voices have called for greater recognition of the media "as sites of the creation of social memory and as a body of available materials for its study," recorded sound has not yet received such consideration. The phonograph's repetitive function acted as a major aid to memory by resounding the patterns of sensibility embedded in commercialized musical formulas from the past. Americans re-experienced and recalled the melodic, harmonic, and rhythmic structures of the past as well as something of the surrounding social and cultural contexts from which they had emerged. The phonograph and recorded sound, therefore, served as instruments in an ongoing process of individual and group recognition in which images of the past and the present could be mixed in an apparently timeless suspension that often seemed to defy the relentless corrosion of historical change. "Record buffs" formed varied communities of memory in response to discs that had been artfully contrived for them.[65]

This "timeless suspension" of images of the past and present are what the cultural sociologist Koizumi Kyōko calls a "memoryscape," one produced by a lifetime of listening to music. Koizumi writes as well about music's remarkable (if not singular) ability to evoke *particular* times and places.[66] This particularity, I believe, is activated by music as an experience and by the characteristics of recordings as capital-driven commodities. As commodities, they must be regularly refreshed in order to stimulate an endless process of consumption. Today, in the United States and most other countries that belong to the International Federation of the Phonographic Industry, new releases "drop" (are released) once every week. A few recordings capture the mass cultural consciousness; a few others are celebrated by various subcultures; but the vast majority essentially go unheard and are quickly forgotten. At the same time, the recording industry attempts to maximize profits by re-releasing older content on new media formats, in remastered versions, or simply in new packaging or compilations. In this way, both novelty and nostalgia are exploited to stimulate demand. By being refreshed so often, popular music becomes strongly associated with certain moments in time and with the personal and collective memories of that moment. Novel when new, yet also keyed to trigger a concrete and specific moment of nostalgia when heard again months or years later, recorded popular music creates imagined communities of listeners whose cultural memories are shaped by structures of temporality and historicity that are generated by the medium and its social contexts. In chapter 4, we will see how radio became the next medium to address and consolidate these already constituted imagined communities of listeners in a new temporal paradigm of "liveness" and immediacy.

4

IMAGINING THE WIRELESS COMMUNITY

THE ARRIVAL OF RADIO

The first radio broadcasts in Japan took place in 1925, five years after the world's first radio broadcasts, in the United States. Japan's first test broadcasts were held in the provisional studio of Tokyo Broadcasting Station (call sign JOAK) located at Tokyo Higher Polytechnic School's library in Shibaura. Regular broadcasts began on March 22 of that year.[1]

In contrast to the phonograph and the telephone, which did not see widespread use and ownership until many years, even decades, after their initial appearance, the radio arrived in Japan during a period when both a more mature consumption economy and a greater receptivity to new technological objects in general ensured that the new medium would enjoy rapid adoption and development, at least in the urban centers.

The acceptance of radio was no doubt helped by the fact that the language reform measures of forty years earlier, to say nothing of compulsory education, had by this time already done their work. It would have been difficult, if not impossible, to establish radio broadcasting as a mass medium without having some form of standardized spoken idiom that would be widely intelligible, at least to a majority of the people within range of the broadcast. It may not be surprising, then, that the initial forays into radio broadcasting were undertaken by established media concerns that shared a deep interest in the existence of a standard vernacular: the newspapers.

FIGURE 4.1 Subjects of the Japanese Empire listening to the Imperial Rescript on Surrender on August 15, 1945, in Yotsuya in Tokyo, Japan. Photo courtesy of Mainichi Newspapers/AFLO.

Major urban newspapers such as the *Tōkyō mainichi shinbun*, the *Tōkyō nichinichi shinbun*, and the *Ōsaka mainichi shinbun* greeted the arrival of the radio in grandiloquent terms. Newspapers immediately saw radio broadcasting as an integral part of their long-term business strategy. In contrast to most of the fourteen other nations that had already made forays into radio broadcasting (the United States was one of the only other exceptions), early broadcasting in Japan was not immediately nationalized.[2] By the same token, broadcasting companies and networks (in the sense that we now think of them) had yet to take shape in Japan, and so it is perhaps obvious that the vacuum was filled by the industrial power of existing media concerns.

In December 1923 the Teishinshō (Ministry of Communications) put into effect the Regulations on Private Radio Telephone Broadcasting Facilities, which established the process by which private companies could apply for broadcasting licenses. Although the ministry wanted to limit the number of stations to one station in each of the three major cities (Tokyo,

Osaka, and Nagoya), it received more than a hundred applications for licenses. Accordingly, the ministry asked the largest and most prominent of the license applicants to share joint control of each of the stations, and although this process went smoothly in Tokyo and Nagoya, the applicants in Osaka remained divided, and the licensing process ground to a halt until the middle of 1924. With the appointment of Inukai Tsuyoshi (1855–1932) as minister of communications in the Katō Takaaki cabinet (formed in June of that year), a move was made to establish the three urban radio stations as nonprofit corporations, thus shutting private, profit-oriented industry out of broadcasting for the time being and sidestepping the vexed issue of license sharing. The Tokyo Broadcasting Station was incorporated in November 1924; the Nagoya Broadcasting Station (JOCK) was established in January 1925; and the Osaka Broadcasting Station (JOBK) opened in February 1925 in preparation for the start of broadcasting some months later. JOBK commenced broadcasting on June 1 and JOCK on July 15.

In the autumn of 1925, the Ministry of Communications formulated a plan to extend radio broadcasting throughout the rest of the country and, as a step in that direction, proposed that the three urban stations be consolidated into a single public corporation, the Nippon Hōsō Kyōkai or NHK. The stations agreed to the consolidation in principle but resisted one aspect of the proposal, which stipulated that the current executives in charge of day-to-day operations at each station be replaced by appointees of the Ministry of Communications. When the final vote on consolidation was taken, police were standing by to ensure that simmering resistance to the plan did not erupt in violence.[3]

On August 20, 1926, the three original broadcasting stations in Tokyo, Osaka, and Nagoya were consolidated into NHK, and it was at this point that radio became a truly national mass medium. This organizational change coincided with an event that further reified the imagined community of the Japanese nation-state and brought radio to the fore as a prime instrument in that reification: the final illness and death of the Taishō emperor. The reports on the emperor's condition were often remarkably detailed, giving hour-by-hour updates on the dying man's body temperature, pulse rate, and respiration. It is significant that the first nationally unifying event of the nascent media revolved around the emperor and, more specifically, around the failing *body* of the emperor. These reports were clinical yet almost conveyed a sense of bedside intimacy.

FIGURE 4.2 Postcard of JOBK in Osaka. Photo courtesy of the Duits Collection.

The public response seems to have been one of wholehearted support and gratitude. Takeyama Akiko contends that this response in turn gave the leadership of the fledgling medium a newfound confidence in the legitimacy of radio as an organ of public discourse on par with the newspapers, and not just as a mere diversion or entertainment. Just as important, it brought radio to the attention of the political leadership as a potentially powerful shaper of public discourse and public opinion. This potential was immediately exploited in the subsequent broadcasts of the Taishō emperor's funeral ceremony and the Shōwa emperor's enthronement. NHK accelerated the process of extending broadcasting to all the provincial capitals throughout Japan in the hopes of completing a nationwide network by November 6, 1928, the date that Emperor Hirohito would be enthroned.

From its very beginning, then, radio was immediately put to effective use consolidating the subjective presence and reach of the imagined community of the nation-state. It accomplished this through the overt means of propagating emperor worship and through a host of other ways that were less obviously nationalistic but probably no less powerful in reifying the sense of nation.

RADIO EXERCISE

Not long after radio broadcasting commenced, one of the most enduring institutions of Japanese broadcasting history was introduced: *rajio taisō*, "radio exercise." The first such transmissions were made on August 1, 1928, by the Osaka Broadcasting Station and continued every day, except Sundays, for one month before coming to a halt. The first radio exercise program that enjoyed a more considerable duration commenced at 7 A.M., November 1, 1928, under the auspices of the Tokyo Broadcasting Station.

Radio exercise originated in the United States in 1925, being broadcast as a public service by the Metropolitan Life Insurance Company in New York. Two Ministry of Communication officials, Inokuma Teiji (?–1942) and Shindō Seiichi (1890–1984), visited the company on two separate occasions: Inokuma left Japan in the spring of 1923 on a research tour through Europe and the United States. He visited Metropolitan Life at a time when

FIGURE 4.3 Cover of the NHK guidebook for radio exercise leaders, 1940 (in celebration of the putative 2,600th anniversary of the foundation of Japan). Photo courtesy of the Duits Collection.

radio exercise was still being developed as an idea, and he sent his findings back to Japan in the spring of 1924. Shindō went on a follow-up visit three years later, saw the exercises in action, and wrote up his findings in the August 1927 issue of the *Teishin kyōkai zasshi* (Ministry of Communications Association magazine). The ministry decided to institute radio exercises based on a hybrid of the Metropolitan model and the exercises used in the Sokol gymnastics movement, which had played a role in Czech nationalism in the late nineteenth century.[4]

Radio exercise was regarded by officials and educators in the prewar and wartime periods as a ritual crucial to the smooth functioning of various Ideological State Apparatuses. The practice was exported to Japan's colonies in Korea and Taiwan as part of broader efforts at Japanification. But after the end of the Pacific War, American Occupation authorities came to view radio exercise as a symbol of militarism and banned it for a time. Ironically, they were banning an American export. They were also banning a three-minute set of light calisthenics and stretches performed to tinkling piano music, exercises so undemanding they can be performed even by small children, the aged, and the infirm. Nothing about the routine itself was preparation for hand-to-hand combat or anything more strenuous than perhaps riding a bicycle to the corner store to pick up some tofu. How could something so innocuous be a symbol of militarism?

Kuroda Isamu points out that radio exercise served several purposes: It was a vehicle for the modernization of time consciousness by encouraging early rising and national synchronization to abstract clock-time. Although the Meiji (1868–1912) government had adopted the Gregorian calendar and the twenty-four-hour clock system in 1873, it took many years before the fractionalization and strict regimentation of time worked its way into the everyday consciousness of common people. Radio exercise thus became one way in which early rising, punctuality, and the efficient utilization of time were reinforced as habits and as a national ethos.

Radio exercise also modernized and "rationalized" conceptions of the body, health, physical fitness, and exercise. Much of this rhetoric was grounded in ideas of national competition and a nagging sense of physical inferiority vis-à-vis imperial or quasi-imperial powers such as the United States, Great Britain, France, and Germany. In its train came the attendant notions of "survival of the fittest" and other social Darwinist ideas. In other words, radio exercise was a vehicle by which to discipline (in the Foucauldian sense) the body in both space and time in the service of state ideology.

Synchronized movement as a form of social control has a long history and is still widely practiced around the world in various military and sporting contexts.[5] Rooted though it may be in the crudest form of behaviorism, it is still surprisingly effective. As Blaise Pascal, Muhammad, Zen meditators, and others throughout history have understood, given enough repetition, kinesthesis becomes psychology: The mind creates post-hoc justifications for the actions of the body. To submit one's body to a voice of authority, to move in sync with a group, to do so every day at set times throughout the day, is to inscribe in the body habits of obedience and a felt, instinctive sense of collective identity.

The relationship between sound and the body is not limited to the case of bodies moving to the commands of a voice. Sound is essentially the perception of vibrations that pass through the air (or other media) in the range of approximately 20 hertz (cycles per second) to approximately 20,000 hertz. With the hearing loss that accompanies age and/or excessive exposure to loud sounds, sensitivity to certain high-frequency bands of sound is progressively lost. At the lower ranges of the audible spectrum, however, the distinction between "hearing" and "touch" begins to blur.[6]

As noted earlier, the human voice occupies a special place in the audible spectrum for the human subject. Jacques Lacan pointed to the invocatory drive, the desire to hear the voice, both one's own and that of others. Theorists such as Guy Rosolato and Mary Ann Doane have fleshed out the meaning of this drive in a Lacanian context, referring to the "pleasure of hearing" the voice as a sensate entity marked by unique characteristics such as volume, rhythm, timbre, and pitch. That is, hearing the musicality of the voice is a pleasure even when it is not used in overtly musical ways. Doane remarks that in psychoanalytic thought, pleasure is a by-product of the gap between a memory, or a trace of a memory—some archaic moment of satisfaction—and a current phenomenon. "Memories of the first experience of the voice, of the hallucinatory satisfaction it offered, circumscribe the pleasure of hearing and ground its relation to the fantasmatic [sic] body."[7]

第三、腕を外と内に廻す運動

1 腕を外に廻す（腕を側より上を通す）。
2 一廻りして腕を側まで振る。
3 腕を内に廻す（腕を交叉しつゝ體前をすり上げ側より下す）。
4 一廻りして腕を體前に交叉する。
5、6、7、8 同様の動作を行ふ。

以上の運動を繰返す。

（注意）腕をよく伸ばして大きく廻す。最後の動作は腕體前交叉のまゝとする。

第四、頭を側に轉し側に屈げる運動

（前半＝側に轉す運動）
1 手を腰にとりつゝ頭を左に轉す（前運動の腕體前交叉より手腰に續く）。
2 頭を正面に復す。
3 頭を右に轉す。
4 頭を正面に復す。
5、6、7、8 同様の動作を行ふ。

（後半＝側に屈げる運動）
1 頭を左に屈げる。
2 頭を起す。
3 頭を右に屈げる。
4 頭を起す。
5、6、7、8 同様の動作を行ふ。

（注意）充分に轉し、屈げ、正面にて輕くとめる。

FIGURE 4.4 Interior of the NHK guidebook for radio exercise leaders. Photo courtesy of the Duits Collection.

ラヂオ體操第三

（大日本國民體操）

第一、膝を屈げ股を前に擧げる運動

1 左膝を屈げ股を前に擧げ股を下す。
2 右膝を屈げ股を前に擧げ股を下す。
3、4、5、6、7、8 同樣の動作を行ふ。
以上の運動を繰返す。

（注意）最後の動作で臂を體側に下す。手足を輕く伸し臂を自然に振り足踏の要領で行ふ。前半は股を低く、後半は股を水平迄擧げる。氣分の高揚を圖る。

第二、臂を側に振り踵を擧げ膝を半ば屈げる運動

1 臂を側に振り踵を擧げる（掌を下に向ける）。
2 膝を半ば屈げ臂を體前に交叉する。
3 臂を側に振り膝を伸ばす（掌を下に向ける）。
4 踵を下し臂を體前に交叉す。
5、6、7、8 同樣の動作を行ふ。
以上の運動を繰返す。

（注意）最初の動作は臂體前交叉から始める。最後の動作は臂を交叉のまゝとする。

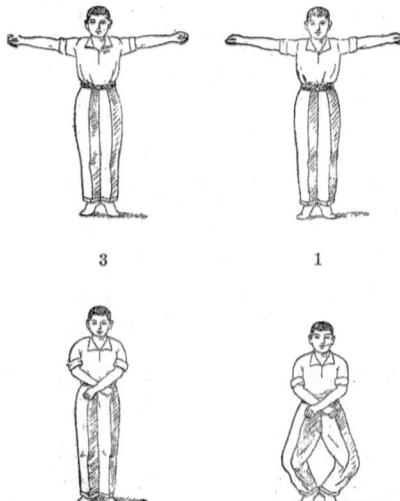

An example of this is found in Tanizaki Jun'ichirō's memoir:

> When I lived in Nihonbashi, I often heard the sound of a samisen as I lay drowsing in the quilted bedclothes, cuddled to my nurse's breast. "Tempura is what I want, tempura is what I want," she would hum softly in time to the samisen's rhythm. "Doesn't it sound like that to you? Tempura is what I want, tempura is what I want.... Doesn't it, Jun'ichi?" And she would peer into my face as my hands pressed against her breast and my fingers played with her nipples. And indeed as I listened, the samisen seemed to be sadly repeating those very words. The two of us would gaze at each other and listen, silently and intently, to the samisen's notes.[8]

The memory trace that triggers this invocatory pleasure is, unsurprisingly, the memories of voices heard in infancy. Rosolato tells us that the infant first understands space (and, indeed, presence) by means of auditory rather than visual information, that visual processing comes later. Furthermore, the voice, unlike the gaze, can travel around and through various obstacles, and thus exercises a greater command over space. In addition—and this is a crucial point—the voice is the "instrument of demand." Even before language is available to the infant, the voice is used to express need and demand various forms of comfort.

It is here that the Lacanian tendency to "dematerialize" the mother's voice and, by extension (and in other ways), her very body, should be revisited and reconsidered. The mother's (or other caregiver's) voice is almost never present without the caregiver's body. The caregiver might be in another room, but the cry is usually met with physical presence: food, a caress, a soothing voice. While voices for the fetus might be acousmatic (that is, issuing from an unseen source) or dematerialized (can we even call them voices at that stage?), voices for the infant usually have tactile and physiological accompaniments, as the passage from Tanizaki illustrates so vividly. Put another way, our earliest memories of voices are bound together with primal memories of embodiment and intercorporeality. While Lacan's late meditations on the Real remediate some of the earlier (over)emphasis on the Symbolic and Imaginary, I think that we can address this issue more directly without dogmatically hewing to Lacan. One of my aims here is to loosen the constricting ideas of sensory isolation and hierarchy—*this* is visual, *this* is aural, vision is more important than hearing, etc.—for a more holistic and, indeed, synesthetic view. For the infant, this requires very little effort, since the senses have yet to be partitioned.[9] Echoes and vestiges of this primal synesthesia—that is, memories and actual synesthesia triggered by various factors—often persist into adulthood, albeit with vast individual differences. The primal memories of the voice are thus never *just* of the voice. We might speculate that this primal bundling of associations is precisely what gives the acousmatic voice its uncanny quality: Every time we hear an acousmatic voice, these bundled associations (which multiply into adulthood, since voices generally are embodied) create ripples of sensory interference when the source is not in view.

In the introduction, I referred to Michel Chion's suggestion that the acousmatic voice exercises the following four powers within the subject's psychic economy: "the ability to be everywhere, to see all, to know all, and to have complete power. In other words: ubiquity, panopticism, omniscience, and omnipotence."[10] This effect is most pronounced in the context of film, in which such a voice is an irreducible surplus to the diegesis on screen; film is a medium in which one can play with showing, partially showing, or not showing the source of the voice. The acousmatic effect is operative in the radio, gramophone, and digital music player as well, though in an attenuated way. As Mladen Dolar explains, "All we see is some technical appliance from which voices emanate, and in a quid pro quo the gadget then takes the place of the invisible source itself."[11] Dolar agrees with Slavoj Žižek that ultimately the voice can *never* be disacousmaticized, its source can never be known, and that every vocal emission is by necessity an act of ventriloquism. According to Žižek,

> An unbridgeable gap separates forever a human body from "its" voice. The voice displays a spectral autonomy, it never quite belongs to the body we see, so that even when we see a living person talking, there is always a minimum of ventriloquism at work: it is as if the speaker's own voice hollows him out and in a sense speaks "by itself," through him.[12]

As my discussion of synesthesia might suggest, I do not entirely agree with these Lacanian or Lacan-inflected descriptions. While acousmatic voices can indeed be unsettling, the insistence on the universally and ineluctably acousmatic nature of voices strikes me now as high-theoretical overreach.[13] If your body is pressed against the body of a person speaking, the origin of the voice is never in doubt, as the vibrations of the sound penetrate from his or her flesh into yours. This is the ultimate tactile grounding of the voice.

I would also argue that voices emanating from the radio exhibit other effects besides being acousmatic, rendering them just as uncanny as acousmatic voices in the cinema: the muffled and metallic quality of the voices due to the inherent limitations of broadcasting and amplification technology, the sense in many cases that one is listening to a "live" voice that is simultaneously being emanated at a great distance, as well as the relative intimacy of the radio listening experience, that direct, almost umbilical link to a voice unmediated by a competing visual presentation.

To return to the question of radio exercise and its perceived threat, we might suggest that, despite the innocuousness of the exercises themselves, this spectacle of large groups of people, young and old, moving in time to the calls of a phantasmic voice was what moved the Occupation authorities to act. Perhaps they recognized that the voice was more than just phantasmic, that the voice-body link enacted and made visual by the ritual was symbolic of the kinds of authoritarianism that they were paradoxically (as authorities) trying to discredit, and that it also made a spectacle of a persuasive operation that they still might have wanted to employ in other forms.

STADIUM OF THE MIND

Everywhere it was practiced, sports broadcasting necessitated the creation of new forms of oral narrative performance, and I stress the word "narrative" because this was clearly a form of storytelling. The sporting events themselves offered the narrative frame and the plot, complete with beginnings, middles, and ends, and the task for the broadcaster was to present that bare sequence of events with enough structure and art to hold the audience's attention to a spectacle they couldn't actually see. At the same time, these broadcasts traded on a rhetoric of immediacy that was based on actuality and, for reasons that will become clear, on a consensual fiction.

In *Theater of the Mind: Imagination, Aesthetics, and American Radio Drama*, Neil Verma subjects that term "theater of the mind"—which has been ubiquitous in discussions of radio drama—to much critical scrutiny, but in the end still finds it compelling enough to make it the title of his book.[14] My section title here is an obvious allusion to and play on that term, one meant to imply an affinity between the ostensibly literary practice of radio drama and the ostensibly journalistic practice of sports broadcasting. But the inherent ambiguity of the preposition "of" in "stadium of the mind," allows it to be interpreted as "a stadium *in* the listener's imagination" but also as "the mind *itself* is a stadium" in which competing ideologies and affective energies play out. Although I don't object to that second reading, I would add that such an agonistic image of ideology is itself highly ideological. We could also analogize ideology to hypnosis, seduction, germination, incubation, and a host of other social and biological processes, all of which are, in their own ways, problematic as analogies for the contradictory, grotesque, yet still thoroughly domesticated and comfortable mechanisms by which ideology works.

Most histories of radio broadcasting in Japan claim that the earliest sports broadcast took place on August 13, 1927, when the Osaka Central Broadcasting Station carried a live broadcast of the opening day of the thirteenth annual National Middle School Baseball Championships held at the Hankyū Kōshien Stadium outside Kobe. But the earliest sports broadcast in the Japanese Empire was in fact that of a grand sumo tournament that took place on June 18, 1927. The station that made the broadcast was JODK, located in Seoul, then known as Keijō. As Yamaguchi Makoto observes, this hardly trivial fact has been strangely overlooked or even suppressed in multiple histories of both Japanese sports and Japanese broadcasting. At least one reference that Yamaguchi cites, *20 seiki hōsōshi* (Broadcast history of the twentieth century), edited and published by NHK in 2001, notes the broadcast in its *nenpyō*, or chronological table, but makes no mention of it in the main body of the text.[15] Whether this was simply an oversight, or an attempt to sustain the fiction that JODK was anything but a Japanese enterprise that broadcast in Japanese and was run by Japanese authorities, is open to speculation.

The earliest sports broadcasts were dogged by multiple difficulties. First, the announcers were accustomed to reading prepared news reports, not improvising commentary on events unfolding in real time. Furthermore, the content of all broadcasts had to be preapproved by the censorship authorities of the Ministry of Communications. JOBK was able to negotiate an exception to the rule in this case, one that involved a ministry censor being present near the announcer to cut off the transmission in the event that "inappropriate" content was aired.[16] This mode of censorship was codified into law in 1930.

The announcer for the 1927 Middle School Championship broadcast by Osaka's JOBK was Uotani Tadashi (1897–?). Uotani had been an infielder for Osaka's Ichioka Middle School and had himself played on the fields of Kōshien Stadium. Before entering the broadcasting company in June of the previous year, he had worked as a bank clerk and before then had been a student at Kwansei Gakuin University. During his year or so at the station, he had received training in the fundamentals of radio announcing, but the decision to put him in charge of the first live baseball broadcast—presumably on the basis of his first-hand experience as a player of the game—had been made barely two weeks before the series was to begin, so Uotani was forced to prepare in haste. He consulted with an *Asahi shinbun* reporter who had recently returned from observing major league baseball broadcasts in the United States, and he practiced by doing mock sportscasts of the elimination games in Hyōgo Prefecture.[17]

Uotani's broadcast was not recorded, but a radio listener transcribed the broadcast using *sokki*, shorthand, and submitted his transcription to *Asahi supōtsu* (Asahi sports), which published it the following month. Uotani's play-by-play tended to focus largely on the direction in which the ball had been hit and not much else. Commentators found noteworthy his frequent use of exclamations, in particular "sora!" (look, there) which he tended to use every time the ball was put in motion. Yamaguchi Makoto hypothesizes that this was an attempt to convey to the listener a sense of immediacy. *Sora* signifies that, at this very moment, something important is happening in the game. The importance of this sense of immediacy, this sense of "liveness" was not something that Uotani articulated explicitly, but it is plausible that he intuited it as one of the features that distinguished radio from other media and helped hold the listener's attention.

This dimension of liveness became cognized, articulated, and debated with the appearance of Uotani's rival at JOAK in Tokyo, Matsuuchi Norizō (1890–1972). Ten days after Uotani went on the air, Matsuuchi went live on August 23 to announce the game between the First and Third Higher Schools at Meiji Jingū Stadium. Matsuuchi was not alone during this broadcast, for the playwright and novelist Kume Masao, who was a commissioned employee of the radio station, was by Matsuuchi's side. The idea was for Kume to write down pithy descriptions of the action on the field, which Matsuuchi would then read on the air. The rationale behind this arrangement is not entirely clear, but unlike Uotani, Matsuuchi had no experience as a baseball player and until then had been a financial news announcer for the station. Kume, though, was a self-proclaimed *yakyūzuki*, or baseball lover, and the station authorities presumably believed that this, combined with his skills as a wordsmith, would make him the ideal partner for Matsuuchi.

Matsuuchi recalled in later years that the arrangement was unworkable and that Kume had been next to useless during the broadcast, in part because he was so distraught over the fact that First Higher School was losing. The Matsuuchi-Kume combo was abandoned after a single game, and Matsuuchi announced subsequent sporting events on his own. However, their tag-team continued in another form, in the pages of various periodicals in which Matsuuchi was forced to defend his particular style of sports broadcasting.

Shūkan Asahi (Weekly Asahi) published an anonymous baseball column entitled "Kanwa kyūdai" (loosely, "Gossip on baseball topics"). The author of the column lobbed the first volley by attacking Kume Masao after reading a *yakyū zadankai* (baseball roundtable) published in *Bungei shunjū* in which Kume had taken part, along with Kikuchi Kan and a number of baseball notables, including Hashido Shin (1879–1936). During the roundtable, Kume gave an erroneous definition of a double-header, in addition to expressing a number of other odd opinions. The author wrote, "I wonder what a hit Kume Masao-kun would be if, instead of directing the baseball broadcasts from Meiji Jingū Stadium, he broadcast to the antennas of like-minded literary friends from the second floor of his house in Kamakura."[18] Two weeks later, the "Kanwa kyūdaiko" ("baseball gossip kid," as he came to be called by Kume and Matsuuchi), turned his sights on Matsuuchi himself, accusing the announcer of getting so caught up in the enthusiasm of the crowd that he fumbled a number of key calls. The crux of Kanwa kyūdaiko's complaints were that both Kume and Matsuuchi didn't know much about baseball—certainly in comparison with Uotani at JOBK in Osaka—and were thus doing their listeners a disservice.

Kume responded in print by arguing that Matsuuchi's style was that of a regular fan who simply reported the games as he saw them.

> A detailed and accurate record of the game can be entrusted to the next morning's newspaper. Readers like Kyūdaiko can peruse the opinions of all the experts at their leisure. But the mission of AK's baseball broadcasts at this point is to provide a lively description [*ikita byōsha*] from a single fan's perspective, baseball as he sees it.[19]

Kume repeatedly uses the phrase *ikita byōsha* throughout his essay, in the process articulating what distinguished sports broadcasting from the descriptions and analyses that could be found in print after the game was over: It was live, it was immediate, and a few mistakes here and there were a small price to pay for that sense of immediacy and real-time participation.

Matsuuchi also responded in *Shūkan Asahi*: "Should we put greater value on an exquisite [*kōchi*] broadcast or a rough-and-ready [*sessoku*] one? This is definitely a dilemma, but in any event I think I'm going to put more effort into making my broadcasts faster rather than more exquisite."[20]

Kume's and Matsuuchi's rebuttals are slightly disingenuous, because at this point Matsuuchi was already developing a highly artful style of delivery that distinguished him from a random fan calling the plays as he saw them. Instead of speeding up his announcing, he became known for a style of delivery similar to that of *kōdan* (oral) storytellers: short bursts in patterns of five or seven morae. This elaborated style in fact slowed Matsuuchi down instead of speeding him up, as was attested to by none other than Kume himself. For the National Middle School Championship that took place at Kōshien Stadium the following year, 1928, Matsuuchi traveled to Kōshien to announce the game for JOAK, while Uotani announced it for JOBK. Here was a chance to compare the styles of the two announcers side-by-side as they called the same games. Kume Masao wrote of the experience:

> Uotani expresses emotionally the action of the game moment by moment. I can praise it by saying it's artistic, but his failing is that he pitches his words too quickly and the broadcast becomes fragmentary; he doesn't systematically explain both teams' [ryōgun] movements and actions. Matsuuchi goes in the exact opposite direction: He methodically describes the outfielders' every move and the batter's psychological state. The problem is that his announcing lags behind the action of the game.[21]

Despite this apparent shortcoming, by 1930 Matsuuchi's style had become so popular that there was a demand for recordings of his broadcasts. But because it was difficult to record on location at the stadium, he would go into the studio and, in a sense, reenact the broadcast he had made a day or two earlier. These records, which went by the generic title of *undō suketchi* (sports sketches) sold well because their audiences appreciated the dramatic and, indeed, literary dimensions of his style, not because they wanted to relive the experience of listening to games whose outcomes they already knew. In a preface to a letter from Matsuuchi entitled "Hōsō no kurushimi" (The pains of broadcasting), the editorial staff of *Bēsubōru* wrote:

> If one were to ask how baseball has managed to become this popular in the last three or four years, one should say that most of it is due to the spread of radio. One can further say that it's due to the top announcer in baseball, the one who, through radio, manages to produce broadcasts that are easy to understand and spark the interest of people even in the farthest provinces. In other words, it's no exaggeration to say that Mr. Matsuuchi is the baseball world's benefactor, one who has popularized the game all across Japan.[22]

As these debates and discussions in print make clear, sports broadcasting did not take place in a vacuum. Radio was one component in a media ecology in which the popular market for print culture was thriving. There were several periodicals devoted exclusively to baseball, such as *Yakyū* and

Bēsubōru, sports-interest magazines, and general-interest periodicals that published reportage (and even fiction) on sports in general and sports broadcasting in particular. *Bungei shunjū ōru yomimono* leveraged its relationship with Kume and Matsuuchi to publish shorthand transcriptions of Matsuuchi's broadcasts. As Hibi Yoshitaka contends, the fact that Matsuuchi's broadcasts were transcribed and published complicates the issue of immediacy that Kume and Matsuuchi foregrounded in the rhetoric of their debates. What happens to the "live-ness" or immediacy of a spoken broadcast that has been transcribed and can be read, reread, and analyzed *as text*? These transcriptions were not simply presented as reproductions of the broadcasts; they were treated as texts incorporated into print media

FIGURE 4.5 "Sports Sketch" recording of Keiō–Waseda Baseball Game announced by Matsuuchi Norizō, 1930. Photograph by the author.

contexts that included photos, drawings, collages, and other visual assemblages.²³

We see from this that for all the rhetoric of liveness and immediacy, sports broadcasts in general, and Matsuuchi's in particular, were commodities that were artfully fashioned according to certain narrative and performative conventions and then reproduced and repackaged across a number of different media platforms.

Kume's and Matsuuchi's rhetorical defense of immediacy set a precedent for sports broadcasting in Japan, a precedent that later come back to haunt Matsuuchi when another man eventually eclipsed him as Japan's favorite sports announcer and went on to announce probably the single most famous event in Japanese sports broadcasting history.

Kasai Sansei (1898–1970) got his start in journalism as a sports reporter for the Jiji Shinpōsha news agency before moving to NHK in 1929. Within a few years he became popular enough as a sports announcer to rival Matsuuchi himself. His delivery was brisk and matter-of-fact, free of the literary and dramatic flourishes that distinguished Matsuuchi's, but at the same time it was more descriptive than Uotani's. He also had a formidable knowledge of the game and its players. Kasai was, in short, the answer to Kyūdaiko's prayers, and his style appealed to other listeners as well. As Takeyama Akiko tells us,

> The debate that arose nearly simultaneously in Japan and the United States over whether it was better for sports announcers to be "entertaining to listen to" or "to convey the course of events accurately" is highly suggestive of the relationship between the radio and the public. As sports broadcasting grew more popular, "accuracy" became more desired than "entertainment," and a shift took place from the Matsuuchi style of announcing to the Kasai style. One can say that this reflected a change in the mentality of Japanese society, which of course constituted the audience for these broadcasts. Matsuuchi's style was a continuation of the type of performance entertainment that the "common people" [shomin] had been familiar with since the Tokugawa period, one that made skillful use of the arts of storytelling [wagei] to captivate the audience. Kasai's style, in contrast, was more descriptive and data-oriented, redolent of the modernity embodied by the urban "masses" [taishū] that came into being in the early Shōwa period.²⁴

I would only add to this that Kasai's popularity was due to more than just his matter-of-fact descriptive style and his mastery of facts and figures. The speed of his delivery and his ability to create that sense of immediacy, that sense of "liveness," were even more powerful than those of his older colleague and rival.

Matsuuchi and Kasai were also at odds in their personalities and temperaments, which made working together as JOAK's top two announcers difficult for both. When the time came for NHK to decide whom to send to Los Angeles for the 1932 Summer Olympics, Matsuuchi and Kasai were the obvious choices. At the insistence of Osaka's JOBK, NHK also included Shimaura Seiji (1906–1992), a rising young star who had begun working at the station only the previous year. The journey across the Pacific on the steamer *Taiyōmaru* was eventful. At one point, Matsuuchi and Kasai got into a drunken shouting match over who would cover which events, and they almost came to blows. The drunken fighting ended once they arrived in Los Angeles—the United States was still under Prohibition at that time—but the tensions between them lingered throughout the trip.

Japan first took part in the Olympics during the 1912 games in Stockholm. Neither those nor subsequent games in Antwerp and Paris elicited much interest on the part of the Japanese people or press. This changed to some extent with the 1928 games at Amsterdam, when Oda Mikio (1905–1998) became the first Japanese to win a gold medal (for the triple jump) and Hitomi Kinue (1907–1931) won the silver medal in the 800-meter, becoming the first Japanese woman to win an Olympic medal.[25] Nonetheless, the Japanese public's interest in the games was still relatively modest. These games were not covered by radio media, only by newspapers, and in any event, radio had yet to attract a sizable portion of the populace.

A more dramatic shift, in both media coverage and public interest, came with the 1932 Olympic Games in Los Angeles. One reason was the fact that many more Japanese homes had radios, thanks largely to the Manchurian Incident of 1931, which had prompted widespread radio purchases by those who wanted to follow the developments of that conflict. The technical facilities for nationwide live broadcasting had already been put into place—in quite a hurry, in fact—in time for Emperor Hirohito's enthronement ceremony in November 1928.

NHK had arranged to use U.S. broadcaster NBC's facilities to transmit live broadcasts to Japan directly from the stadium. NBC negotiated the deal under the assumption that live broadcasts would be possible because they had been made during the Winter Olympics earlier that year in Lake Placid, New York, but the summer games' organizing committee decided late in the planning to forbid any kind of live broadcast of the games for fear that it would cut into ticket sales.

Since NBC no longer had a financial incentive to install live broadcasting equipment in the stadium, it reneged on the deal, and the NHK contingent was forced to jot down notes and rush to the studios of nearby station KFI, where they filed radio reports made to sound as if they were coming directly from the stadium. These broadcasts were called *jikkan hōsō*, "broadcasts that feel live." Although the announcers apparently made every effort to make these broadcasts "feel live," they weren't always successful. Matsuuchi, in particular, tended to stretch the events out temporally; so much so, in fact, that a 100-meter dash—which usually took only about ten seconds—wound up lasting a full minute from the moment that he said the race began to the moment he reported the winner crossing the finish line.

We see thus with both the *jikkan hōsō* broadcasts and the *undō suketchi* recordings a kind of simulated or fabricated immediacy. The consumers of these broadcasts and recordings were aware that they were not literally "live," yet their desire for the "feeling" of liveness, for the *jikkan*, was enough for them to play along with the fiction.

The tenor of the Los Angeles broadcasts was often unapologetically nationalistic, reflecting a rising tide of international competition and tension as well as Japan's increasing self-assertiveness (and isolation) in the aftermath of the Manchurian Incident. The following are Shimaura's notes for the broadcast after Japan swept the top three places in the 100-meter backstroke:

> First place, Japan. Second place, Japan. Third place, Japan. The day that Japan has long yearned for has finally arrived. Now, thanks to our three heroes, Kiyokawa, Irie, and Kawazu, we can feel overwhelming pride at the sight of three Japanese flags fluttering high in the sky as the "Kimigayo" anthem plays in the background. . . . The entire swimming team of Japan, occupying one corner of the stands, stood up and, at the team captain Takaishi's signal, gave three cheers of "Banzai!" Let us join in our friends' cheer, for now Japan has conquered the entire world. "Nippon banzai!"[26]

The NHK broadcasting team sent to cover the 1936 Olympics in Berlin was reduced to only two announcers: Kasai Sansei and his JOAK colleague Yamamoto Teru, four years his junior, (1902–1998). They were accompanied by their director Tanomogi Shinroku (1899–1968).

On the morning of the 200-meter women's breaststroke, which took place on August 11, the eleventh day of the games, Kasai told Yamamoto he was exhausted and asked him to announce the event in his place. As the only two announcers, they had been working nonstop since arriving in Berlin, announcing events, researching athletes from other countries, and preparing for the next day's broadcasts. They were also fed up with the bland German food and the exorbitant taxi fares. But both men also knew that Maehata Hideko (1914–1995), who had won silver in the 200-meter at the Los Angeles Olympics in 1932, had a very good chance of winning the gold this time around; knowledgeable observers figured the race to be a two-way fight between Maehata and Germany's Martha Genenger (1911–1995). Good *kōhai* (junior colleague) that he was, Yamamoto insisted that the event was too important, and Maehata's chances of winning too good, for anybody other than Kasai to announce it.

Kasai relented, but his physical indisposition was only the first sign of trouble that day. The shortwave transmitter that the German authorities had provided for sending the broadcasts back to Japan broke down. Another was provided, but it transmitted on a different frequency, and the team had to send an urgent telegram to Tokyo asking JOAK to take the necessary measures to receive the transmission. The telegram arrived only two hours before the broadcast was to begin.

The race had originally been scheduled to begin at 3:40 P.M. local time, which would have meant that the live broadcast would begin at 11:40 P.M. in Japan, in time for the midnight broadcasting cutoff imposed by the Ministry of Communications. As it happened, the women's breaststroke event was delayed right up until almost 4 P.M., or midnight in Japan. This Cinderella scenario is the reason why Kasai began the broadcast with the following plea: "Please don't turn off the switch . . . it's already time, but please don't turn it off, just wait. Please just wait." It sounds as if Kasai is addressing the listening audience, asking them not to turn off their radios. He's doing that too, but more pertinently he's pleading with the Ministry of Communications officials and the JOAK technical staff overseeing the broadcast in Tokyo. He's asking them to bend the rules in order to broadcast live to the nation a moment of potential national triumph. The Ministry of Communications allowed the broadcast to proceed.

The transcript of Kasai's broadcast is too long to reproduce in full here, but the last couple of minutes should be enough to give a sense of how frenzied Kasai became near the end. The Japanese word *ganbare* (keep going/fighting, hang in there) is here translated as "Go!":

> Genenger's advancing. A slim, a slim lead, Maehata has a slim lead.
>
> Go! Maehata, go! Go! Go! Fifteen, fifteen, fifteen, slight lead, slight lead, slight lead.
>
> Maehata! Maehata, go! Go! Go! Genenger's advancing. Go! Go! Go! Go! Go! Go! Go! Go! Maehata, Maehata's lead, Maehata's in the lead, Maehata's lead.
>
> Maehata, go! Maehata, go! Leading, leading, five meters left, five meters left, five meters left, three meters, two meters, ah! Maehata's lead...
>
> She won! She won! She won, she won! She won! She won! Maehata won! She won! She won! She won! She won! She won! Maehata won! Maehata won! Maehata won! Maehata has won, Maehata has won! Maehata has won, Maehata is victorious. It was razor-thin, it was razor-thin, but Maehata is victorious, Maehata has raised the Rising Sun high, the Rising Sun.

The recording that we have of the race was made without official authorization by a Polydor Records employee named Yuji Tomio (1908–?), who used a newly developed Western Electric recorder to press a test record of the broadcast directly from his radio. By an interesting coincidence, Yuji Tomio's father, Keigo, was the first Japanese to successfully produce a disc recording, of General Nogi Maresuke, in 1907.

There actually are two other recordings of this event. The first was discovered by Yuji Tomio in 1990 when he went to visit Hyōdō Hideko (née Maehata Hideko) at her home. She had a cassette tape dub of a recording of the broadcast that was different from the one Yuji Tomio had made—it was considerably longer, including portions of the broadcast before and after Yuji's Polydor version. Maehata couldn't remember the provenance of this recording, which was known in the household as *maboroshi no tēpu*, "the phantom tape." Yuji made a copy of the tape and took it to NHK to see if they had a similar recording or a record of such in their archives, and none was found. The identity of the person who made the recording is still unknown. Noise and other acoustic signatures suggest that it might have been made directly from the shortwave transmission sent from Germany. Although there were many amateur radio operators in Japan at the time, consumer recording technology was hard to come by, so it's likely the recording was made, again without authorization, by somebody in the recording industry, or perhaps even somebody associated with military communications.[27]

The second, less mysterious, recording was not a *jikkyō hōsō* at all. Employees of Asahi Records, unaware that Yuji was recording the live broadcast, took down shorthand transcripts of the broadcasts of numerous Olympic events and then *reenacted* those broadcasts for recording. Thus, this recording didn't even qualify as a *jikkan hōsō*: it was an *undō suketchi* produced from the transcript of a *jikkyō hōsō*. Nonetheless, Asahi tried to obscure that fact by referring to it as *kesshō jikkyō* (live from the final round), but this "liveness" is clearly fabricated from multiple layers of mediation.

Back to the recording: Kasai, who was famous for his crisp, clear, coolheaded style, very clearly lost his cool, which provoked a stern rebuke from some commentators at the time. The poet and scholar Toki Zenmaro (1885–1980), who was also an editorial writer for the *Tōkyō Asahi shinbun* and a member of NHK's Broadcast Terminology Committee, argued in the official NHK periodical *Hōsō* that Kasai had lost his journalistic objectivity and failed to provide "scientific observation" of the competition. Many complained that Kasai said nothing about the third- and fourth-place finishers or how close they may have been to the leaders. Shimaura Seiji bluntly dismissed the broadcast with "That kind of thing isn't live sportscasting" (*Anna no wa jikkyō hōsō ja nai*). Others accused Kasai of *ōen hōsō*, "broadcast cheerleading." Some who watched the newsreel of the event afterward claimed that Kasai had even exaggerated how close the race had been.

But other voices were more appreciative. According to a *Yomiuri shinbun* article,

> In the end, she won. Miss Maehata was victorious. That moment was a killer broadcast [*satsujinteki hōsō*] that took every Japanese person's breath away. With the 200-meter women's breaststroke, Kasai became

"Kasai the Japanese" [*Nihonjin Kasai*]. Clutching his mike 9,000 kilometers away, "Kasai the Japanese" stirred the hearts of all Japan.[28]

The reference to this as a "killer" broadcast is not entirely figurative. One listener, a newspaper bureau chief in Hamamatsu, Shizuoka Prefecture, came home drunk from a banquet and became so excited listening to Kasai's frenzied narration that he collapsed and died.[29]

As we can see, opinions were divided. Kasai himself was chastened enough by the criticism that he became embarrassed by the broadcast and almost never listened to the recording. In later years he even visited the grave of the man who had died listening to the live broadcast, to pay his respects and perhaps to atone. But if posterity has the power to vindicate, as it is commonly assumed to do, then Kasai was vindicated. The SP record of this broadcast sold 110,000 copies after its release by Polydor, an unprecedented figure at the time. "Maehata, *ganbare!*" is possibly the most famous phrase in Japanese sports broadcasting history. And undisguised broadcast cheerleading has—at least in recent years—become quite common.

Takeyama Akiko speculates as to why Kasai might have lost his head the way he did:

1. The air in Nazi Berlin was filled with nationalist fervor, with endless cries of "Heil Hitler!" and other unrestrained expressions of national pride.
2. The overwhelming force of the German people's worship of Hitler made Kasai mentally agitated. Whenever Hitler appeared, the stands would literally tremor at the force of their cries of "Heil! Heil!"
3. These expressions of nationalism, militarism, and anti-Semitism made Kasai acutely conscious of himself as Japanese.

Although all of these are compelling possible reasons, in an interview many years after the event Kasai himself gave a much more mundane explanation: "It never occurred to me to announce the event in that way, but Nishida and Ōe from the track-and-field team were next to me at the broadcasting table. They were cheering her on with 'soore, ganbare, soore, ganbare' ('that's it, keep fighting'), and I basically wound up joining in with 'ganbare, ganbare.'"[30]

This, too, must be taken with a grain of salt because in the broadcast immediately before the women's 200-meter breast stroke, the 4 × 200-meter men's relay, Kasai can twice be heard saying *ganbare*—relatively calmly, but in that race the Japanese men finished ahead of the second-place U.S. team by a full 11.5 seconds and also set a new world record. Indeed, Japan was absolutely dominant in swimming at the 1936 Olympics, winning four gold medals and eleven medals in total, as against four gold and five total for the Netherlands, and two gold and eight total for the United States.

Takeyama posits one additional factor:

4. The athletes were encouraged at home to win at all costs, for "the sake of their country." As Maehata herself recalled of that time, "All of Japan's attention was focused on me. Of course, athletes today experience a great deal of pressure as well, but back then there was the added burden of all of that nationalism. There really is no comparison between then and today. At the time, I felt that if I didn't win, I would want to die."[31]

"All of Japan's attention was focused on me" (*Nihonjū ga watashi ni chūmoku shite ita no desu*). Here was something entirely new, something made possible for the first time by the medium of radio: the sense that an entire nation could be focused on the actions of a single individual, in real time. In reality, of course, millions of Japanese didn't have radios, didn't happen to be listening to that broadcast, or simply couldn't have cared less. But we know from this statement that, at the very least, the reification of the national community was undoubtedly complete: The nation was listening as one.

The political and ethical ramifications of nationalism in a colonial context, or in the context of a nation like Japan in 1936, which had joined the ranks of imperial powers but was still marginalized for racial, economic, and geographic reasons, are extremely complex. Japan was still reeling from the attempted coup d'état of the February 26 Incident earlier that year, and many turned to the games to restore their sense of confidence in their nation and its institutions. Nationalistic fervor was pandemic, and

FIGURE 4.6 Recording insert of Kasai Sansei's recording of the 800-meter relay at the 1936 Berlin Olympics. Photograph by the author.

the fever that marked the 1932 Los Angeles games was exponentially amplified in the Berlin games, which came to serve as a showcase for Hitler's Germany. Although Germany and Japan did not sign the Anti-Comintern Pact until nearly four months later, on November 25, 1936, Joachim von Ribbentrop (1893–1946) and Ōshima Hiroshi (1886–1975) were already working out the details of the pact in October and November 1935,[32] and ties between Germany and Japan had been close for some time. Thus the Japanese contingent was greeted in Berlin as favored allies. A taxi driver in Berlin even asked the NHK broadcasting team for a Japanese flag to put on the hood of his taxi, saying that he wouldn't get stopped by the police for speeding if he were flying the Japanese colors. In that sense, Kasai's cheerleading in a head-to-head competition against Japan's German ally seems a little misplaced, but it must also be read in the context of German (as well as other European and American) racialist discourses that were implicitly and often explicitly demeaning to the Japanese.

On its surface, Kasai's broadcast appears to be immediacy reduced to its barest essence: exclamation, exhortation, and repetition, delivered live to a transfixed national audience. *Ganbare, ganbare, ganbare ganbare*, pure incantation, pure poetry of nationalism. But we must ask: To whom is the imperative *ganbare* addressed? In strictly rhetorical terms, the apostrophic addressee is, of course, Maehata, the competitor in the pool. But because she is in the pool, Maehata cannot hear the exhortation, and furthermore, it is safe to assume that she is already trying as hard as she can to win. For an exhortation to work, the recipient must presumably hear it, unless it is a kind of magic or action at a distance. Yet we know from her remarks afterward that Maehata had already internalized the commandment, that she already knew that nearly all of Japan was listening. I am tempted to speculate that the addressee in this case is not the audience per se, or the authorities whom Kasai implored not to turn off the switch, but the Lacanian big Other. The message is not so much an exhortation *to* the big Other to *ganbaru* as it is proof, in performance, that Maehata is trying hard, that I, Kasai, am trying hard, that we all are trying hard, that *minna ganbatteiru* (everyone is trying), because if anything, the injunction to *ganbaru* already has come primordially from the big Other itself.[33]

As John Durham Peters reminds us in *Speaking into the Air*, radio broadcasting was "not embraced until wireless technology had been in use for a quarter of a century."³⁴ Early developers of that technology were more interested in point-to-point, or person-to-person, communication. The omnidirectionality of wireless transmissions was seen as a defect. Peters argues persuasively that the subsequent history of radio broadcasting represented an ongoing attempt to simulate some kind of direct communication.

> Liveness in radio was the effort to break the connection between death and distance.... A sociologist in 1928, predicting a greater future for the radio than the phonograph, made the explicit equation of simultaneity with life and recording with death: "The radio does not transmit 'dead' material as does the phonograph, but present and 'living' events." In a "live" performance, the body is present in the flesh. "Live" means that contingency is still possible, that the energy is actual, and that a new and singular event can take place. Here again, in the bowels of the new machines of simulation, the old marker of authenticity—the mortal body itself—reappeared.³⁵

The live broadcast of the physical competition of those mortal bodies adds another facet to Peters's argument. In this broadcast, multiple vectors of contingency, energy, and affect converge, emanating from the athletes, from the crowd, from the announcer, from the track-and-fielders cheering on their teammate, from the Ministry of Communications bureaucrat, from the idiosyncrasies and failures of the technical apparatus itself, from the listening audience, and from the young Polydor employee surreptitiously recording it all and thus, in a sense, killing the killer.

But beyond death there is an afterlife, and this broadcast enjoys an afterlife in the form of its bootleg recording and again, in the form of a full transcript in *Bungei shunjū*.

This "killer broadcast," this *satsujinteki hōsō*, became remediated, reinscribed, and reproduced, attaining thereby a power just as lethal through the mechanisms of repetition compulsion and commodity fetishism. These mechanisms, so tightly conjoined with technologies of reproduction, are arguably the most plausible rejoinder to the rhetoric of immediacy that animated early discourses of radio in Japan and the United States. At the same time, these mechanisms would likely not have kicked in had the affective potential of the live moment not been so dramatically realized. I must leave suspended, then, the question of whether the immediacy of live broadcasting can somehow transcend the logic of commodity to reveal an actual social relation, a message that has actually been received by its addressee. All I can discern is a hand in a glove, a doubly or triply or multiply mediated immediacy, a "live" moment that is reified and then relived and relived again in a spectral, vertiginous spiral that extends into the present.

NANIWABUSHI

In August and September 1925, the Tokyo Broadcasting Station conducted a poll of its subscribers to determine what kind of programming they wanted to listen to. Nearly 33,000 people responded to the poll, and table 4.1 gives a fascinating and fairly accurate glimpse of the state of auditory culture in Japan at the time.[36]

As we shall see, the relative popularity of these different types of programming changed over time, especially with *naniwabushi* becoming increasingly popular in the 1930s. No type of program enjoyed a commanding lead in popularity in 1925; no category scored in the double digits, and ten different categories were clustered in the 4.4- to 3.0-percent range. Noteworthy, however, is that the top three slots are occupied by narrative genres and that broadcast stage plays and even the reading of movie narratives are not too far behind.

Naniwabushi originated in the Kansai region during the late Tokugawa period (1603–1868) as a form of street entertainment. The origins of the form are a hybrid of *shōmyō* and *wasan* Buddhist chanting, with elements of *saimon* 祭文 Shinto ballads and *sekkyōbushi* 説経節 narrative ballads. This hybrid came to be known as *chongare* 弔歌連 (also pronounced *chongari* and *chobokure*), which became popular in the early nineteenth century thanks to the efforts of a (possibly apocryphal) performer named Naniwa Isuke. Another performer by the name of Kyōyama Kyōansai (?–1890) added elements of the *gidayū* and *biwa* performing traditions, creating a form known as *ukarebushi* 浮連節. Although this form was first performed by street performers, over time it moved indoors to small huts within the precincts of temples and shrines. The term *naniwabushi*

TABLE 4.1 Results of Listener Preferences Poll, Tokyo Broadcasting Station, 1925

Programming	%	Programming	%
Radio drama ラジオ劇	4.4	Violin バイオリン	2.2
Rakugo 落語	4.4	Brass band 吹奏楽	2.1
Kōdan 講談	4.0	Koto 箏曲	2.0
Gidayū 義太夫	3.8	Vocal recitals 独唱	1.9
Stage plays 放送舞台劇	3.7	Daikagura Lion dance 太神楽	1.9
Nagauta 長唄	3.5	Symphonies シンフォニー	1.9
Satsuma biwa 薩摩琵琶	3.2	Utazawa 哥沢	1.8
Naniwabushi 浪花節	3.1	Mandolin マンドリン	1.7
Shinnai singing 新内	3.0	Dramatic recitation 脚本朗読	1.7
Children's songs 童謡	3.0	Cello セロ	1.7
Children's stories 童話	2.9	Seasonal poetry 景物詩	1.6
Movie storylines 映画物語	2.9	Jazz band ジャズバンド	1.6
Chikuzen biwa 筑前琵琶	2.8	Lyrical music 抒情曲	1.4
Orchestral music 管弦楽	2.8	Opera オペラ	1.4
Tokiwazu ballads 常磐津	2.8	Sekkyōbushi 説教節	1.4
Kiyomoto jōruri 清元	2.8	Icchūbushi 一中	1.0
Chaban farce 茶番掛合噺	2.7	Tomimotobushi 富本	1.0
Harmonica ハーモニカ	2.7	Organ オルガン	0.9
Folk songs 民謡	2.7	Katōbushi 河東	0.8
Shakuhachi 尺八	2.6	Ogiebushi 荻江	0.5
Kouta 小唄	2.4	Sonohachibushi 薗八	0.4
Piano ピアノ	2.2	Other その他	0.7

appears as early as 1830 (although written as 難波ぶし), but it is not known if the style designated by that term has any direct connection to the *naniwabushi* of more recent times. The term in its current orthography was first publicly used in 1872 by the Kyōmushō (Ministry of Education).

The first wave of *naniwabushi*'s popularity came at around the turn of the twentieth century, in large part due to the sensational rise of the legendary balladeer Tōchūken Kumoemon, whose recordings sparked the landmark copyright case discussed earlier. The second wave came in the charged political atmosphere that followed the Manchurian Incident.

Table 4.2 shows the results of a poll conducted by NHK in 1932 asking listeners what types of entertainment programming they wanted most to listen to, and it reveals that *naniwabushi* was the most popular type of programming nationwide, by far.[37] It is only fitting that these results appeared in an NHK poll, since radio was the prime mover behind *naniwabushi*'s resurgent popularity in the early 1930s after a fallow period brought about by the loss of audiences to the new medium of cinema.

The form of vocal literature known as *naniwabushi*, through the agency of the new medium of the radio, created what Hyōdō calls a "vocal unison" across the entire nation of Japan during the early years of the Shōwa period (1926–1989):

> These melodious voices, which absorbed and dissolved the logic of the legal system, were the essence of the *naniwabushi* mentality, a mentality described in terms of "Japan's native ethos of duty and human feeling." These narratives, whether they were revenge tales, Robin Hood-type stories [*kyōkakumono*], or sentimental tales [*ninjōmono*], were permeated with the voice of *naniwabushi*, and their morality, while inciting a sense of violent revolt against the existing order and hierarchy, at the same time helped construct the sensibility required for fascism in a Japanese key.[38]

One of the key "texts" (or rather, a body of texts around a common theme) in the construction of this sensibility was the Forty-Seven Righteous Samurai of Akō (*Akō gishi*), a story perhaps best known in its incarnations as the bunraku and kabuki plays *Kanadehon chūshingura* (or commonly just *Chūshingura*). Hyōdō and Henry Smith contend that *naniwabushi* can claim responsibility for the "Gishi boom" of the last years of the Meiji period. In a very real sense, the ubiquity of this story in Japanese culture today can be traced back to the concerted efforts of *naniwabushi* singers (and their nationalist patrons) during the art form's heyday in the late Meiji and then subsequently when *naniwabushi* made a comeback in the 1930s thanks to radio. As Hyōdō and Smith write, "In

TABLE 4.2 Results of 1932 NHK Listener Poll

	First Place	Second Place	Third Place	Fourth Place
Kantō	Naniwabushi (49.0%)	Kōdan (17.9%)	Rakugo (14.3%)	Biwa (12.2%)
Kansai	Naniwabushi (53.0 %)	Rakugo (27.9%)	Kōdan (10.7%)	Biwa (9.0%)
Tōkai	Naniwabushi (49.6%)	Gidayū (11.6%)	Rakugo (10.0%)	Kōdan (9.8%)
Chūgoku	Naniwabushi (41.2%)	Biwa (12.7%)	Gidayū (11.6%)	Kōdan (9.8%)
Kyūshū	Naniwabushi (47.9%)	Yōkyoku (12.4%)	Gidayū (12.2%)	Biwa (12.1%)
Tōhoku	Naniwabushi (29.8%)	Minyō (26.7%)	Kōdan (9.0%)	Biwa (8.6%)
Hokkaidō	Naniwabushi (23.3%)	Minyō (19.8%)	Yōkyoku (8.9%)	Biwa (6.6%)

this way, the Chūshingura phenomenon progressed to a new plane, now far more widely known throughout Japan than ever before and deeply embedded in all of the leading modern media technologies, especially phonograph records and, in time, radio and television."[39]

RADIO NOISE

Of all of the writers of modern Japan, the one who paid the greatest attention to the sounds of modernity was Nagai Kafū—probably because he hated them the most. Of the many aural banes of his existence, radio was the worst. The sound of his neighbors' radios and phonographs drove him from his house evening after evening to the *bokutō* (the part of Tokyo east of the Sumida River), where the courtesans were forbidden to use such devices. This passage from *Bokutō kidan* (*A Strange Tale from East of the River*), published in 1937, makes evident Kafū's exasperation with the by-then ubiquitous convenience:

The rains ended, the hot weather came, and, because the windows were open, sounds not heard in other seasons began to come to my ears. The sound that disturbed me most was that of the radio next door, beyond a thin board fence.

Waiting for the cool of evening, I would turn on the light at my desk; and at exactly that moment, it would begin, strident and somehow cracked, and it would not die away until after nine o'clock. I was particularly tormented by political orators with west-country accents, by singers of *naniwabushi*, and by readings that made one think of amateur players, broken by snatches of Western music. And the radio alone did not seem to be enough. Morning and night there were phonographs playing popular music. In the summer, I would hurry through dinner, or even dine out—I would flee the house at the stroke of six o'clock. Not that there were no radios to listen to even after I went out. The clamor from houses and shops along the way was even more deafening; but it was mixed with the sounds of the city, automobiles and streetcars, and I found less to bother me when I was out walking than when I was alone in my study.

With the end of the rains, the progress of my *Whereabouts Unknown* was interrupted by the neighbors' radio. I had done no work on it for ten days and more. There seemed to be a possibility that I would quite lose interest in it.[40]

The noise of the radio is so maddening that Kafū's fictional alter ego cannot even make progress on his novel. Like so many other technological innovations, the radio had unintended consequences: people could now unwittingly (or perhaps not so unwittingly) torment their neighbors with the electrical sounds emanating from their radios and phonographs.

The passage of time did nothing to lessen Kafū's torments, as we see from a series of entries in his diary, *Danchōtei nichijō*, from 1946:

July 24: Fled to the shade of a tree to escape the radio.
July 25: It's impossible to read or write in this heat with the sound of the radio next door. Every day in the afternoon I leave the house and go to the greenery of Katushika Hachiman or the Shirahata Tenjin grounds

and return around sunset. The radio doesn't stop until past ten at night. The torture of the past few days doesn't need mentioning.

August 1: Unable to stand the sound of the radio at night, I took a walk in the darkness to visit Kogawa.

August 2: The radio next door creating a racket again tonight.

August 3: Already in the morning, the radio next door is blaring. Head aching unbearably, I step out to visit Kogawa. In the afternoon, Kogawa stops by to talk. As I sit at my desk after dinner, once again the radio starts up. Pen and notebook in hand I walk to a grove in Suwa Shrine and sit on a rock. As I write a few lines in the dark of night, I am suddenly besieged by mosquitoes. I walk home along the national highway. I roll out my futon, stuff cotton into my ears, and try to sleep.[41]

The Swiss writer Max Picard shared Kafū's distaste for the sonic intrusions of the radio:

Radio is autonomous noise itself. It has occupied all space: man has been pushed to the edge of space and he can only worm his way through a few remaining gaps and crevices in space.

At six in the morning he is called to early morning physical jerks, at 6:20 to a piece of music, at 7 to news from all over the world, then again to music. At 8 he is called to prayer. At half past eight he is surrounded by recipes for housewives, at 9 by Bach and so on. The radio machine does not seem to be in the least dependent on man at all. It is as though it were just listening to itself all the time. A pianoforte piece by Chopin is answered by some jazz and this in its turn by a talk about vitamins. Radio seems to be engaged in a conversation with itself. Man has been pushed on one side; he is simply a machine-hand attending to the radio noise-machine.[42]

Picard saw radio as part of the larger problem of humanity's atomization under the sign of modernity, as a contributor to the disjointedness and discontinuity that strips human beings of their ties to one another and to the past—even to their own personal past, which is drawn into and lost in the whirlpool of chaotic streams of unrelated impressions. This discontinuity and disjointedness, in Picard's view, was precisely what allows totalitarian regimes (particularly Hitler's Nazism) to take power even in putatively democratic polities:

> From this outer jumble, then, Adolf Hitler could easily sneak into the inner jumble; in this disjointedness he could show himself beside anything because he fitted anything: such as he was, he fitted into anything disjointed.
>
> And as again and again he showed himself in this jumble, he became more distinct than the other parts of the chaos; one got used to him and accepted him as one accepts a toothpaste which turns up again and again in the chaos of advertising pages. Soon he appeared as the only reality in a world wherein everything else manifested itself only to vanish again immediately.[43]

It's easy, and perhaps a little tempting, to dismiss both Kafū and Picard as hypersensitive curmudgeons, Luddites, or antimodernist reactionaries. Yet they speak from the perspective of those who witnessed the transition to modernity, those who didn't need to imagine the world before it became saturated with these maddening new noises and fleeting, disjointed impressions because they had lived in it. In a Gadamerian sense, that kind of authority is one to which we have no real answer: It gives us pause, it makes us uneasy. Who are we to know, ultimately, exactly what modernity has made of us? We can only imagine how Schopenhauer, Carlyle, and Sōseki—who could barely stand the noise of the preindustrial and early industrial ages—would have fared today. But we don't need to imagine what Schopenhauer would think about the modern subject's brutish indifference to such sonic assaults—our brains, it seems, have been rendered "rough and coarse."

VOICE AND VOID

Although the radio was utilized as an effective means of social and political control, it's a fascinating paradox that the voice of the head of state and the father of the metaphorical nation-family, that is, the emperor, was not allowed to be broadcast. It is popularly believed that the emperor's voice was never broadcast until the *gyokuon hōsō* (lit., "broadcast of the precious sound") announced Japan's surrender in the Pacific War. But according to Takeyama Akiko, Hirohito's voice was in fact inadvertently broadcast during the live broadcast of a state military parade in December 1928.[44] The radio station responsible was severely upbraided for that lapse, and in the future, the utmost care was taken to ensure that the emperor's voice was never broadcast again until the end of the war.

This refusal to broadcast the emperor's voice suggests some underlying assumptions about broadcasting, about voices in general, and, it goes without saying, about the emperor system. It is first and foremost an element of showmanship: what is kept hidden is mysterious, what is mysterious becomes invested with a manner of numinous power. As Yoshimi Shun'ya put it, the emperor's voice had to remain a kind of a void (*kūhaku*),[45] but a void is never really a void, for it inevitably becomes the projecting screen of fantasy.

Mladen Dolar posits two characteristic functions of the voice in totalitarian regimes. The first model is that of Hitler, whose very voice alone was what made him the Führer. His voice itself was the law. Dolar quotes Adolf Eichmann, who famously said, "Führerworte haben Gesetzkraft" (the words of the Führer have the force of law). In contrast, Joseph Stalin's voice was meant to be monotonous and free of rhetorical power and affect. Stalin read from an interminable prepared script that succeeded in doing nothing other than putting the audience to sleep. Dolar writes: "The Führer's words, supported by the immediate charismatic presence of the voice, were immediately legislative . . . while the Stalinist ruler endeavors to efface himself and his voice; he is merely the executor of the text, just as he is the mere tool of the laws of history, not their creator."[46]

The case of Hirohito presents a third possibility, one that may have eluded Dolar's purview of cultural reference. The oversight is understandable but is made all the more remarkable by the fact that the voice, as an *objet petit a*, is in fact always already subject to the vanishing act that it systematically underwent in the emperor system. The unheard voice was precisely "the lack, the remainder of the real that sets in motion the symbolic movement of interpretation, a hole at the center of the symbolic order, the mere appearance of some secret to be explained, interpreted, etc."

We get a clear sense of this when we read the testimonials of those who heard that first broadcast:

> I could hear the anguish in His Majesty's feeble and halting voice, and I had to hold back my tears. (Abe Yoshishige, philosopher)
>
> My first feeling was of relief: he sounded much more cheerful, youthful, and energetic than I had expected. He spoke without the slightest pause in a healthy, natural voice animated by awareness and intelligence. It was as if he were talking to us like any normal person would; it was completely to be expected, I suppose, but at the time it felt like something miraculous. (Nagayo Yoshirō, writer)
>
> The poor quality of the recording and His Imperial Majesty's distinctive pronunciation made it difficult to understand what he was saying, so I focused all of my attention on his every word. (Itokawa Hideo, engineer)
>
> We could hear tears in the emperor's stammering voice, a voice we were hearing for the first time. Everyone in the company was sobbing. (Takemori Kazuo, author, who was in Dalian, China, at the time)
>
> Although His Majesty's voice didn't break, I could still somehow sense the grief and solemnity in it and couldn't help but feel an ominous foreboding. Near the end of the speech, all I could hear clearly were the words "my subjects" [*nanji shinmin*] repeated again and again. I realized that I was one of the subjects being addressed, and although I barely understood everything else that was being said, that alone was enough to make my eyes well with tears of gratitude and awe. (Koyama Eiko, twenty-five at the time)
>
> What a clear voice! I was filled with a sense of gratitude, down to the last hair follicle. This, this was humanity at its loftiest heights, and the dulcet voice passing through the earthly matter of those vocal cords was a divine sound [*tenrai no hibiki*] showing us the path of truth. (Tokugawa Musei, *benshi* and voice actor)
>
> The emperor's voice seemed to tremble a number of times. It also seemed to be filled with sadness. (Eguchi Kan, novelist)

FIGURE 4.7 Original disc of the Shōwa emperor's declaration of surrender, NHK Museum of Broadcasting. Photograph by the author.

When I heard it for the first time, His Majesty's voice had a limpid youthfulness about it. He spoke the words as if he were reciting poetry, and there was an almost superhuman [*ningenbanare*] quality to his voice that I have never heard before or since. (Ozaki Shirō, novelist).[47]

The emperor's voice, rendered into a phantasm by the very mechanism of its recording and broadcast, thus became an auditory Rorschach test for his subjects, a screen onto which they could project their own individual reactions to the emperor, the emperor system, and ultimately the big Other itself, from the matter-of-fact observations of the engineer Itokawa to the hyperbolic mysticism of the famed *benshi* Musei. What they heard through the crackling static, in the end, was whatever they wanted to hear.

5

GHOSTLIER DEMARCATIONS, KEENER SOUNDS

Early Japanese Radio Drama

> *If we sit and talk in a dark room, words suddenly acquire new meanings and different textures. They become richer, even, than architecture, which Le Corbusier rightly says can best be felt at night.*
> —MARSHALL MCLUHAN, UNDERSTANDING MEDIA: THE EXTENSIONS OF MAN

On the evening of August 13, 1925, the Tokyo Broadcasting Station (call sign JOAK) broadcast a radio drama entitled *Tankō no naka* (In a coal mine). Although it wasn't the first radio play ever to be broadcast in Japan, it was the first to be designated as a radio *drama* (*rajio dorama*), as opposed to a radio *play* (*rajio geki*) or some other name. *Tankō no naka* was a translation by playwright and director Osanai Kaoru (1881–1928) of a radio drama entitled *Danger*, written by novelist and playwright Richard Hughes (1900–1976) and commissioned and produced by Nigel Playfair (1874–1934) for the BBC. That radio piece had had its premier in London on January 15, 1924, and is widely considered the first play written in the United Kingdom specifically for the medium of radio.[1]

Danger is set in a coal mine in Wales. A young couple, Jack and Mary, and an old man, Mr. Bax, find themselves lost in the mine after an electrical failure. Since the action is set in complete darkness, the announcers introducing the play for both the London and the Tokyo broadcasts advised their respective audiences to turn off their lights as they listened in. Tokyo Broadcasting Station at the time was housed in a building in central Tokyo, atop a twenty-six-meter-high hill called Atagoyama with an impressive view of the surrounding streets and buildings. Producer Kobayashi Tokujirō later recalled that after the announcer had finished his introduction, "if you looked outside the window, you could see the lights in the houses down below going off one by one."[2] A magazine reporter present during the broadcast wrote that there was "an unusual tension in the air, like Paris bracing itself for a night attack from a German Zeppelin. All the homes listening to the radio were shrouded in darkness."[3]

The image of thousands of households turning off their lights together to dream as one is haunting. This dreaming is not the collective dreaming of an audience in the cinema; instead, the audience listens together, but what they see is the product of their own mind's eye and is thus private and individual. The psychologist Hugo Münsterberg (1863–1916) suggested that many of the conventions of cinematic art, such as close-ups and flashbacks, were analogous to universal modes of mental representation. In that sense, cinema, though a new medium, presumably meshed easily with spectators' innate habits of visual thinking. Radio drama, in contrast, offered something more subtly but even more radically new: disembodied voices enacting a dramatic narrative. If cinema can be analogized as a kind of collective dreaming, radio drama might be thought of as a kind of collective hypnosis, or perhaps even as a medium (in both senses) to a spectral world.

BEGINNINGS

In Japan, radio drama had the misfortune of coming into being just as the Taishō period (1912–1926) was ending. It had only a few years to develop before the rising tide of militarism cast a chill over all aspects of cultural production. Although radio drama enjoyed something of a golden age in Japan between the end of the Pacific War and the widespread adoption of television, that golden age was remarkably brief. Radio drama therefore is the rare and possibly unique case of a major art form that was born and then, for all intents and purposes, died, all within living memory. Yet like the spectral presences it vivifies for its listeners, it lives on in disparate forms in disparate corners of the Earth, as well as in the digital recesses of the internet.

The transition from the thinking and conventions of stage drama to radio drama was not quick or easy. Many of the earliest radio dramas were nothing more than slight alterations of stage pieces, and even many of the early plays written originally and specifically for radio broadcast did almost nothing to make conscious use of the medium. As Nishizawa Minoru's comprehensive analysis of the earliest Japanese radio dramas asserts, many of them were little more than chamber dramas, simple dialogues in rooms. The potential for a radio drama to be set in any place and time, to go far beyond what can readily or feasibly be represented through images, was only occasionally exploited. Some of this was due to the very primitive state of sound-effects technology, but much of it was due to the playwrights' refusal or inability to "think outside the stage" and exercise a specifically auditory imagination.

Because of the centralization of early Japanese broadcasting, the history of Japanese radio drama is generally better documented than the history of radio drama in the United States. Nonetheless, there still is some ambiguity about exactly what constituted the very first "real" Japanese radio drama. The following are some of the candidates, according to Nishizawa:

1. The first drama of any kind was broadcast was on April 29, 1925: *Daichi wa hohoemu* (The Earth smiles).
2. The first drama to be broadcast after the beginning of *regular* broadcasting: July 12, 1925: *Kiri hitoha* (A falling paulownia leaf), an adaptation of the 1894 play by Tsubouchi Shōyō.
3. The first dramatic broadcast adapted for radio: July 19, 1925: *Taii no musume* (The captain's daughter), based on the novel *Gendarm Möbius* by the German poet and novelist Victor Blüthgen (which also was made into a silent film in Germany in 1914).
4. The first radio drama selected from an open competition for amateurs: October 9, 1925, the musical drama *Wakare no Urashima* (Farewell at Urashima).

5. The first broadcast of an original radio drama script by an established author: November 26, 1925, *Fūfu* (Husband and wife), a radio comedy by Nagata Hideo.

Table 5.1 lists all the dramatic broadcasts of Tokyo's JOAK between late April and December 1925.[4]

Each of these productions attracted much interest as well as new business to the nascent medium. The day after the broadcast of *Kiri hitoha* with the famed kabuki *onnagata* (woman impersonator) Nakamura Utaemon performing, the number of applicants for new radio subscriptions tripled. Then after the broadcast of *Taii no musume*, the number of applicants doubled again.[5]

Although it's difficult to say with certainty what the first "genuine" radio drama may have been, the identities of the two people who helped launch the genre in Japan can be affirmed with more confidence: Nagata Mikihiko (1887–1964) and Hattori Yoshio (1882–1939).

Nagata Mikihiko was born in Tokyo in what was then called Kōjimachi Ward, now Chiyoda Ward. His father was a physician in private practice, and he grew up in comfortable circumstances. He entered the English literature department at Waseda University, but in 1909 temporarily broke off his studies to travel to Hokkaido, where he worked variously as a railroad worker, coal miner, and itinerant entertainer. Nagata returned to Tokyo two years later and graduated from Waseda. Just as important was his literary debut that year in the literary journal *Subaru* (The Pleiades) with his serial novel *Mio* (Waterway), which was followed the next year by *Reiraku* (Downfall), which appeared in *Chūō kōron*. He became friends with Tanizaki Jun'ichirō, and the two young writers spent much of the summer of 1912 indulging in the pleasures of Kyoto's Gion entertainment district. These adventures provided the material for Nagata's short-story collection, *Gion*, published in 1913. The two young men came to be dubbed the Tanbiha (Aesthetes) because of their self-consciously decadent tendencies. Not long after that summer of debauchery and camaraderie, the two young authors had a falling out, as comrades in debauchery are wont to do, but Nagata's taste for Gion remained undiminished. In 1915 he published *Gion yawa* (Late night talks in Gion), which was followed by a number of other Gion-related works.

TABLE 5.1 JOAK Dramatic Broadcasts Between Late April and December 1925

Date	Title	Type	Author
April 29, 1925	*Daichi wa hohoemu* (The Earth smiles)	Movie dialogue	Yoshida Hyakujō
May 10, 1925	*Sayaate* (Rivals in love)	Broadcast stage play	
May 30, 1925	*Kunisada Chūji*	Radio play	Yukitomo Rifū
June 14, 1925	*Hototogisu* (Cuckoo)	Radio play	
July 4, 1925	*Eijigoroshi* (Infanticide)	*Shingeki*	Yamamoto Yūzō
July 12, 1925	*Kiri hitoha* (A paulownia leaf)	Stage play	Tsubouchi Shōyō
July 19, 1925	*Taii no musume* (The captain's daughter)	Radio play	Nakauchi Chōji
July 28, 1925	*Kanashiki henro* (The melancholy pilgrim)	"Radio lyric opera"	Nagata Mikihiko
August 13, 1925	*Tankō no naka* (In a coal mine)	Radio play	Based on *Danger* by Richard Hughes, translated by Osanai Kaoru
August 20, 1925	*Kuregata* (Toward nightfall)	*Shingeki*	Kubota Mantarō
October 9, 1925	*Wakare no Urashima* (Farewell at Urashima)	Radio drama	Kurokawa Senpachiya
November 26, 1925	*Fūfu* (Husband and wife)	Radio comedy	Nagata Hideo
November 28, 1925	*Futocchō* (Fatty)	Radio drama	Sawa Katsuzō
December 19, 1925	*Sumidagawa* (The Sumida River)	Radio drama	Hongō Shuntairō

FIGURE 5.1 Photo of Nagata Mikihiko, featured in *Musen to jikken* (Radio experimenter), June 1925.

On June 11, 1925, Nagata went to visit his friend Hattori Yoshio at the provisional radio broadcasting center in Shibaura (the Tokyo Broadcasting Station moved to its permanent base at Atagoyama on July 12). The programs he listened to while there included a *kōen* narrative recital (*Kurimoto igaku hakase* [Doctor of medicine Kurimoto]), a *naniwabushi* performance, and a *nagauta* performance (*Aki no irokusa* [The varied colors of autumn]). A month later, he wrote in the magazine *Josei* (Woman): "As I was being drawn, body and all, into an endless brocade of fantasies, I listened to the beautiful, plaintive cry of the strings emerging from the speakers like choked-up sobs, to the auditory illusion of a beautiful, living voice. I was spellbound and breathless."[6]

Before this, Nagata had exhibited a strong interest in cinema and photography as well. In addition to being a best-selling author, he worked as a consultant to Shōchiku Kamata studio, and in 1928, when his serial novel *Kaen no tsuzumi* (Drum of fire) was being made into a film by Shōchiku, he wrested directorial control away from the studio-assigned director, Yasuda Norikuni.[7] Nagata had a professed love for all things new, and radio, as the newest media technology at the time, clearly stoked his imagination.

Hattori Yoshio is an almost-forgotten figure whose influence on the subsequent development of Japanese radio would be hard to overstate. After working for a time at the *Jiji shinpō* (a liberal newspaper founded in 1882 by Fukuzawa Yukichi), he went to work as the advertising director for the cosmetics firm Itō Kochōen. In 1916 Itō Kochōen had started a publishing company, Genbunsha, which published several magazines and newspapers, including *Shinengei* (New performing arts), for which Hattori also wrote drama criticism under the pen name Katashira Rōjin. This publishing venture was part of a cross-platform marketing plan similar to that of Itō Kochōen's main competitor, Mitsuwa, and was not much different from the branding and cross-marketing strategies employed by conglomerates and partner businesses today. Hattori then began working as the assistant to Count Ogasawara Nagayoshi (1885–1935), president of the Kokuseiin National Statistics Bureau. He stayed for only five months, because in April 1925 he joined the just-formed Tokyo Broadcasting Station and in June of that year was named its broadcasting director. In August 1926 the Ministry of Communications decided to consolidate the Tokyo (JOAK), Osaka (JOBK), and Nagoya (JOCK) stations into the newly formed Nihon Hōsō Kyōkai (NHK). When Hattori stepped down as JOAK's broadcasting director, Nagata decided to leave with him. As Takeyama Akiko outlines in the following list, Hattori achieved a great deal in the fourteen months that he held his position:

1. He put in place a program production staff. He hired Uchiyama Rizō and Kobayashi Tokujirō from Genbunsha to handle literary and dramatic programming, and from the *Chūgai shōgyō shinpō* (precursor

of today's *Nikkei shinbun*), he hired Machida Kashō to program Japanese music and Senō Kōjirō to program Western music.
2. He was a leader in helping create radio drama.
3. He established a system of "honorary artistic staff" to attract performers.
4. He established an English-language education program.
5. He helped establish the Nihon Symphony Orchestra, precursor of the NHK Symphony Orchestra.[8]

In those early days of 1925, Hattori made sure that some form of spoken narrative had a place in radio programming, but he had not yet formulated a clear plan of the shape those programs should take. Nagata thus set about convincing Hattori that the simple reading of literary works and stage plays into the radio microphone was not the best use of the new medium.

> I realized that broadcasting stage plays just as they were over the radio was rather difficult and, indeed, quite ill-advised. Just as movies have screenplays made specifically for film, radio plays [*rajio geki*] must have scripts written specifically for radio. In the future, I would like radio drama to achieve perfection as a new art form.[9]

One way to achieve that perfection, in Nagata and Hattori's estimation, was to assemble a group of specialists—writers, broadcasters, musicians, actors—who would explore the possibilities. The result was the Rajio Dorama Kenkyūkai (Radio Drama Research Group), composed of twenty-five members, including Nagata, Hattori, Osanai Kaoru, Nagata's brother Hideo (1885–1949), Kubota Mantarō (1889–1963), Yoshii Isamu (1886–1960), Yamamoto Yūzō (1887–1974), Satomi Ton (1888–1983), Kikuchi Kan, and Kume Masao. This is how the group was described to reporters at a press conference:

> To put it boldly, creating a drama that takes place solely in the realm of hearing is to create an art form that has never existed before. Just as cinema has finally gained a foothold as a new art form, so too must the "radio play," in all its various guises, come to fruition. For that to

happen, research must be undertaken by people who not only truly understand and love radio but who also yearn for and are committed to art. The aim of our research group is precisely that, to undertake a lively inquiry into radio play criticism and production and, of course, to develop and further the careers of radio authors in general.[10]

In 1925, the group put out a series of radio plays, the *Rajio dorama sōsho* (The radio drama library, published by Shunyōdō), which became the founding documents of radio drama practice in Japan.[11]

1. Nagata Mikihiko: *Kanashiki henro* (Melancholy pilgrim), *Fukushū* (Vengeance), and *Kiri* (Fog).
2. Kubota Mantarō: *Kuregata* (Dusk) and *Tsukiyo* (Moonlight).
3. Nagata Hideo: *Mekura no kōrikashi* (The blind usurer), *Fūfu* (Husband and wife), and *Senpu no ko* (My ex-husband's child).
4. Osanai Kaoru: *Tankō no naka* (In a coal mine) and *Inu* (The dog), based on Chekhov's short story "The Lady with the Dog."
5. Yoshii Isamu: *Saigo no seppun* (The last kiss), *Gekijō iriguchi no hanjikan* (Half an hour at the theater's entrance), and *Kamome no shigai* (The seagull's carcass).

None of the original Japanese works is today considered a masterpiece of radio drama. In fairness, however, we must point out that even Hughes's *Danger*, which is rightly celebrated as an innovative essay in the new form, also doesn't break free of a single-point auditory perspective or the general conventions of a one-act drama. Together, these plays represented a diverse set of approaches to the problems and possibilities of the genre. The concerted effort to produce original dramas for the radio was quite remarkable. Although the United Kingdom, which had a head start, broadcast 1,300 radio plays (including repeat broadcasts and sketches) between 1923 and 1928, only 55 "originations" (the BBC term for plays written specifically for the radio) were actually written during this period.[12]

Nagata Mikihiko's *Kanashiki henro* is not so much a drama as a kind of musical for the radio. It is one of the few radio dramas from this period (or from the entire prewar and wartime period, for that matter) for which a recording survives. This recording also happens to be one of the oldest extant recordings available in the public NHK archives, dating from

July 28, 1925. When listening to the recording, one is struck by the effective use of sound effects such as a temple bell and birdsong to create a sense of ambience, but the structure of the work isn't especially dramatic. It's also hindered by a repetitive and not particularly inspired theme song. Nagata later had a successful career as a song lyricist, and one gets the sense in this work that he was more interested in crafting songs than drama.

The Radio Drama Research Group was less notable for the quality of the actual plays it produced than for the discourses it generated on what exactly made good radio drama. The discussion and debate on the matter continued for several years and split into two groups: the "dialogue" camp and the "sound-effects" camp. The foremost proponent of the "dialogue" camp was Osanai, the translator of *Danger*.

Osanai Kaoru was born in Hiroshima, son of an army surgeon. After his father's early death when Osanai was five, his family moved to Tokyo, where he developed an appreciation of literature in high school and began experimenting with writing and translation. He graduated from the English literature department of Tokyo Imperial University in 1906. The next year, with the financial backing of a friend, he started the coterie magazine *Shinshisō* (New thought), which was devoted to publishing translations and criticism of Western plays. Although the magazine lasted for only six issues, it made a considerable impact. In 1909 Osanai founded the Jiyū Gekijō (Free Theater) with kabuki actor Ichikawa Sadanji II (1880–1940), who had just returned from studying in Europe. The company's first production was Mori Ōgai's translation of Ibsen's *John Gabriel Borkman*. The company staged plays by Ibsen, Chekhov, and Gorky. Between 1909 and 1911 Osanai serialized a novel, *Ōkawabata* (The lower reaches of the Sumida River). Between 1912 and 1913 he traveled throughout Europe, visiting Moscow, Berlin, and London, among other cities. He was especially impressed by the work of the Moscow Art Theater (going to see twice its production of Gorky's *The Lower Depths*) and even being invited to the home of the actor/director Konstantin Stanislavski. The Free Theater continued its activities until 1919. That same year, Osanai worked together with Komura Kin'ichi (1883–1930), Nagasaki Eizō (1881–1953), Kubota Mantarō, and Yoshii Isamu to establish the Kokumin Bungeikai (The National People's Art Association). In 1920 Osanai was hired as a consultant to Shōchiku to create a school for actresses. He became much more involved with the studio than that, however, when he took a role in and produced *Rojō no reikon* (*Souls on the Road*) based on a story by Gorky and directed by Murata Minoru.

As this brief biography makes clear, Osanai approached radio drama in 1925 with a wealth of experience writing for the stage, and his perspective was fundamentally dramaturgical, and perhaps even conservative, even though he was a progressive pioneer in Japanese theater circles proper. Despite being a founding member of the Radio Drama Research Group, he is quoted as saying, "I seriously doubt that radio drama will ever mature into a real art."[13] His conservatism extended to the approach he thought the director of radio dramas should take:

> With the radio, the characters are nothing more than their dialogue, so one can't neglect the slightest detail. The clarity of the words must always be preserved, even if in some cases that means sacrificing intonation or inflection to a certain degree. The worst thing possible when listening to a radio drama is for the words to be unclear. That's the one thing you must pay the most attention to.... When it comes to directing radio drama, it's my personal opinion that sound effects shouldn't be ignored, but the first thing you have to think about is the actors' lines.[14]

Osanai's position makes sense from the perspective of a traditional playwright and dramaturge, but it also seems to neglect the novel possibilities of the genre.

One of the more interesting arguments in favor of sound effects came from a slightly later practitioner of radio plays, Mafune Yutaka (1902–1977). Mafune attended Waseda University, where he studied English and Irish theater, but he dropped out to join a leftist agrarian movement. He later wrote short plays, such as *Itachi* (The weasel, 1934) and *Hadaka no machi* (The naked city, 1936), as well as number of radio plays such as *Nadare* (Avalanche, 1936) and *Gekiryū* (Torrent, 1939). Mafune wrote the following reminiscence for an NHK radio drama anthology that appeared in 1956:

> When I wrote this radio drama [*Nadare*], not many original radio dramas had appeared, and we didn't know much about what was being

written abroad. So the first thing I had to consider was what on earth a radio drama was supposed to be.

Since it's a drama, it has to be like a play. But there's no point whatsoever to imitating a stage play: You have no makeup, no costumes, no props, no facial expressions, no stage decor, no form or movement.

All you have are voices. All you can appeal to is the ear. It's a theater that's received by that most sensitive of the senses, hearing. In that case, isn't it closer to music than to theater? These were the very difficult questions with which I grappled. But what I knew for sure was that, as a form of expression that only came into being in this century, it was neither this nor that, and everyone had to struggle with it in his own way.

My solution at the time was this: The stage is much better for the exchange of the dramatic language of human relationships. Since radio addresses the sense of hearing exclusively, it has to express something that the stage can't, namely, the drama of the relationship between people and nature. The sense of hearing apprehends nature simply through its sounds. So I would try to unfold my drama through the quality of the sounds.

Thus, in radio drama, sounds should take the leading role and the actors' dialogue should be its accompaniment. If you make the various sounds that nature produces the very heart of the play, while the drama of the human voices and words provides the accompaniment, you will have a kind of theater unique to radio.

This piece, *Nadare*, is the product of that thinking. The people in the sound-effects department really went to great pains to create the sounds for the broadcast of this play. It may seem pretty unremarkable by today's standards, but back then, sound equipment wasn't as developed as it is today, and I clearly remember how hard the sound-effects engineers had to work to create the echo of a valley or of the mountains, or the sound of an avalanche, in order to put together a "theater of sound," piece by piece.

Until the war began, *Nadare* was broadcast almost once a year with the roles performed by various *shingeki* and *shinpa* actors; but more interesting than the "drama" was the progress made in the sound effects year after year. Even today, I clearly remember that the fascination with a "theater of sound effects" always won the day.[15]

Mafune's decision to couch his defense of sound effects in the rhetoric of human beings' relationship with nature is somewhat problematic. All the sound effects themselves are the products of human ingenuity and artifice, and it isn't clear, at least from his argument, what the exact relationship between human beings and nature is (in the case of an avalanche, one imagines antagonism, but clearly there are other possibilities) and how it is to be dramatized. Yet, at a minimum, Mafune does recognize that radio as a medium has resources to be exploited in addition to limitations to be observed, and when we actually hear a well-produced radio play with evocative soundscapes, Mafune's argument becomes much easier to grasp. On the radio, human beings and their surroundings are flattened into a single ontological dimension, the audible dimension of sound, and we as listeners are immersed in that realm, with no choice but to "believe" what we hear.

"HOW-TO" MANUALS AND AMATEUR PLAYWRIGHTS

Thanks to the many radio play contests that were open to amateurs, radio drama was in some ways a democratic genre. One of the consequences of such a relatively open field of cultural production was the proliferation of guides to writing such dramas. The earliest example of such a work was a Japanese translation of *Théâtre radiophonique, mode nouveau d'expression artistique* (Radio theater, a new mode of artistic expression) by Pierre Cusy and Gabriel Germinet. The book was published in Paris in 1926 and in Japanese translation in 1929. It is conservative in its outlook, arguing for the essential similarity between radio drama and theater, perhaps, as Anke Birkenmaier maintains, in order to lend radio drama the prestige of an ancient art.[16] The same year that *Théâtre radiophonique* appeared in France, Gordon Lea published *Radio Drama and How to Write It* in Great Britain. Although Lea's book appeared at the same time, it wasn't translated into Japanese until 1939. There were also homegrown examples of the genre. *Rajio dorama no tsukurikata, narabi ni rajio doramashū* (How to write radio dramas, with an anthology, 1938), by Hayashi Nikuta, was probably the earliest.

Long before such guides appeared, however, amateurs were submitting their forays into the genre to competitions sponsored by both broadcasters and radio-related publications. One can only imagine what the average quality of the submissions might have been (few of the losing entries survive), but the winning plays provided early Japanese radio with some of its best content. The very first radio drama proper, as defined by Nagata Mikihiko himself, was entitled *Sumidagawa* (The Sumida River), which was the winning selection of an open competition sponsored by the *Nikkan rajio shinbun* (Daily radio times), chosen out of more than five hundred entries.

Sumidagawa was written by Hongō Shuntairō (this was a pen name: his real given name was Takeo), a twenty-year-old editor for the Kenbunkan publishing company, where he worked on the *Shinseinen* (New youth) magazine for teenaged boys. The play was broadcast on December 19, 1925. The two lead voice actors in the play's broadcast were Ōya Ichijirō, a noted *shinpa* actor, and Murata Kakuko, an actress affiliated with the Imperial Garden Theater. Nagata wrote that these two actors "skillfully expressed the individual nuances of the lines in a way that only radio could make possible, and set the new genre of radio drama in an extremely fruitful direction."[17]

Sumidagawa is a period drama that takes place in what seem to be the waning days of the Tokugawa period (1603–1868). The action takes place entirely on a lighter carrying coal along the Sumida River in Edo at dusk. The characters are Genzō, the boat's skipper; Gen'ichi, his son; Yōhei, the elderly skipper of another vessel; and Onatsu, Genzō's wife. The play is short and the story is simple: Onatsu has gone on shore without Genzō's permission. It's apparently not the first time that such a thing has happened, and Genzō, assuming the worst, wants nothing more to do with her. Gen'ichi, however, pines for his mother. Their lighter comes upon Yōhei's boat, barely visible in the gloaming. Yōhei tells them that Onatsu, full of contrition, wishes to come back. He begs Genzō to forgive her and tells them that she's waiting for them on Shirahige Bridge. They pass under the bridge where Onatsu is, in fact, waiting, but Genzō ignores her pleas for forgiveness; distraught, she throws herself into the river. The play ends with Genzō and Gen'ichi trying to pull her from the water, leaving the audience to guess whether or not they succeed.

Melodramatic though it may be, as a radio drama the piece has much to recommend it. Because so much in radio is left to the listener's imagination, the play is able to create a period feel—that of old Edo—at very little cost and effort in the way of sets, costumes, and props. Indeed, the only means available to create that period feel is language—specifically, dialogue. The language of *Sumidagawa* is slightly antiquated (for the time) Edo dialect, with references to Tokugawa-era place-names (Shamisenbori, Shirahige Bridge) completing the sense of periodicity. Just as important, the platform of the moving boat creates a moving auditory perspective that paints a sonic "picture" of the old town while also vivifying the action.

Hongō Shuntairō wrote three other radio dramas: *Kurosawa kyokubadan* (The Kurosawa circus, May 28, 1926), *Sōmatō* (Revolving lantern, July 22, 1926), and *Shinya no kyaku* (Late-night visitor, December 15, 1927). He died in 1928 from causes unknown, at the age of no more than twenty-two or twenty-three.

THE 500-YEN DRAMA

Hattori's successor as broadcasting director of JOAK was Yabe Kenjirō (1885–1962). Japan was in the midst of a severe recession, and Yabe was under pressure to increase the number of subscribers, since Japanese radio at the time didn't air advertising and its only revenue came from subscriptions. The total number of subscribers to NHK was approximately 340,000 (compared with 280,000 for the three independent stations combined a year earlier), but more subscribers were canceling than signing up. Yabe's plan was to commission famous playwrights and novelists to write original radio dramas. The fee per play was 500 yen, which in the depressed economy of the time was reportedly enough money to build a small house. The plan generated the hoped-for public relations sensation, and over the next two years, ten of these "500-yen dramas" were produced and aired:

Although the series generated much publicity and the plays produced were generally more assured and interesting than the fledgling efforts of the Radio Drama Research Group a couple of years earlier, they were, on the whole, not as satisfying as their high commissions promised. Although

TABLE 5.2 JOAK's Five Hundred–Yen Radio Dramas

Author	Work	Date
Satomi Ton	Aru fūfu (A husband and wife)	May 23, 1927
Matsui Shōō	Saō no iede (Shakespeare leaves home)	June 10, 1927
Osanai Kaoru	Chinkyaku (A rare guest)	June 28, 1927
Nagata Hideo	Denpō (Telegram)	August 21, 1927
Yoshii Isamu	Ame no yowa (Talk on a rainy night)	September 29, 1927
Kubota Mantarō	Ukiyodoko shōkei (Sketches from the barbershop of the floating world)	November 29, 1927
Kishida Kunio	Ganbaharu-shi no jikken (Mr. Ganbahal's experiment)	December 29, 1927
Kikuchi Kan	Karera no kibō (Their hopes)	March 1, 1928
Yamamoto Yūzō	Kiri no naka (In the fog)	May 6, 1928
Nakamura Kichizō	Onna ni maketa otokotachi (The men who lost to women)	May 14, 1929

some of these works were anthologized long after, and at least one (*Ukiyodoko shōkei*) was later turned into a television drama, Yamamoto Yūzō's *Kiri no naka* is the only one of the group that ambitiously and effectively made use of the medium.[18]

The son of a dry-goods merchant, Yamamoto was born in Tochigi City. After he completed the equivalent of elementary school, his father sent him to apprentice at a dry-goods shop in Tokyo's Asakusa district, but after a year he ran away and returned home. His mother convinced him to return to Tokyo to continue his schooling. After an irregular accelerated middle school course, he passed the entrance exam to the prestigious Dai-ichi Kōtō Gakkō (First Higher School), an extraordinary feat for a provincial whose schooling had been interrupted for a year. Since the First Higher School was in fact the preparatory division of Tokyo Imperial University, and although Yamamoto failed a year and was held back there, he managed to be admitted to the university itself, where he studied German literature. While at the university, he, Akutagawa Ryūnosuke (1892–1927), and Kikuchi Kan published the third series of the *Shinshichō* (New intellectual currents) literary magazine. Yamamoto translated three plays by Strindberg and was a playwright himself, noted for *shingeki* works like *Eijigoroshi* (Infanticide, 1920), *Sakazaki Dewa no kami* (Lord Dewa, 1921), and *Dōshi no hitobito* (The comrades, 1923).

Kiri no naka takes place on a Japanese freighter on the Kamchatka sea-lane, steaming toward Petropavlovsk. Yamamoto establishes the scene in a few short lines at the beginning of the play:

A freighter at sea.
We begin on the ship's bridge.
A steam whistle intermittently blows, "poh, poh."
The gentle sound of the engine can be heard from the boiler room below.
THIRD MATE: When on earth is this weather going to clear up? This is some pretty thick fog, isn't it?
CAPTAIN: It's especially thick tonight.
THIRD MATE: Yes, sir. This is my first time on the Kamchatka sea-lane, but from what I hear, the fog is always really bad. We haven't had a single day without fog since leaving port, have we?
CAPTAIN: Yeah, it's always bad in the summer.
THIRD MATE: At this rate we'll be pretty late getting into Petropavlovsk.
CAPTAIN: We have no choice. We can't very well speed up under these conditions.

The story is about a newly recruited cabin boy, Tsuruoka, who for unknown reasons commits suicide by jumping overboard. Third Mate Sugino, to whom we're introduced in this opening section, had struck the young man shortly before his death and later blames himself for the suicide. Racked by guilt, Sugino hallucinates that Tsuruoka is actually alive and has come to visit him in Sugino's darkened cabin from his hiding place somewhere aboard the ship. This "Tsuruoka," heard but not seen, reassures Sugino that he's alive and well and that Sugino's beating him wasn't the reason for his disappearance. This auditory hallucination is soon replaced by another one, a voice claiming to be Sugino's "good friend." This voice warns him that he's imagining Tsuruoka to be alive simply to assuage his own guilt, that he's too much of a coward to accept responsibility for his actions. Sugino grows panicked and impatient, and he asks the voice to go away for good. He then starts banging on the door of his cabin, at which point the play ends.

Yamamoto's play highlights another possibility of the sightless medium: the ability to traffic in the fantastic as Tsvetan Todorov described it, as the realm of epistemological hesitation between the uncanny (reducible to rational explanation) and the marvelous.[19] The play doesn't completely exploit that, but it does offer evidence that this possibility for the genre had not been completely overlooked.

LEARNING CURVES AND MISSED OPPORTUNITIES

The early history of radio drama in Japan poses some interesting questions. With few exceptions, the established authors of the day were not, at first, the ones writing the plays that made the most effective use of the medium. We have already seen that many established authors, even those who tried their hand at the genre, regarded it with doubt and sometimes even disdain. The "500-drama" commissions, intended to spur the cream of the literary crop to new heights of inventiveness, turned into little more than easy pay for established authors who didn't take the task very seriously. Another possible explanation is that established authors were so deeply immersed in the conventions of existing (notably dramatic) forms that they were simply unable to embrace the new possibilities. Whatever their origins, the unwillingness or inability of established authors to create the masterpieces of the new medium left the gates open for amateurs. The majority of the amateurs' efforts were probably worse, on various levels, than those of the professionals, but probability ensured that a number of them would break through in original and effective ways. Just as users generate a large percentage of the content available on the internet today, the new technology of radio afforded listeners the opportunity to create their own content in the 1920s—albeit through the gatekeeping and intermediary functions of the cultural elites in the publishing and broadcasting industries.

Early radio dramatists in Japan were also slow to adapt and adopt cinematic conventions such as montage and superimposition, and they made few attempts to incorporate modernist literary techniques such as stream of consciousness. Radio is especially well suited to the representation of interior monologue. As Peter Lewis writes, "Since we do not see the actor speaking, the words seem to come straight from the mind, not the mouth."[20] We can only speculate what turns early Japanese radio drama might have taken if the people writing radio plays included Shinkankakuha (New Perception) modernists like Kawabata Yasunari (1899–1972) and Yokomitsu Riichi (1898–1947) or surrealist poets like Nishiwaki Junzaburō (1894–1982) and Hagiwara Kyōjirō (1899–1938). We can only imagine what Tanizaki Jun'ichirō, who later played on the themes of sound and blindness so brilliantly in *Shunkinshō* (*A Portrait of Shunkin*, 1933) could have done with the genre if he had tried. One wonders why he never did and whether his falling out more than a decade earlier with Nagata, who was so central to the early development of the radio drama, might have had something to do with it. Striking, too, is the almost complete absence of female writers from the early forays into the genre. Enchi Fumiko (1905–1986) wrote one of the finest examples of early Japanese radio drama, *Atatakaki tochi nite* (On a warm plot of earth, 1931), a few years later, but she was a rare exception to the rule of almost exclusively male authorship. Clearly, the composition and social dynamics of the Radio Drama Research Group exerted a significant influence on the subsequent evolution of radio drama in Japan, and the sociological questions raised by that fact deserve further scrutiny. In any event, we are left with an acute sense of missed opportunities: Had a more diverse range of authors been attracted to (or lured into) the medium, we can imagine that the results might have been as impressive as the brilliant achievements of Japanese cinema in those years. One difference, of course, is that by that time, films had been produced in Japan for nearly three decades; it took nearly that long for Japanese radio drama to flower fully. Was this due purely to social and historical factors, or do new media intrinsically have such lengthy learning curves?

Stories that employ fantastic or supernatural elements were also largely missing from the early crop of Japanese radio dramas. It's difficult to imagine why, because radio drama is the perfect medium for tales of the supernatural or unsettling. Even *Kiri no naka* leaves the audience with the impression that the strange, disembodied voices that Sugino hears are the products of his feverish conscience. The relative absence of the supernatural is made more conspicuous by the fact that premodern Japanese literature is rich in supernatural themes, which were also present in the modern literary context of early radio drama practice.[21]

VOCAL CAPITAL: AN ARCHEOLOGY OF EARLY JAPANESE VOICE ACTING

The arrival of radio in Japan manifested new forms of performance that were not merely variants of old forms stripped of their visuality. Vocal performance for radio made demands specific to the medium itself, as well as specific to different genres within it. Sports broadcasting developed different conventions from radio drama, which in turn differed from news reading and educational fare, but each was an instance of deliberate performance shaped by multiple and dynamic social contexts and expectations.

Narrative ensemble genres—primarily early radio drama, early talkie animation, and the early and abortive attempts at dubbing feature films—all used actors who remained invisible to the audience, but they differed in their materiality, reception contexts, and institutional contingencies. Most obviously, radio relies almost exclusively on sound for the construction of narrative (I say "almost" because many broadcasts had supplementary printed matter), whereas the imaginative freedom of animation was potentially even richer than that of live-action film. Feature-film dubbing, though, presented technical, economic, and cultural challenges that were never fully overcome in the prewar period.

Nagata Mikihiko didn't want to limit the activities of the Radio Drama Research Group to simply the writing of radio plays. He also set about recruiting and training aspiring voice actors. In August 1925 he began advertising auditions, which continued through the rest of the year and into 1926. Applicants for these auditions included students, clerical workers, and trained stage performers. A story from the September 5, 1925, morning edition of the *Yomiuri shinbun* featured a male Korean applicant who had taken the Japanese name Nishimura Gyōson. He had just moved to Tokyo from Seoul in March and was working at a printing press. In his written application, he expressed admiration for Nagata and a hope that voice acting would lead to a better life. The writer of the story applauds his efforts while gently poking fun at his letter of application, which he describes as *taihen muzukashii* ("very difficult") because it's filled with rare Chinese compounds that Nishimura presumably learned as a student of classical Chinese. The story doesn't reveal whether he was selected, but given that his name doesn't appear again in subsequent records or news items, it's safe to assume that he wasn't. The attention lavished on his case suggests that he was the only colonial subject who attempted to find work as a radio actor in the metropole, while the attention paid to what was perceived to be his linguistic otherness hints at both the status of the voice as marker of identity and the intensely linguistic nature of the medium. The story doesn't mention whether Nishimura had an accent, but again, his recent arrival suggests that he probably did, and the reference to his excessively literary and sinicized mode of written expression could have also been a veiled hint that the grain of his voice was also insufficiently Japanese.

In the same story, Nagata complains that there weren't enough women applicants and appealed to readers to apply in greater numbers. He notes that a radio actor's voice is her capital (*rajio geki no haiyū wa koe ga shihon de*) and that he can't have too many actors with the same voice (*onaji koe no hito ga ōkucha komaru*).[22]

This insistence on vocal distinctiveness is sensible and obvious in the medium of radio and the genre of drama because vocal characteristics are the only means of distinguishing one speaker from another. Most people have little trouble with this in direct, unmediated settings, even with similar voices, but the low fidelity of early radio's sound reproduction necessitated greater vocal distinctiveness. Issues of reproducibility may also explain why Nagata was so keen to find and select women voice actors for the early classes of the Radio Drama Research Group's training program, as higher voices tended to transmit better than lower ones. However, Nagata made no mention of regional dialect and accent, linguistic elements that could also have contributed to the distinctiveness of characters.

The curriculum was divided into three categories: theater history and dramatic recitation, taught by Nagata himself; vocal music, taught by choral conductor Harada Jun (1882–1946); and voice training and music theory, taught by the composer Yamada Kōsaku (1886–1965). We can see from this curriculum that Nagata was invested in the idea of musical/lyrical radio drama, and many of his own earliest forays into the genre, such as the lyric drama *Kanashiki henro*, attest to that.

The September 25, 1925, *Asahi shinbun* reported that as of that date, the first wave of applicants numbered around twenty, and that around ten of them had been selected for training. Applications were being accepted on a rolling basis, however, and advertising for the course continued at least as late as December, even after training began. One of the new trainees was supposed to be selected to perform a supporting role in a September 29 broadcast of a radio play entitled *Mekura no kōrikashi* (The blind usurer), adapted by Nagata Hideo. However, that broadcast was canceled on September 26 after one rehearsal (which took place before that trainee could even be selected) when the Ministry of Communications objected to a scene in the play in which a man is choked to death. The ministry decided that the sounds of strangulation would be "problematic from the perspective of social education" (*shakai kyōikujō komaru*),[23] since radio listening was a group and household activity, and people with presumably delicate sensibilities—like the very young, the very old, and women—would be listening.

By mid-October of that year, the first class of voice actors was ready for its debut. Their first broadcast was of a lyric drama with music by Nishino Teruo and written and directed by Nagata. Although this broadcast had unfavorable reviews, the fledgling voice actors had better luck with their second attempt, *Futocchō* by Sawa Katsuzō, the prize-winning entry in an *Asahi shinbun* radio drama competition for amateur authors.[24]

Although the training program put in place by Hattori and Nagata foundered after JOAK was incorporated into NHK and they left the station, it was only a matter of time before the new management returned to the conclusion that it needed a stable of dedicated voice actors. Instead of training neophytes, however, JOAK seized upon the dissolution of Tsukiji Shōgekijō's (Tsukiji Little Theater) legacy troupe Shin-Tōkyō to sweep up all twenty members, including Aoyama Sugisaku, Tomoda Kyōsuke, Shiomi Yō, Tamura Akiko, and Higashiyama Chieko, into the newly formed Tōkyō Hōsō Gekidan (Tokyo Broadcast Acting Company). This core group was supplemented by members of other acting troupes.[25]

Another training course for aspiring neophyte voice actors did not appear until April 1941, with the establishment of NHK's Seiyū Gekidan (voice actor troupe). This class of approximately thirty students underwent a two-part training program lasting from June 1941 to March 1942 for the first part, and April 1942 to March 1943 for the second part, all taking place in a training center established expressly for that purpose. The center was under the direction of the head of NHK's entertainment division, and the actors were trained by the actor Aoyama Sugisaku (1889–1956) and the playwright Sekiguchi Jirō (1893–1979), among others. Applications were open to both men and women between the ages of eighteen and thirty-five who had at least a middle school education and were able to reside in Tokyo for the duration of the training course.[26] By this time, the appeal of musical drama had faded, and the training focused exclusively on the use of the speaking voice.

The first use of voice acting in a Japanese animated film came with the 1933 short *Chikara to onna no yo no naka* (The world of power and women), directed by Masaoka Kenzō (1898–1988). The film was commissioned by Shōchiku president Kido Shirō on the heels of the success of Shōchiku's first talkie, *Madamu to nyōbō* (*The Neighbor's Wife and Mine*). Although voice actors had been practicing their trade in radio drama for nearly eight years by this time, this very first animated talkie was voiced primarily by screen actors, with the voice of the main character performed by the comedian and vocal impersonator Furukawa Roppa (1903–1961). Roppa's powers of vocal mimicry were made legend in August 1932, when he substituted for an ailing Tokugawa Musei (1894–1971) during a live radio performance that lasted forty minutes and during which none of the listeners could tell that they weren't listening to Musei.[27]

After this initial, commercially successful attempt at an animated talkie, the voices in subsequent animated shorts were only infrequently credited by name. In one short from 1939, *Benkei tai Ushiwaka* (Benkei versus Ushiwaka), directed by the aforementioned Masaoka Kenzō and animated by Kumakawa Masao (1916–2008), the only voice credit goes to the director. The reason may be that in this period, many or even most of the characters in anime were children voiced by children. Thus, there could be any number of reasons, from the legal to the economic to the cultural, why they might not be credited.

The third case was film dubbing. Fox made the first attempt to dub an American film into Japanese with *The Man Who Came Back* (1931), directed by Raoul Walsh and starring Janet Gaynor and Charles Farrell.[28] Unable and possibly unwilling to commission a dub in Japan, Fox hired Nakazawa Ken (1883–1953), a professor of Chinese and Japanese literature and Japanese language at the University of Southern California, to write and direct a translation. A first-generation immigrant from Fukushima,[29] Nakazawa recruited local Japanese American non-actors to voice the parts, most of whom were originally from Hiroshima and spoke in a Hiroshima dialect further altered by years of living abroad. Nakazawa wrote a two-part article for the December 3 and 4 editions of the *Asahi shinbun* in which he complained at length about the almost insuperable difficulties of translating for dubbing (the title of the article is "Nihongo no fukikomu: Nanto muzukashii shigoto yo!," or "Dubbing Into Japanese—What a Difficult Job!").[30] Japanese critics and audiences complained in turn, first, about the unnaturalness of foreigners speaking Japanese and, second, about the incongruity and unintentional humor of their speaking Hiroshima dialect. Subsequent efforts were made during the prewar period to dub imported films. They generally didn't find much favor among urban moviegoers, but Paramount scored a success in 1935 in the Japanese provinces with its dubbed version of Harold Lloyd's 1930 *Feet First*.[31] The relative success of this effort (again, a success that was limited to provincial theaters) may have been due to the dubbing, which was carried out in Japan by PCL, Paramount's distributor. After this, PCL went to work dubbing Paramount's *Four Hours to Kill!* (1935, titled *Seimei no zattō* in Japanese).[32]

One work that straddled animation and dubbing was the Chinese film *Tie shan gongzhu* (Princess Iron Fan, 1941). The first feature-length animated film to be produced anywhere in Asia, it was imported into Japan in 1942, and the lead characters were voiced by famed former *benshi* Tokugawa Musei and Yamano Ichirō (1899–1958).

As these cases show, the approaches to voice acting taken in these three genres were conditioned more by institutional considerations than by anything else. In radio drama, where production and decision-making were centralized, a more formal approach to radio actor training was adopted. In the dubbing of Western films, which was decentralized, transnational, and carried out by private industry, the approaches were more diverse and seemingly haphazard. Early animation seems to have partially skirted the issue by minimizing dialogue, frequently using nonprofessional children, and only rarely crediting the vocal talent. Radio drama was the only medium in which a concerted effort was made to train and professionalize specialist voice actors. This did not begin to change until the 1960s, when the five major studios decided to stop providing content to television stations and those stations turned to imported films and television shows. Although NHK's policy was to subtitle foreign content, the commercial stations opted for dubbing, which created an explosion in demand for voice actors, many of whom could maintain a livelihood from this kind of work alone. The unprecedented success of the movie version of *Uchū senkan Yamato* (*Space Battleship Yamato*, 1977), which outperformed even *Star Wars* at the Japanese box office, inaugurated the era of the *seiyū* (voice actor) idol and the subsequent creation of an extensive voice actor–training infrastructure in dozens of schools.

OTOZUKURI: ONTOLOGY AND *TECHNE* IN EARLY SOUND EFFECTS

Japanese has at least four terms for sound effects: *gion* (imitative sound), *onkyō kōka* (acoustic effect), its variant *kōkaon* (effect sound, sometimes just *kōka*), and the loanword *saundo efekuto*. The earliest example of *gion* I could find dates from 1892[33] and refers to imitative sounds in the context of music. References to *onkyō kōka* begin in the 1920s with the arrival of radio. This terminological variability is of some historical and linguistic interest, but it also unveils a conceptual tension that is obscured by the uniformity of the English term "sound effect": Are these sounds meant to be imitative of "truly existing" sounds or to create aesthetic or phenomenological "effects" not necessarily moored to a recognizable reality? The wind in the trees, or phasers set to stun? In practice, of course, sound designers (a term dating from the late 1970s that might have puzzled most of the artists I discuss later) and editors produce both types of "sound effects," but the blurring of the distinction between the two raises questions about the discourses of realism that have arisen around sound cinema from its earliest days. More than dialogue or even extradiegetic music, the sound effect as phenomenon and practice creates problems of representation with their own histories and local manifestations. Sound effects thus played significantly different roles in radio and early sound cinema.

As in corresponding arenas of cultural production in Europe and the United States, when questions of sound (and sound effects) arose in Japan, questions of realism, verisimilitude, and even ontology were quick to follow. The desire for greater verisimilitude and believability (which were not always the same) of sound effects led to the increasing professionalization and specialization of these practices, along with greater concomitant economic investments in them.

Sound effects in Japan began with traditional theater and reached an early high point of refinement in the kabuki theater of the nineteenth century. The primary tool for sound effects used by the offstage musicians was the *taiko* drum, which was creatively employed to represent diverse natural sounds. It could approximate different types of water, including rain, flowing rivers or streams, and sea waves. It could represent weather, including wind, storm gusts, and thunder. It could also be used to suggest more delicate, subtle sounds, such as those of falling snow and echoes. Other sources of sound effects in kabuki included *tsukeita* wooden clappers, flutes, and more elaborate, specialized contraptions that came into use after around 1830, near the end of kabuki's so-called golden age. As Yamato Sadaji points out,[34] and as any modern-day kabuki-goer can discern, these sonic representations are symbolic rather than realistic. This symbolic representation was, and remains, acceptable in the context of the general conventions of artifice in which kabuki operates.[35]

With the arrival of naturalistic modes of theatrical representation based largely on European models, stage producers and technicians were forced to develop new techniques and seemingly closer approximations. The first wave came in the late nineteenth century with the *shinpa* (new school) style of theater developed by Sudō Sadanori (1867–1907) and Kawakami Otojirō (1864–1911), first as a form of agit-prop theater and then gradually transforming into very old-school melodrama. A second wave came in the 1910s, with a style even closer to Western naturalism that came to be known as *shingeki*. One of the influential groups that embraced this naturalism was the aforementioned Jiyū Gekijō, founded by Osanai Kaoru and the kabuki actor Ichikawa Sadanji II, which was inaugurated with a performance of Ibsen's *John Gabriel Borkman* in 1909.

Osanai later played a central role in the third and arguably most important stage of sound-effects development in Japan, which began with the arrival of radio and radio drama in 1925. A year earlier, in 1924, Osanai had founded a new troupe with its own dedicated theater, the Tsukiji Shōgekijō to continue the *shingeki* movement he had helped set into motion fifteen years earlier. The sound effects developed for *shingeki*, and particularly those developed at the Tsukiji Shōgekijō, were more sophisticated and realistic than those that had been employed in kabuki, *shinpa*, or even earlier *shingeki* productions. They also attempted to represent a multitude of objects not found in older theatrical styles, such as steam locomotives.

The sound-effects technician and historian Iwabuchi Toyō identifies three people as the founders of his own profession in Japan: Nakamura Hyōzō IV (1889?–1982), Kobayashi Tokujirō (1899–1977), and Wada Sei (1893–1970). Nakamura was a bridge figure who carried over traditional kabuki sound-effect know-how into the worlds of *shinpa* and radio drama as well. He served simultaneously as the music master for Sawamura Gennosuke's theater company, in the production team at the Shōchiku Theater, as well as in the music departments of Inoue Masao's (1881–1950) Inoue Engeki Dōjō and Mizutani Yaeko's (1905–1979) Geijutsuza, two prominent *shinpa* theaters of the time. In his later years and until his death at the age of ninety-three, he worked in the music department of Gekidan Shinpa.[36]

Kobayashi Tokujirō, the second member of Iwabuchi's sound-effects triumvirate, was a member of the Radio Drama Research Group and served as the producer or director for many of the early radio dramas produced by JOAK.

It wasn't long before the need for sound effects became apparent. According to Yamato, the July 19, 1925, broadcast of *Taii no musume* (The captain's daughter), adapted from the novel *Gendarm Möbius* by the German poet and novelist Victor Blüthgen, was the first work produced for the radio that called for a sound effect—in this case, a fire bell.[37] The producers of the broadcast looked around for an acceptable approximation and wound up using a real fire bell. Because the studio was small and the sound of a real bell would be too loud for the microphone to pick up properly, the stage assistants opened the door of the studio and rang the bell as they walked through the hall. The sound of the fire bell thus escaped into the surrounding area, and alarmed neighbors called the fire department. Later experiments revealed that banging the rim of a kettle was an even better approximation than the real thing for the purposes of radio. Yamato suggests that this episode revealed two of the fundamental challenges of sound effects, which persist to this day: First, the sound of the real thing often *does not* sound like the real thing when broadcast or recorded; and second, it's often difficult to gauge the right amount of distance to place between the sound source and the microphone.[38]

The cast and crew for *Tankō no naka* were drawn from Osanai's Tsukiji Shōgekijo and included the sound-effects supervisor, Wada Sei, the third and perhaps most important member of Iwabuchi's trio of sound-effects pioneers. Wada was given credit by name in the notice for the broadcast alongside the producer, director, playwright, and actors, suggesting that his contribution was considered important.

The production called for a number of different sound effects: The sound of a pickax was created by striking together two storm-door rollers; the explosion in the coal mine was represented by striking piano wires and a kettle drum; and the sound of the mine flooding was created by loosening the cap of a gas cylinder in a tub full of water. The echoes one would imagine being produced in a coal mine were approximated by positioning two large *taiko* drums next to the microphone, a method that was arrived at through a long process of trial and error.[39]

Wada Sei happened to have been a high school classmate of Kaeriyama Norimasa (1893–1964), the film critic and director who helped found the Pure Film Movement in the 1910s. Wada's collaboration with Osanai later led to an even more direct connection to film when Wada provided the sound effects for Osanai's early attempt at a talkie, *Reimei* (Daybreak), which was filmed in 1927 but never released because of technical problems with the sound technology employed, the "Mina Talkie" system, which was based on the DeForest Phonofilm. This abortive attempt was, to the best of my knowledge, Wada's sole foray into film sound, but his influence nevertheless was felt through more indirect channels over time. At a minimum, Wada can claim to be the first Japanese sound-effects technician to work in both radio and sound film.

Wada was also responsible for the steam locomotive effect to which I referred earlier, which became a memorable episode in *shingeki* theater history. During a performance of Kishida Kunio's (1890–1954) play *Seimei o moteasobu otoko futari* (Two men who toy with life) in October 1929 at the popular Meiji-za, Wada devised a way to recreate the sound of a passing locomotive using oxygen cylinders and a large variety of train and ship whistles. These sounds were so convincing that the large audience burst into applause the first time they heard the effect and did so repeatedly the seven or eight times that the effect returned throughout the play. Sound effects had essentially taken a starring role.

By that point, Wada was no longer working for JOAK in Tokyo. As I previously recounted, in 1926 the three major urban radio stations in Japan were consolidated under the umbrella of the Nippon Hōsō Kyōkai, or NHK. When Hattori, JOAK's programming director, left the station, Nagata and the rest of the Radio Drama Research Group (including Osanai and Wada) went with him, and the group disbanded. Osanai died in 1928 at the age of forty-seven. Wada's triumph at the Meiji-za led to another opportunity, however, because the broadcasting director of JOBK in Osaka, Kemuyama Jirō (1884–1964), was present at that performance and decided that Wada was just the person his radio drama department needed. He pursued Wada aggressively, and in the following year, 1930, Wada finally joined JOBK as a regular employee.

Meanwhile at JOAK, the interest in sound effects took its own course. In 1928, the station started using multiple microphones and a mixer. In January 1929, the station hired its first dedicated sound-effects specialist, Kimura Hajime (real name, Arakawa Toshio), who went by the nickname "Pin-san." Although he was the station's only designated "*kōka* man," he was helped by several jack-of-all-trades stage assistants, the same technicians who had previously been responsible for sound effects as well.

Soon after this, in 1930, sound effect recordings started to be imported from abroad, first from RCA in the United States and then from other companies and countries, such as Germany. In 1931, domestically produced gramophone disc recorders and electrical players first appeared. That same year, an effects technician at JOAK named Yugeta figured out how to use electric amplification to cut disc records from recordings made on a wax cylinder Dictaphone.[40] The portability of the Dictaphone allowed it to be carried into the field, where the sounds of actual objects and natural phenomena could be recorded, but the volume produced by the Dictaphone itself wasn't adequate for broadcast purposes. The ability to record the sounds of nature on-site and then mix in those sounds instead of inventing contraptions to approximate those sounds came as a welcome development and was quickly put to use, but it wasn't a panacea: As noted earlier, using the actual source of a sound often wasn't effective. Microphones and speakers didn't have the sensitivity and range that they do today, and the sound coming out of radios and phonographs had a narrow frequency and dynamic range.

In July 1930 Kobayashi Tokujirō put together a "sound-effects review" entitled *Natsu hakkei* (Eight scenes of summer) with minimal dialogue and in which "sound effects are the protagonist." Broadcast on July 25, the review featured seasonal sounds such as a passing rain shower, the croaking of a frog, fireworks, a motorboat, and even *minage*—the sound of somebody jumping overboard to die. The *Yomiuri* article describing the broadcast also explained how the sounds were produced.[41]

In the 1930s two radio dramas were notable for pushing the boundaries of sound-effects techniques: The first was *Bakuon* (Roar) by Itō Shōzan (or Shōzō), which was produced in 1935. Kimura Hajime recounted the challenges this radio drama presented to him and his crew:

> The microphone we used then was a Reisz with an octogonal carbon diaphragm and marble housing; unlike today, we didn't use multiple mikes, and of course, the studio was small. This drama called for a lot of sound effects, and what made it difficult was the many scenes with location changes.
>
> The drama starts with a dog barking in the middle of a rainstorm then moves from outside to inside. We had few effects records in those days, so we did it all live with contraptions, whistles, etc. So when we were moving from outside to inside, we had to move the sounds as we were making them from near the mike to farther away. In a scene set in a moving car, the passing background noises—chickens, a tatami-weaving machine, etc.—were all made by effects technicians running this way and that. For the roar of an airplane, we attached a rubber propeller to a small motor and, by adjusting the pressure with which we held it against a drum, were able to create the changing sounds of a plane performing aerobatics.[42]

Another masterpiece appeared in 1936: *Nadare*, by Mafune Yutaka, whom I identified earlier. This drama proved so popular that by the end of 1937, it had already been rebroadcast twice, which, in that age of live broadcasting, entailed two full new stagings.[43] By the time the theater troupe Gekidan Kaze performed a stage adaptation in 1971, it had been rebroadcast more than a dozen times.[44]

In February 1936 JOAK established a Gion Kenkyūkai (sound effects research group), which met every Tuesday and Friday. Kimura Hajime taught the younger effects technicians about the fundamentals, and the group also explored and experimented with new possibilities.[45] The group originally had eleven members, including Kimura, with others, such as Iwabuchi Toyō, joining in later years. By 1937 Japanese sound-effects technicians were producing their own sound-effects records.[46]

All this suggests that the real hotbed of sound-effects innovation in Japan in the late 1920s and 1930s was radio. In that sightless medium, anything that doesn't sound in effect doesn't exist; it can be referred to, but if no sound is ascribed to it, it has no presence. This is obviously very different from cinema, where things generally have a presence by being visible.[47] Of course, there can also be off-screen or acousmatic sounds, and indeed, some early examples of early Japanese sound cinema make extensive use of off-screen sound, but for the most part presences in cinema are seen, or seen *and* heard, and, more rarely, just heard. Perhaps for this reason, sound effects were not as urgent a priority in the early Japanese sound cinema as they were in radio. Even if sounds were thin or barely audible, this was tolerated—if noted at all—because sound and image reinforced each other. Needless to say, this didn't stop early technicians from relentlessly pursuing greater verisimilitude in the sounds they were recording, employing technological advances as they appeared for that purpose.

Attempts were made to produce talkies after Osanai's 1927 *Reimei*, but the first truly successful all-talkie is generally considered to be Gosho Heinosuke's (1902–1981) *Madamu to nyōbō* (*The Neighbor's Wife and Mine*, 1931) produced by Shōchiku, with sound recording by the Tsuchihashi brothers, Takeo and Haruo, using their namesake Tsuchihashi recording system. This film, in particular, seems to revel in the use of off-screen sound.

Sound-effects know-how did transfer between radio specialists and film specialists, but the transfer was not very extensive. The institutional structures of the two industries made the sharing of personnel unusual (though not impossible), and the techniques developed by individual groups were considered proprietary knowledge jealously guarded from both other industries and competitors in the same industry. Thus, even though Tokyo's JOAK and Osaka's JOBK were united under the

NHK umbrella and didn't compete for the same audience, the effects technicians at one station didn't share their most recent inventions with their colleagues at the other station. Once a technique had been in use for a while, however, it would eventually be made public, usually in trade magazines but sometimes even in mass publications.

Radio-effects specialists were unlikely to take positions at film studios, as the studio system encouraged hiring young recruits and training them in-house. Just as important, radio technicians enjoyed job security and generous pay. Iwabuchi reports that a radio-effects technician at JOAK in Tokyo in the 1930s, who, on average, was twenty-three years old, could net a monthly income of 300 yen in base income, bonuses, and outside freelance work at a time when 30 yen a month was sufficient to live quite comfortably.[48] In contrast, sound-effects technicians in studios such as Nikkatsu and Daiei, while not badly paid, were still subordinate members of sound recording departments and didn't enjoy a great deal of prestige within their organizations. Conditions were more favorable at PCL, the forerunner of Tōhō, but not enough to lure radio employees away from their comfortable posts. If anything, film sound-effects technicians were trying to find employment at radio stations. One who succeeded was Yamaguchi Jun (real name: Yamaguchi Kinpei, 1905–1979), who started out as an effects technician for the Tsukiji Shōgekijō, moved on to become a sound recordist at PCL, and then brought that combination of skills as an effects technician working for Wada Sei at Osaka's JOBK.[49]

One cinematic realm where the demand for sound effects was high was, not surprisingly, animation. During the Pacific War, several highly accomplished sound animation films, often with overt propagandistic goals, were produced. One of the most impressive of these, more generally and from the standpoint of sound effects, was *Momotarō no umiwashi* (*Momotarō's Sea Eagles*), directed by Seo Mitsuyo (1911–2010) and released in March 1943 by Geijutsu Eigasha. According to Yamato, the production pamphlet for the film lists Kimura Hajime ("Pin-san," the first dedicated effects specialist at JOAK) as the sound-effects director for that film.[50] Although Yamato had been Kimura's assistant at JOAK, he had never heard about that experience directly from Kimura himself, but he does report that in 1953 Kimura took him to a private studio in Hamachō in Tokyo where they were part of a group of freelancers adding sound effects to an animated film from abroad.[51]

Although sound effects didn't command much respect or prestige in the studios, some film critics did recognize and appreciate their importance. The film critic Sasaki Norio (1902–1972) devotes a section to sound effects in his influential 1931 study *Hassei eiga kantoku to kyakuhonron* (On directing and writing sound films).[52] The July 1931 issue of *Eiga jidai* features a special section on talkies with an article by Kawabata Masao (1905–1982), who later became best known for writing detective fiction and science fiction under the pen name Minamizawa Jūshichi, entitled "Gion tōkī" (Talkies with sound effects), in which he mainly bemoans the poor quality of the then-existing sound effects. Kawabata begins by pointing out that every object has its own unique sound: animate objects produce their own sounds while inanimate ones produce distinctive sounds by being struck, rubbed, etc. This argument for what we might call an audio-ontological specificity leads Kawabata to establish a rather high bar for what counts as a believable sound effect. He sees hope, however, in work being done by German acoustics scientists (whom he does not name), who were analyzing the sonic waveforms of commonly occurring sounds in order to one day be able to create sounds simply by generating the proper combination of sound waves, a dream that did not become a reality for sound-effects designers until the postwar period when sophisticated technologies of synthesis and sampling appeared.[53] The composer Itō Noboru (1903–1993) discusses sound effects at length in a piece published in the September 1931 issue of *Eiga kagaku kenkyū* entitled "Ongaku oyobi onkyō kōka ni kan suru kōsatsu" (Thoughts on music and sound effects). *Onga geijutsu no hōhōron* (Theory of sound film art), a widely read 1933 translation by Magami Gitarō (1902–1971) of Aleksander Andrievskii's 1931 *Postroenie tonfil'ma*,[54] also tried to situate sound effects (or simply ambient noise) within a larger theory of sound film aesthetics. It's somewhat surprising, however, how little attention the early technical manuals on talkie production devote to sound effects proper, as opposed to recording. I'm thinking here of works such as *Tōkī to tennenshoku eiga* (Talkies and color movies) by Kaeriyama Norimasa and others (1931);[55] *Tōkī no sekkei to seisakuhō* (Talkie planning and production) by Hirata Masuo and Muramatsu Yoshinaga (1934);[56] and *Saishin tōkī no seisaku to eisha no jissai* (Newest practices of talkie production and projection) by Nakagi Teiichi and Yoshida Masayoshi (1935).[57] The primary consideration in most of these practical manuals is, not surprisingly, dialogue. Indeed, it is difficult to find a noteworthy dedicated sound-effects technician in the Japanese cinema before the postwar period and the arrival of Minawa Ichirō (born 1918), who did the sound effects for Kurosawa Akira, arguably the Japanese director most attentive to such details. Minawa also did the sound effects for Honda Ishirō's (1911–1993) *Godzilla* of 1954.[58] The latter film raises issues of genre that could form their own chapter, but one obvious observation is that science fiction, as a genre that imagines nonexistent realities, must fabricate the audible signs that give those imagined realities some kind of sonic presence. *Chanbara*, sword-fighting films, in contrast, represent realities that are not entirely unreal but that cannot be enacted for the purposes of a film—for example, that of a sword cutting through flesh. Despite the long history of the genre in Japan, Kurosawa was the first director to use such a sound, in the 1961 film *Yōjimbō*, which was then used extensively in the 1962 sequel, *Tsubaki Sanjūrō* (*Sanjuro*). Kurosawa thought it odd to have a body cut open with no accompanying sound, so he tasked Minawa with finding a way to represent that sonically. After some experimentation, Minawa settled on cutting through a plump chicken filled with *waribashi* (disposable chopsticks) using a long, slender, *yanagiba* (sashimi knife). Although Minawa had already perfected the technique by the time of *Yōjimbō*, he claims to have used it sparingly and at low volume out of a sense of residual restraint left over from the days of Occupation censorship, when any explicit depiction of bloody violence would have come under scrutiny. By the time of *Sanjūrō*, this reluctance seems to have been overcome.[59]

Perhaps it's merely a coincidence, but it's worth noting that Kurosawa showed a somewhat greater-than-average interest in radio and radio drama from the time of his youth. According to his autobiography, he owned a crystal radio set from the age of sixteen,[60] and in 2010, a radio drama entitled *Yōki na kōjo* (The cheerful factory) that he had composed and that was broadcast during the war was discovered at the Tsubouchi Memorial Theater Museum at Waseda University.[61]

On the whole, however, during this immediate postwar period, directors such as Kurosawa were the exception, not the rule. The sound recordist Ōtani Iwao recalls that when he was working on Mizoguchi Kenji's (1898–1956) films in the 1950s, Mizoguchi never once requested a particular sound effect: "In those days we didn't know about sound effects.... He never made any requests. I would think through it all myself and add the sound effects. Mizoguchi-san never gave me any direction."⁶² It is remarkable and telling that already more than two decades into the sound era, a director as demanding and detail-oriented as Mizoguchi still couldn't be bothered to call for specific sound effects. Despite this seeming indifference—which, for all we know, he felt precisely because of Ōtani's own care and creativity—Mizoguchi's films from this period use sound in ways that were subsequently highly regarded. Noël Burch, for example, describes *Chikamatsu monogatari* (*A Story from Chikamatsu*, 1954) as "a film that even today remains at the very forefront of experimentation in the relations of sound and image."

> The particular quality of Japanese music . . . with its predominance of abrupt percussive sounds and its eminently "graphic" structures obviously made it easier to create some form of interaction between sound effects and music. Yet, even granting the advantage Japanese music confers, Mizoguchi's sound track is a unique achievement in the history of cinema. In a scene in which the hero hides in an attic, a succession of sounds with a distinct rhythm of their own created by the wooden bowls from which the hero has been eating, then by a ladder banging against the wall, provide the first notes (of somewhat indeterminate pitch) in a musically orchestrated structure that goes on to incorporate instruments with tone qualities similar to those of these "natural" sound effects.⁶³

The skillful, dialectical use of diegetic sound (whether recorded during filming or added afterward) is an issue somewhat orthogonal to the more narrowly ontological questions that I have been discussing. Mizoguchi's reported indifference to sound effects per se were not necessarily—indeed, were by no means—indicative of a desultory attitude toward the aesthetic stakes of sound and the importance of the relationship between sound and image. Rather, it's possible to speculate that Mizoguchi was content to delegate the details of how the sounds were produced to specialists while focusing his attention on how the elements fit together in the final product. It's also possible that he wasn't fully aware of just how much artifice was necessary to create sounds that sounded "real."

In contrast to film-oriented discourses, sound effects were a central concern in almost every theoretical and practical tract devoted to radio drama. There was, not surprisingly, a lot of attention paid to the practical techniques of sound production necessary to produce specific effects. When reading the memoirs of effects technicians like Yamato and Iwabuchi, one is struck by the loving care and fascination with which they describe even techniques that had already been rendered obsolete before they started working in the field themselves, as well as the understandable pride they take in their own inventions and innovations. In addition to this sense of professional pride must be included a genuine curiosity on the part of audiences about how the sounds they heard on the radio were produced. There was an element of magic in sound effects (they were, quite literally, sonic illusions), which unsurprisingly made audiences want to know how they were achieved. Unlike illusionists, sound-effects technicians were happy to comply, at least up to a point. For example, the "Kodomo pēji" (Children's page) of the March 5, 1933, *Asahi shinbun* contains a half-page feature entitled "Tane o akasu to bikkuri suru rajio no gion no shōtai" (You'll be shocked when we reveal the secrets of radio sound effects). As the title promises, the article centers on the unexpectedness of the sound sources: for example, using dried beans to create the sound of rain and waves. The following year, JOAK effects technicians put on a live demonstration of sound effects at the Hibiya Kōkaidō (Hibiya Public Hall).[64]

All these public revelations were couched in terms of wonderment at the ingenuity of the techniques presented, but they also raise some unspoken questions: Why, on the radio, don't things sound like themselves? How does the medium sever the supposedly intrinsic connection between an object and the very specific sounds that—according to Kawabata Masao, for example—belong to it? The very possibility of sound effects questions the very indexicality of sound recording, anticipating in nontrivial ways the types of questions that would be raised by Photoshop-altered photographs seven decades later. Of what, if anything, do recording media prove the existence?

In the reminiscence about *Nadare* that I quoted earlier, Mafune Yutaka's valorization of the sounds of nature over others seems to be rooted in the commonplaces of traditional Japanese aesthetics and, indeed, seems to hark back to the origins of sound effects in kabuki theater itself. What is apparent is not a tension between the categories of nature and artifice so much as a sly refusal to uphold that binary in the absolute terms in which it is often understood.

The filmic spectator, in contrast, is presented with visual and auditory streams that are, in most cases, coconstituting and interdependent. The connection between early film sound and film realism has been much discussed in the past two decades, but as James Lastra points out, there are multiple "realisms," none of which ever quite escape the orbits of representation/semiosis/inscription into ontology proper. And as Michel Chion observes, the balance of "ontological"—that is, representational—anchoring is unstable: Sometimes the image does most of the work, and sometimes the sound, but usually the former.

> The figurative value of a sound in itself is usually quite nonspecific. Depending on the dramatic and visual context, a single sound can convey very diverse things. For the spectator, it is not acoustical realism so much as synchrony above all, and secondarily the factor of verisimilitude (verisimilitude arising not from truth but from convention), that will lead him or her to connect a sound with an event or detail. The same sound can convincingly serve as the sound effect for a crushed watermelon in a comedy or for a head blown to smithereens in a war film. The same noise will be joyful in one context, intolerable in another.[65]

Radio drama wasn't afforded the same margin of error. Either a sound had to be immediately legible (immediately because it was sure to be followed by another one, leaving precious little time for auditory parsing and interpretation), or the dialogue would have to explain what it was, an awkward and undesirable solution. Thus there was a greater demand for verisimilitude, whether "true" or conventional.

To return to the issue of terminology with which we started, Iwabuchi states that the term *gion* was first used in the context of sound effects (rather than musical imitative sounds) by the musician and composer Fukuda Sōkichi (1893–?).[66] Fukuda migrated to radio after losing his job as a silent-film accompanist during the transition to talkies. Since early radio dramas didn't feature musical accompaniment (they were broadcast live, and there was already enough that could go wrong, as well as a shortage of microphones), he became an effects technician. According to Iwabuchi, Fukuda was the first to refer to his job as *gion gakari* (person in charge of imitative sounds), and the term soon spread, but it was unpopular with effects technicians, who felt that it reduced their position from that of partner in the creative work of aesthetic expression to that of mindless imitators of the already-existing. They also preferred the more modern ring of *kōka* and the fashionable exoticism of *efekuto*. Radio-effects technicians were always referred to as *kōka man* or *efekuto man*, whereas their counterparts in the film world were disparaged as *gion gakari*, usually against their will, if they were called anything at all, instead of simply being thought of as junior members of the recording department.[67]

In his 1929 essay "The Art of Sound," René Clair made the oft-cited prediction that "if *imitation* of real noises seems limited and disappointing, it is possible that an *interpretation* of noises may have more of a future in it."[68] The art of sound effects represents precisely this practice of interpretation, but what for Clair was the future of motion pictures was at that time already, in a sense, the present of radio drama. What is somewhat surprising is just how long it took for Clair's prophecy to be realized in cinema: It was not until the 1950s in Japan, with the sound design of Kurosawa and Minawa, and arguably not really in a widespread and full-throttle fashion in Hollywood until the 1970s with the rise of the science fiction and horror blockbusters of George Lucas and Steven Spielberg and the immaculately sound-designed collaborations of Francis Ford Coppola and Walter Murch, that cinematic sound effects really came into their own. Although these developments were driven by generic demands and technological innovations such as Dolby Stereo, it's worth noting that these directors all counted Kurosawa as a seminal influence on their own filmmaking.

6

SOUND AND MOTION

THE SLOW INVASION

The transition from silent to sound cinema in Japan was both a film-historical and a discursive event. The late 1920s and early 1930s saw an efflorescence of writing about talkies both practical and theoretical: how they worked (mechanically), how they should be made (aesthetically), how they should be acted, and how they should be understood in multiple contexts, including film art and the larger contexts of media ecology and social economy. This discursive activity took place in several sites, including trade magazines like *Kinema junpō* and critical journals like *Eiga hyōron*, which in turn fed into book-length tracts and treatises. Although numerous translations of works, and selections of works, from German, Russian, and English played a central role in framing many of the issues in Japan, Japanese who wrote on the subject were often aware that they faced their own specific theoretical questions and would likewise need to generate their own answers.

This talkie-theoretical discourse began well before talkie production became a feasible reality in the Japanese film industry itself (taking foreign talkies as its objects of scrutiny), and it proliferated further when Japan began producing its own sound films. As in many other countries, this discourse on sound cinema and sound in cinema gradually faded away so that, by the early 1940s, sound had become normalized and was no longer a topic of sustained commentary. This situation persisted until the 1980s renaissance in film sound studies, first in Europe and the United States and then in Japan.

As film scholarship of the last two decades has demonstrated, there was never a truly "silent" cinema: Almost all cinematic exhibition was accompanied by some kind of sound making, whether live musical accompaniment, live narration/commentary, live sound effects, or the playing of recorded music.[1] Audiences apparently found it discomfiting to watch films in relative silence.[2] This was especially true in Japan, where the figure of the *katsudō benshi* or *katsuben* film narrator was ubiquitous. *Benshi* narrators exercised extraordinary creative control over the film's reception.[3]

Synchronized-sound film in Japan arrived in stages. Its adoption was slowed by a number of factors: the resistance of the *benshi*, who had a clear—even existential—economic stake in the existing order; the high cost of equipping cinemas with the necessary technology, especially electrically amplified speakers that could fill very large metropolitan theaters (some of which could seat more than a thousand spectators); an economic situation that went from recession to depression during the very period when sound film was being adopted elsewhere (a circumstance that only intensified the drag generated by the first two factors); and, finally, an economic model of film production that was based on producing a large number of films, which made the relatively more expensive sound productions almost prohibitive.[4]

Table 6.1, compiled by Nagato Yōhei, shows the known experiments with and productions of sound film in Japan in the early years of cinema.[5] The first synchronized sound feature to be made was *Reimei* (Daybreak), directed by the famed *shingeki* pioneer Osanai Kaoru, whom we encountered in chapter 5. *Reimei* was produced in 1927, the same year as *The Jazz Singer*. Unlike *The Jazz Singer*, which used the Vitaphone sound-on-disc system, *Reimei* used an optical soundtrack directly on the film. Optical soundtracks eventually completely replaced sound-on-disc as the preferred system of sound reproduction, so in that regard, *Reimei* was ahead of its time. The film never saw general release, and it subsequently sank into an obscurity from which it has never recovered, and

TABLE 6.1 Known Experiments with and Productions of Sound Film in Japan in the Early Years of Cinema

Year	Disc	Optical
1896	Bruhl Fréres begin importing the Kinetophone.	
1900	July: *Sumō no katsudō shashin* (Sumo moving picture) exhibited at the Kinkikan in Kanda with the referee's voice played back on a phonograph.	
1902	September: *Sumō no katsudō shashin* shown at the Fukagawaza with "loudspeakers accompanying the picture." Yoshizawa shōten exhibits the *hassei katsudō dai shashin: Kinetofuon* (speaking moving picture: Kinetophone) at the Meiji-za.	
1908	January: *Sanja matsuri no tekomai* (*Dance of the Sanja Festival*) shown at Denkikan with a loudspeaker behind the screen. December: *Yūsei katsudō shashin: Kuronofuon* (Voiced moving picture: Chronophone) exhibited at the Mizaki-chō Tōkyō-za.	
1909	September: *Yūsei katsudō shashin (mono o iu shashin)* (Voiced moving picture [a picture that talks]) *Toyotake Roshō no gidayū eiga* (Toyotake Roshō's *gidayū* film) shown at Opera-kan.	
1913	September: Yamato Onei Kabushiki Gaisha shows *Chūshingura* at Asakusa Teikokukan. Nihon Kinetofuon Kabushiki Gaisha begins importing the Kinetophone from America. December 6: Nine works for the Kinetophone are shown at the Teikoku Gekijō.	

Year	Disc	Optical
1914	January: The "Animatophone" is exhibited at the Mikuni-za. July: Seven Japanese short films for the Kinetophone are released.	
1917	Nihon Kinetofuon goes bankrupt.	
1925		Mina Talkie Minagawa gets license to use De Forest's patented Phonofilm technology. July: Phonofilm shown at Shinbashi Enbujō.
1927		January: Minagawa founds Shōwa Kinema Co. September: *Daybreak* and seven short films are shown at Tōkyō Kaikan.
1928	*Tokyo March* planned as a talkie but doesn't succeed. Masao Tōjo invents the Eastphone. September: Establishes Nihon Tōkī Kabushiki Geisha.	
1929	March: Nihon Tōkī produces seven short test shorts. June: Makino completes *Modoribashi*. August: Nikkatsu completes *Hachisuka koroku*. October: Nikkatsu completes *Ukina zange* (Confession of a scandal).	July: Shōwa Kinema is renamed Hassei Eiga Kabushiki Kaisha, and Minagawa Phonofilms is renamed "Mina Talkie." November: Mina Talkie releases *Taii no musume* (The captain's daughter).

(continued)

TABLE 6.1 Known Experiments with and Productions of Sound Film in Japan in the Early Years of Cinema (*continued*)

Year	Disc	Optical
1930	February: Chiyogami Eiga completes *Osekisho* (The checkpoint). May: Shōchiku Kamata completes *Daitokai rōdōhen* (The big city: Labor, sound edition). June: Teikine completes *Nani ga kanojo o sou saseta ka* (What made her do it?). September: Teikine completes *Komoriuta* (Lullaby). Teikine's Nagase Studio burns down, and Tōjō's materials are lost.	January: Mina Talkie releases *Kanaya koume* (Koume of Kanaya). March: Nikkatsu Uzumasa and Mina Talkie coproduce *Furusato* (Hometown). December: Mina Talkie releases *Nakayama shichiri* (Seven miles to Nakayama)

probably never will, because no prints or negatives are known to have survived.

The oldest surviving Japanese part-talkie is Mizoguchi Kenji's 1930 *Fujiwara Yoshie no furusato* (Fujiwara Yoshie's hometown, hereafter *Furusato*). Nagato Yōhei makes a case for including Mizoguchi's earlier 1929 film *Tōkyō kōshinkyoku* (Tokyo march) in the canon of sound-oriented films because its theme song—that is, the SP record of its theme song—sold more than 250,000 copies and helped inaugurate the age of popular recorded music in Japan.[6] The film itself was based on a novel by the author and publisher Kikuchi Kan (1888–1948). Chika Kinoshita argues for *Tokyo kōshinkyoku* to be analyzed as a multimedial phenomenon—text, film, recording—representative of the economic and institutional formations active in Japan in the late 1920s and 1930s.[7] As we saw earlier with radio drama and sports broadcasting, this transmedial strategy was common across different forms of cultural production and spectatorship, and Kikuchi Kan was one of its most enthusiastic practitioners. Although *Tōkyō kōshinkyoku* was a silent film, it enjoyed a parallel life, as well as an afterlife, in the realm of recordings.

Indeed, well before sound came to the movies, the movies came to sound. Gramophone records of both film theme songs and *benshi* narrations of silent films were popular commodities that allowed filmgoers to relive their viewing experiences. In many cases, they were a listener's *only* experience of a film, which might seem odd from our perspective but not in a popular film culture in which the *benshi* were stars just as big as the actors and directors and in which many viewers went to see a film for the *benshi* instead of the film itself, or anybody who might have made or appeared in it.[8]

MADAMU TO NYŌBŌ

Claims for Gosho Heinosuke's (1902–1981) *Madamu to nyōbō* (*The Neighbor's Wife and Mine*, 1931) being the first "real" talkie or first "full" talkie oversimplify somewhat the fact that films before it made significant use of sound, as well as the fact that it still took months, if not years, before regular sound film production became both economically feasible and artistically mainstream. Ozu Yasujirō (1903–1963), for example, waited until 1936 to direct his first talkie, *Hitori musuko* (*The Only Son*), despite working for the studio, Shōchiku, that produced *Madamu to nyōbō*.

Madamu to nyōbō, in brief, is about a playwright, Shibano Shinsaku (played by Watanabe Atsushi), struggling with writer's block. He and his very traditional wife (played by Tanaka Kinuyo) move to a house in the suburbs, where he hopes he can find peace and quiet and finally finish a play he's been working on. The couple is low on cash, and a deadline is looming. One day a jazz band comes to rehearse in the house next door, creating a din that prevents Shibano from working. He goes next door to complain but is soon mollified when the lady of the house invites him in to have a drink and listen to the band rehearse. The drink, the sex appeal of "the neighbor's wife," and the music gradually seduce Shibano into embracing this new, modern lifestyle, one marked by the potent signifier of "speed." The number that the band is rehearsing is, in fact, called *Supīdo hoi* (something like "Speed, hoy!" or "Speed, yes!") and the film's other theme song is called "The Age of Speed."

According to Satō Tadao, although Tanaka Kinuyo (1909–1977) already was an established silent movie star, she was almost passed over for the role of the writer's wife because she spoke Japanese with a Shimonoseki (that is, Yamaguchi Prefecture) accent. In due course, however, it was precisely this accent that proved to be one of Tanaka's enduring assets in the sound era, as it imparted to her voice, in Satō's words, a "coquettish eroticism" (*amattareta iroke*) in the ears of filmgoers nationwide.[9]

We see here again the tension between the desire to use new auditory media as vectors of language standardization, and the potential to use them as showcases of linguistic difference. Actors embodied these differences as products of different linguistic communities, and they had to choose how to resolve that tension in their performances—either by going with the grain of normative nationalism (and against the grain of their own vocal habits) and mimicking standardized speech, or by going against that grain and expressing their own regional identity. Every performer had to negotiate that tension differently. Even though Tanaka's Shimonoseki accent might have sounded "coquettish" and "erotic" to other Japanese ears (it probably didn't elicit quite the same reaction from Shimonoseki natives), other regional accents conjured up different, often less "positive," associations and would certainly need to be attenuated or erased for widespread consumption.[10]

PCL

A significant industrial milestone in early Japanese sound film was the creation of Photo Chemical Laboratory (PCL) in 1933. The company was an outgrowth of a firm established in 1929 by Masutani Rin (1892–1967, probably best known today as a mentor to Sony cofounders Morita Akio and Ibuka Masaru) and Uemura Yasuji (1897–1971) to study film developing and emerging sound-recording techniques. In 1932, the company built two sound stages to rent out to other studios, and in 1933 it embarked on its own first production, *Ongaku kigeki—horoyoi jinsei* (Musical comedy: Tipsy life). This was the first in a series of musicals that pushed both the new medium and the genre in new directions.[11] PCL scored a series of successes, including *Odoriko nikki* (Dancing girl's diary, 1934) and *Enoken no seishun suikoden* (Enoken's tale of youthful drunken folly, English title *Romantic and Crazy*, 1934), which helped launch the comic performer Enomoto Ken'ichi (1904–1970) from fame in Tokyo to an even larger national stage.

PCL entered the ranks of full-fledged studios in 1936 when it issued a call for applications to its assistant director training program. A mere five candidates were selected out of a pool of five hundred applicants. Of these five, one was a graduate of Tokyo University, another was a graduate of Kyoto University, a third was from Keiō University, and still another was from Waseda University. In other words, they represented the four most famous and elite universities in Japan. Only one of the five was not a graduate of a prestigious institution (having attended the humble Keika Shōgyō Kōtō Gakkō, or Keika Commercial Junior High School), but only he went on to become a director of distinction: Kurosawa Akira.[12]

In 1937, PCL merged with JO studio (formed in 1933 and based in Kyoto) to form the Tōhō Film Company, which merged again in 1943 with the Tōkyō Takarazuka Theater (a subsidiary of the Osaka-based Hankyū Railway Company) to form Tōhō Company, Ltd., the corporate entity with which we associate the Tōhō films of the postwar golden age.

DISCIPLINING SOUND

Because I have already discussed sound effects as a transmedial phenomenon in chapter 5, I will focus in this chapter on questions of music and dialogue, two ubiquitous forms of expression that seemed well understood but that became newly problematized in the context of sound film. First, however, I will describe the lay of the talkie-theoretical land and list a few of its key texts.

The Japanese film world had a tradition of film-theoretical discourses long before the arrival of sound,[13] a product of the convergence of a thriving film culture (between four hundred and five hundred films produced per year during the late 1920s)[14] and an equally thriving print media culture. That a healthy volume of written discourse would be generated over the arrival of sound was only to be expected.

Between 1927 and 1939 the flagship trade journal *Kinema junpō* alone contained 120 articles with the words "talkie" (86) or *hassei eiga* (talking picture, 34) in their titles. This is a rough count and undoubtedly underrepresents the degree of interest, since the issue of sound also comes up in articles whose headlines, and thus ostensible focus, point elsewhere. A broader search of periodicals in the National Diet Library digital collection yields 409 title-word hits for "talkie" and 77 for "talking pictures" in periodicals between 1927 and 1939, and 357 hits for "talkies" and 93 for "talking pictures" in book chapter titles during that same period.[15] While these numbers are not especially meaningful outside a comparative context—such as, for example, the relative percentage of film articles devoted to sound, or that percentage relative to corresponding percentages in the discursive outputs of other film-exporting industries such as those of the United States and France—they are evidence enough that the topic attracted considerable attention.

Many of the most influential books on the subject were translations of the work of foreign filmmakers and critics. In the previous chapter I mentioned *Onga geijutsu no hōhōron* (Theory of sound film art), Magami Gitarō's translation of Aleksander Andrievskii's 1931 *Postroenie tonfil'ma*.[16] Sasaki Norio's 1931 *Hassei eiga kantoku to kyakuhonron* (Sound film direction and screenwriting) is a somewhat unusual medley of Heinz Umbehr's *Der Tonfilm: Grundlagen und Praxis seiner Aufnahme und Wiedergabe* (The sound film: Principles and practice of recording and playback),[17] Walter Pitkin and William Marston's *The Art of Sound Pictures*,[18] and Hans Kahan's *Dramaturgie des Tonfilms* (Dramaturgie of sound film).[19] It is worth noting, just as a curious historical publishing practice, that none of these editions prominently listed the names of the authors of the original German, Russian, or English texts. In other words, they were not marketed as *translations* but as edited, annotated, and reworked *translated selections*. The editor/translator was essentially credited as a coauthor—and on the cover at least, as the sole author—while the original authors' names were hidden away deep in the text.

There was no shortage of domestic theoretical production, either. The most famous volume of early writings on sound cinema was *Tōkīron* (Talkie theory), composed of essays by Ishimaki Yoshio, Yamanouchi Hikaru, Mori Iwao, Iwasaki Akira, and Shimizu Kō. Ishimaki's essay

"Hassei eiga kigyō no taisei" (Trends in the sound film industry) describes the economic and industrial history of sound-film development in Hollywood, with a short section devoted to the film industry in Germany. Yamanouchi's "Sobuēto dōmei ni okeru tōkīron" (Talkie theory in the Soviet Union) is an exposition primarily of the writings on sound film by Sergei Eisenstein and Vsevolod Pudovkin, with passing mention of a few other Soviet filmmakers. Mori's "Nihon eiga tenkōroku" (A record of Japanese cinema's conversion) is based largely on Mori's experiences as the writer of the original story for Mizoguchi's *Furusato*. Iwasaki's "Tōkī to musan kaikyū" (Talkies and the proletariat) argues that the talkie is an art form of the bourgeoisie, one that came into being when it did—not earlier, and not later—because of economic conditions in Hollywood. The greatest challenge facing sound cinema was that the introduction of national languages had made cinema less international, which could be addressed through the musical or "review," a genre that could cross linguistic boundaries more easily. That said, for the twenty-seven-year-old Iwasaki, the greatest problem with talkies was how capital intensive they were, making them difficult for the proletariat to employ as they had done with less expensive silent film. Shimizu's "Tōkī no shōrai" (The future of the talkies) draws on European modernism, primarily Russian formalism, to speculate on the future development of sound cinema.

Another substantial intervention was the monograph *Tōkī igo* (After the talkies, 1933) by the critic and poet Iijima Tadashi (1902–1996), whose ambitions were both historical and critical-theoretical. Iijima invoked two organizing principles: Gaston Rageot's (1871–1942) notion of *cinématisme*, and speed. *Cinématisme* should not be confused with the cinematism elaborated by Paul Virilio, although Virilio has read Rageot and seems to have taken his idea as the basis for his own.[20]

Speed was a common theme in the late nineteenth and early twentieth centuries when the introduction of rail travel, followed by automobiles and airplanes, rendered it one of the defining conceptual tokens of both modernity and modernism. This discourse experienced a revival with the introduction of sound film: As we saw earlier, much of *Madamu to nyōbō* is devoted to the topic. This seems like a puzzling development when one considers that the introduction of an optical soundtrack onto the print necessitated a standardization of projection frame rates (to the well-known twenty-four frames per second). This in turn demanded precise—and therefore mechanically driven—cameras and projectors, which, if anything, slowed down the perceived speed of movement in the frame. The paradox offers something of a resolution if we look back at *Madamu to nyōbō*, which situates the discourse of speed in music, specifically jazz.[21]

THE SOUND OF MUSIC

Japanese discourses on sound film extended to the specialized genre of film music as well. I would like to take a closer look at the work of the theorist Nakane Hiroshi (1893–1951).

In an essay from February 1931, Nakane writes the following:

> Sound cannot simply be an effect: It has to be one of the principal elements constituting a talking picture. In the case of the talkies, image and sound . . . should be considered equal partners and assigned equal value. This, however, is a matter of quality and not of quantity. It is a matter of the expressive function of each element.[22]

At a time when some film theorists were falling back on variants of specificity theory to keep the auditory essentially subordinate to the visual in the film text, Nakane offers the provocative suggestion that the two should be given equal importance in the creation of cinematic meaning. It is probably significant in this regard that Nakane was not originally a film critic or theorist but a music critic. I have found very little information about Nakane's early life and education, but we do know that he was a musician and a member of the *Ongaku to bungaku* (Music and literature) coterie magazine founded by the pioneering music critic Ōtaguro Motoo (1893–1979).

Although Nakane had a musical background and possessed a keen musical sensibility, his approach to the theory of talkie music did not favor music at the expense of the image or other auditory elements such as dialogue and sound effects. While insisting on the *equal* importance of sound in relation to image, Nakane was an aesthetic pragmatist who wanted to maximize the expressive potential of sound by any means necessary, including means that we might term "minimalistic."

Tōkī ongakuron (On music for the talkies) is a collection of essays and critical analyses published by Nakane, mainly in *Kinema junpō* but also apparently in other unnamed venues, between February 1931 and August 1932. Nakane first began writing about cinema at the invitation of *Kinema junpō*'s president and cofounder, Tanaka Saburō (1899–1965), who told Nakane that the advent of talkies made the magazine feel an urgent need for somebody who could specialize in sound and music.

The volume was published in October 1932 by Ōraisha as the seventeenth installment of its Eiga kagaku kenkyū sōsho (Researches in film science library), an outgrowth of its journal *Eiga kagaku kenkyū* (Researches in film science). This highly influential series included the work of both Japanese theorists, such as Iwasaki Akira's seminal *Eiga to shihonshugi* (Film and capitalism, 1931), as well as translations of luminaries such as Vsevolod Pudovkin, Sergei Eisenstein, and Léon Moussinac. The book includes laudatory prefaces by the Tōhō cofounder and sound-film theorist Mori Iwao (1899–1979) and the composer Yamada Kōsaku. It is difficult to assert this with certainty, but Nakane's volume may have a claim to being the first book-length study dedicated to sound-film music anywhere in the world: Leonid Sabaneev's *Music for the Films* did not appear until 1935, and it is, in any event, much more of a practical guidebook for aspiring composers;[23] Kurt London's *Film Music: A Summary of the Characteristic Features of Its History, Aesthetics, Technique; and Possible Developments* was published in 1936.[24] Much had been written about scoring and accompanying silent film, of course, and shorter interventions had already appeared on sound-film music, but Nakane was possibly the first—certainly one of the first—to lavish such substantial critical-theoretical attention on the changing nature of film music in the sound era.

Nakane contends that for most audiences, the basic appeal of the talkies was in their "naturalness" (*shizensei*). When we see people talking in ordinary life, we hear them at the same time. We generally hear the sounds that objects make at the same time that we see them. For the fidelity of this kind of representation to be complete, Nakane observes, three conditions must be met:

1. Sound and image must be synchronized.
2. Sounds must have the same balance, nuance, and dynamic range that they naturally have.
3. There must be a sense of auditory perspective as objects move through space.

Nakane was, of course, familiar with Eisenstein, Pudovkin, and Alexandrov's statement on sound, and its arguments against auditory naturalism. Indeed, Nakane's somewhat limited exposure to film theory seems largely confined to the Soviets' work. While highly sympathetic to Soviet film and film theory, he was also attentive to popular appetites and believed that sound and music could be deployed to artistic effect even within the limitations of naturalism and synchronization. Although "naturalness" is what originally draws popular audiences to the talkies, Nakane argues that it is not, and should not, be the final objective of sound-film art. While he acknowledges that the resistance to sound makes perfect sense from the perspective of theorists who are used to thinking of film as a visual medium, he sidesteps their objections by defining the talkie as a new art form in its own right.

The aesthetic possibilities of the talkie can be realized, however, only when sound and music are used with appropriately artistic restraint. The aesthetic problem is not one of synchronization but of overuse:

> The talkies are a new art form, and must have their own, new aesthetics. Music cannot just be used for effect or to create a mood—it has to have an independent function and be seen as an important structural component. This doesn't mean it should be overused, but rather that it should be harmonized as organically as possible with the action on screen.[25]

The main problems that Nakane identifies in the sound films of his time are excessive dialogue and excessive music. These are symptomatic of what he terms the "pioneering" (*kaitakuteki*) period of sound film, during which new possibilities are embraced with no sense of moderation.

It is perhaps not surprising that Nakane, as a trained musician, blames much of this on this fact that filmmakers and audiences generally didn't have the musical training necessary to apply and appreciate sound with understanding and sensitivity. With this maneuver, Nakane turns the liability of his status as a relative outsider to established filmic discourse into an asset—he has, he implies, something that the world of film theory needs. At the same time, although auditory sensitivity must thus be cultivated, Nakane goes to pains to clarify that what is needed is not formal musical training per se so much as a cultivated attentiveness to sound and music, the ability truly to feel it even if one does not necessarily understand it. In the meantime, he proposes filmmakers would do well to rely more on the expertise of musical specialists—film composers and theorists—when deciding how and when to use sound and music.

Nakane felt that music has a singular, mysterious ability to captivate people's hearts, as well as an unparalleled capacity to infiltrate and propagate itself into other art forms. As an example, he discusses at length the role of music in both the theater and the silent cinema, whose exhibition almost single-handedly sustained live ensemble music in Japan. This mysterious power of music, Nakane writes, comes from the fact that "in its formal construction and the morphology of its performance, music is built upon an extraordinarily mathematical and organic foundation, but what it expresses are extraordinarily free and abstract feelings and notions."[26]

The power and versatility of music that allow it to be employed extensively in arts like theater and silent film also often lead it to be viewed as an intrusion into or nuisance (*jamamono*) in those very same arts. Nakane himself basically makes the same charge when he observes, as noted previously, that even when music is used appropriately in talkies (in the sense of the right *kind* of music), it is almost always used excessively.

He then appropriates a musical analogy for sound's role in the talkie: We may think of the image as the melody and of sound as the harmony or counterpoint. Nakane credits the Soviet theorists with being the first to theorize film sound in this way, and he marvels at the fact that they were able to do so even before actually producing a single sound film. But he departs from them, as I noted, by suggesting that one can still employ counterpoint against the image within naturalistic limits. He also suggests other musical forms as templates for the sound/image relationship, including canon, fugue, theme and variations, and sonata form. He proposes that we extend the analogy even further and think about sound and image in symphonic terms that incorporate multiple timbres.

He offers the following scene from Josef von Sternberg's *Morocco* (1930) as a particularly effective example of his idea of sound/image counterpoint:

> The flute and drum continue unabated throughout Tom and Amy's conversation, reminiscent of a nighttime Oeshiki festival, a mysterious combination of tone, melody, and rhythm. And then comes a silence like death.
>
> The heartbreaking piano and forte tones of the flute and drum actually have nothing to do with what's happening on screen. They're also not simply an effect meant to convey the atmosphere of Morocco's streets at night.
>
> The uncanny music that arises from the soft and loud notes of the flute fill the unfamiliar streets with a sense of foreboding—we see Adjutant Caesar, burning with jealousy, and the vicious Arab who has been hired by Caesar to kill Tom—and all these elements blend in a three-dimensional way that hints at the disaster that is about to occur. This is all expertly rendered using methods that I would call symphonic.[27]

Despite his appreciation for *Morocco* (which was, after all, directed by the German Sternberg), Nakane's aesthetic and political sympathies lead him to take positions that are, on balance, critical of American talkies and highly appreciative of Soviet talkies. He acknowledges the crucial technological contributions of the United States to the perfection of sound cinema, but he recycles the charge that most American talkies are nothing more than *sōga* or "noisy pictures," and attributes much of this to the breathless pace of profit-driven studio production. In contrast to this, he prizes Soviet talkies above even those of Germany and France, and prophesies that only nationalized production on a Soviet scale can bring together the material and artistic resources (including first-rate composers such as Dmitri Shostakovich) necessary for what he teleologically terms the "perfection" of the sound film.

Nakane devotes a chapter and several close readings to what he calls "talkie operettas and operas." By "talkie opera," he means grand opera that has been adapted for film. Although filmic opera adaptations are as rare now as they were when Nakane was writing, they have been sporadically produced and even enjoyed something of a vogue in the 1970s and 1980s, so his speculations were not entirely unprophetic. Interestingly, Nakane surmises that Giuseppe Verdi's grand operas, like *Il Trovatore* and *La Traviata*, would not work as films but that Georges Bizet's *Carmen* would, though he doesn't explain exactly why. He thinks smaller-scale Italian operas such as Pietro Mascagni's *Cavalleria Rusticana* would also work. He sees possibilities for adaptations of Richard Wagner and Richard Strauss but wonders at the financial and logistical difficulties and again concludes that a Soviet-style production infrastructure would be necessary.

More relevant to the mainstream of film history is Nakane's discourse on the talkie operetta. Musicals were, of course, a staple of early sound film because they exploited the new possibilities to the hilt: "all singing, all dancing, all talking." Their popularity presented something of a theoretical conundrum for Nakane, however, in that musicals depart significantly from the naturalness and, by extension, the naturalism that he posits as the first source of the talkies' appeal. Nakane objects to stereotypical moments in musicals, such as when a man and woman, engaged in naturalistic dialogue about their love for each other, suddenly break out into song and then just as suddenly return to dialogue. An operetta, in contrast, maintains a high degree of stylization and exaggeration from beginning to end, and this internal consistency is what redeems it. Nakane admired the work of Ernst Lubitsch and René Clair and considered the musicals of the former, in particular, to be exemplars of the talkie operetta.

Nakane also lavishes considerable attention on a slightly more marginal genre, the *jissha eiga*, which today generally refers to live-action films, but which in Nakane's time was a term for actuality films. He was very excited by the possibilities that talkies afforded for photorealism and also auditory realism. "The sounds of waves, of storms, the gurgling of water, the calls of boatmen, the songs of farmers . . . all of these can now be freely and realistically expressed through sound."[28] Unlike musicals or talkie operettas, actuality talkies are entirely consonant with his theory of verisimilitude appeal. Nakane professes the deepest interest in *jissha* films and films that include documentary elements and complains that they don't appear frequently enough in cinema programs.

Nakane was largely dissatisfied with the scoring of the documentaries and actuality films he had seen. The musical accompaniment of most documentary films ignores the realism of the sounds captured on the soundtrack and doesn't try to establish an organic relationship with them. As in the silent age, the music's only objective is to create a mood or to accompany the progress of the action. He offers the example of *Among the Man-Eaters* (*Chez les mangeurs d'hommes*, 1930), a documentary by André-Paul Antoine (1892–1982) about cannibals in Vanuatu, about which he writes, "It's unbearable to have European-style music come in right at the moment when your sense of hearing is captivated by the chorus of primitive aboriginals [*genshiteki na dojin*]. You can't help but feel indignant at the stupidity of it all."[29] Despite his somewhat derogatory choice of words and the fact that he was himself steeped in the European musical idiom, we can detect in this and other flashes of impatience a painful recognition of the power of sound and music to accompany and heighten, but also to silence. Even though he doesn't make this claim for himself, I believe that Nakane's theory offers us both an aesthetics and an ethics of film sound.

At the same time, one does not get the sense that he felt himself to have been silenced; he comes across as a confident and cosmopolitan interlocutor in a transnational discussion in which he has an inalienable right to participate. This was quite normal for Japanese film writing of the period, even if not for those writing under Japanese colonial rule. Nakane's admiration for Soviet theory is palpable, but he doesn't hesitate to disagree with it; he doesn't wring his hands over any supposed deficiencies in Japanese production methods or film criticism, but neither, even more tellingly, does he resort to any manner of defensive chauvinism.

Whatever their sins of teleology, many of Nakane's insights were so prescient that they closely resemble contemporary trends in film-sound theory after the work of Michel Chion. In that regard, they may not hold for us some of the *frisson* of the more puritanical image theories, but neither are they precursors of any so-called Hollywood style, which even now tends to use music to a degree that Nakane would likely consider excessive and in ways symptomatic of an inability or unwillingness to *listen*.

Finally, Nakane offers us, or at least me, a tantalizing possibility: What becomes possible when a theorist of one medium is called upon to theorize another, when that other form incorporates elements of the theorist's primary expertise? As a composite medium, film lends itself well to this kind of border-crossing intervention, sometimes to the chagrin of dedicated film specialists. I think, however, that we would be wise to remain open to the potential for cross-pollination and theoretical short circuits that such interventions afford, as well as the fields of asymmetric power that are established whenever a border is crossed.

IMAGINED COMMUNITIES, INVENTED PASTS

The introduction of sound posed a raft of challenges both technical and aesthetic. Of these, the problems presented by the sudden explosion of spoken language in the filmic text were some of the most vexing.

Actors, who until then needed only to be photogenic and act with an expressiveness bordering on pantomime, now needed to learn how to speak effectively, in terms of accent and delivery, and also to enable their voices to be picked up by primitive microphones. Screenwriters needed to learn how to write effective dialogue, whether that was meant to be "realistic" (and realism, as we have seen, was the privileged mode in the discourses of sound cinema) or dramatically expressive. Directors and editors needed to put this dialogue together in ways that felt natural—too long or too short a pause between utterances could ruin the pacing and rhythm of a film as much, or more than, a badly timed cut. Practitioners of the nascent art of film music composition had to figure out new types of counterpoint between word and music. None of these new skills could be learned overnight; indeed, the "skills" had to be newly crafted out of existing practices before they could be learned.

The linguistic textures themselves had to be addressed, most overtly in regard to questions of regional and historical variations. On the one hand, actors were not tabulae rasae that could simply be told to speak a certain way at will. As the living embodiments of specific historical and geographical contingencies, they brought with them traces of stubborn heterogeneity that had survived the standardizing impulses of the previous half century. On the other hand, dialogue writers had to create new languages that were widely intelligible in the context of a film and that also were suggestive of particular times and places, as well as of gender and class. Like radio and stage drama before it (and, indeed, like the "vernacular"[30] fiction that came even earlier), the arrival of sound turned cinema into a workshop where new languages were forged. This was true for the representation of regional differences and for the creation of an imagined past: *jidaigeki*, or period drama, had been a staple of Japanese silent cinema from its very beginnings[31] and had reached its first artistic peak within that aesthetic framework. The introduction of sound made it necessary, essentially, to *create* a new spoken language, one that sounded historically accurate enough that it wouldn't elicit disbelief but also modern enough that it could be understood by audiences entirely by ear and in real time.

"THE SMELL OF THE SOIL"

Japanese is usually divided into three main dialect groups—Eastern, Western, and Kyushu—within which are further subdivisions and sub-subdivisions numbering in the dozens. While these regional variations are marked by a high degree of mutual intelligibility (certainly more than that between, say, Mandarin and Cantonese), some of the differences are marked enough to create significant barriers to understanding. The differences extend to accent, lexicon, and sometimes to grammatical features. This rich diversity was precisely what necessitated language standardization in the Meiji period (1868–1912) in the first place, since the differences, in both degree and kind, were significant enough that they could present barriers to communicating and to subscribing to the newly constructed national identity.

Perhaps no films from the early sound-film era exemplify the perils and possibilities of the use of regional language as well as a pair of films directed by Mizoguchi Kenji in 1936: first *Naniwa erejī* (*Osaka Elegy*) and then *Gion no shimai* (*Sisters of the Gion*).

Naniwa erejī was Mizoguchi's first collaboration with the screenwriter with whom he made most of his arguably finest—and certainly best-known—films, Yoda Yoshikata (1909–1991). Yoda was a native of Kyoto whose ear was finely attuned to the nuances and accents of the Kansai region. This was one reason why Mizoguchi decided to work with him, for he knew that only a native speaker of the dialect would be able to write dialogue that would meet his own exacting standards of realism. While this opened up new possibilities, it also sparked in Mizoguchi an obsessive perfectionism that pushed both casts and the crews to their limits. The performers in these films recount how lines of dialogue would be changed the night before a scene was shot or even on the very same day. Not having enough time to relearn their lines, the actors would have to read cues written on chalkboards off-screen. Multiple takes would have to be shot, because non-Kansai-native actors had trouble remembering their lines and also delivering them with the proper intonation.[32]

In addition to his tremendous creative gifts, Mizoguchi was a clear and forceful writer, with a cast of mind that I dare call scholarly. Some of the most acute commentary on the question of film dialogue comes from his own pen. In a series of short, often occasional pieces written in the late 1920s through the 1930s, he approached the issue of language in sound cinema from a number of different angles.

From the beginning, Mizoguchi embraced the arrival of sound. In addition to attempting one of the first part-talkies, he wrote critically of those who resisted adopting sound. In an article for the *Osaka Asahi shinbun* from April 21, 1929 (that is, after the release of *Tōkyō kōshinkyoku* and before that of *Furusato*), he wrote:

> The people who cry that the advent of sound film will make cinema revert back to the forms of stage theater do not understand cinema's potential; they're like a flock of patients in a ward of ignorance. Not only do they want to halt cinema's development—I wouldn't say it's an exaggeration to call them reactionary vermin who would demolish all scientific progress.[33]

For an established silent film director like Mizoguchi to issue such a stinging polemic is a bit surprising. His pronouncements could be acerbic, but the "reactionary vermin" he decries here still counted among them a number of accomplished filmmakers. In any event, that Mizoguchi already at this point embraced sound without reservation is left beyond doubt. Sasō Tsutomu speculates that Mizoguchi was familiar with the thinking of Osanai Kaoru and Sergei Eisenstein on the possibilities of sound and that this was why he was open to it. He had also seen many of the successful early American talkies. I'm inclined to think that

Mizoguchi was intimate enough with his chosen medium that he didn't need the theoretical arguments of Osanai and Eisenstein to sway him: He could see and hear the results coming out of Hollywood and use his own imagination as a filmmaker.

Having committed himself early out of the gate to the relatively new medium, Mizoguchi was also one of the first to begin the still preliminary process of thinking about exactly what form film dialogue should take. Here, in full, is a short note he published in the April 1930 issue of *Eiga ōrai* entitled "Tōkī no kotoba to butaigeki no serifu to" (Talkie words and stage play lines):

> I'm still new to talkies, so there isn't much I can say, but as I was working on *Furusato* I sensed repeatedly that there's a difference between dialogue in a talkie and lines in a stage play. They're extremely dissimilar: Lines are the essence of a play, but in talkies, the words step all over the techniques for developing the plot, like intertitles, fade-ins, and fade-outs. Thus the words in talkies cannot simply be [thought of as] an extension of play lines. I think talkie dialogue can neither be like stage dialogue nor be like everyday conversation but must take a new form. As to what that form should be, without having had a full screening [of *Furusato*] yet, the effect of what we have now still isn't clear.[34]

This is one of the earliest written observations by a Japanese filmmaker or critic that the language used in film dialogue is, must be, different from the language of the stage and the spoken language of everyday life. Dialogue must be made to fit in and work together with the other elements of the filmic text, visual and auditory. While this note is quite preliminary, the insight is valid, and it was only the beginning.

As he started making full talkies in earnest, Mizoguchi's thinking about dialogue grew deeper and more nuanced. Furthermore, he became concerned—one might even say preoccupied—with the question of dialect in a way that no other filmmaker had been until that point.

Perhaps Mizoguchi's longest, most searching meditation on the question of language appeared in the summer 1938 special issue of the *Sandē Mainichi*. Even at this late date, two years after the releases of *Gion no shimai* and *Naniwa erejī*, Mizoguchi was still preoccupied with the question of dialect and how it could be incorporated into cinema.

Mizoguchi begins by pointing out that, until then, the question of language in film and stage drama had been researched only in a lax and haphazard (*hōman na*) manner: "For example, one can say that almost no films have been made that use standard Japanese and dialects freely, having chewed on and digested them both. Kansai dialect might make a sudden appearance in one act of a play, but almost without exception, the character speaking it is being ridiculed as a comic figure."[35] He goes on to point out that if one wanted a rustic or bumpkin, for example, invariably the character would speak in the dialects and accents of Ibaraki and Tochigi Prefectures.

Mizoguchi observes that these "bad habits" of misusing dialects were themselves part of an old tradition that dated back to kabuki theater in the Tokugawa period (1603–1868). But to continue doing this in modern theater and cinema was, as he bluntly put it, "a disgrace" (*chijoku*).[36]

> Strictly speaking, it's quite difficult to find a standard language that encompasses the homeland we call "Japan." With all the hue and cry today about the need to regulate the national language and writing, all we hear in plays, in films, and on the radio is the language of Tokyo, with some "Edo dialect," "Yamanote speech," and "Shitamachi speech" mixed in. In that sense, the language we speak ultimately never takes even one step away from being a colonial language.[37]

Because this "colonial language" is intelligible across Japan, dramatists and filmmakers use it without question. According to Mizoguchi, it takes a great deal of courage and determination to represent regional linguistic variations in all of their diversity and richness.

What follows is something like a socioeconomic theory of language:

> Interpreted in the broadest sense, dialects are languages that are brought into being, cultivated, and sustained by each region's productive aspect. By no means are they representative of a region's consumptive aspect. We can say that they are symbols of farms, small businesses, and industries, and of other local people who are engaged in production. Even as the culture of the center progressively infiltrates local cultures and words are mixed together, leading to a jumble that is then subjected to a process of pruning and selection, dialects retain forever vestiges of the

words that came into being as a result of their respective regions' productive aspect.[38]

Mizoguchi states that the only reason he focuses so much on dialect in films is to convey "the smell of the soil" and to portray the social and economic specificity of each region. That's why he used Osaka dialect in *Naniwa erejī* and the languages of the Murayama Basin in Yamagata for *Aa furusato* (Ah, my home, 1938). "From north of Fukushima to Shōnai Heiya, there remain euphonious words filtered through the language of the samurai. The language of northern Kanto, right next door, is wildly different, making clear the distinctiveness of each region."[39]

He observes that there is still much work to be done in understanding dialects, and he urges linguists to study them in greater depth.

> The Murayama Basin dialect I'm using in my current film has, of course, been transformed into film dialogue. But what I'm trying to do here is put into practice my theory that today's playwrights and screenwriters must dispense with their indifference toward language and, if they do decide to use dialect, must carefully dissect its workings as a tool of living expression.[40]

One might detect in Mizoguchi's argument here the influence or trace of both folklorist Yanagita Kunio's (1875–1962) localism and Marx's materialism. Although Mizoguchi was not, strictly speaking, a Marxist, his younger brother Yoshio was. Yoshio died under mysterious circumstances in April 1938, shortly before this essay was written, and it isn't difficult to imagine that his brother's life and beliefs were much on Mizoguchi's mind.[41] Because Yanagita's folklore studies already had a firmly established place in the mainstream intellectual imagination, they could have been part of Mizoguchi's somewhat idiosyncratic worldview. What's most striking about Mizoguchi's defense of regional language, however, is his willingness, at the height of Japan's colonial project, to use the word "colony" in a way clearly derogatory to the standardized language, to metropolitan culture, and, by implication, to the central authority that foisted that language and culture onto every part of Japan. Whereas Yanagita's work may have been politically ambiguous (sometimes in the worst way), Mizoguchi here seems to be treading a dangerous, almost radical line, especially with the not-so-subtle touch of placing the almighty signifier "Japan" in quotation marks. Such moves could easily be thought to challenge both the orthodox discourse of the *kokutai* (national body) and the logic of empire in ways that might be tolerable in an unknown critic (if barely, or at all) but that could be seen as potently dangerous in a major film director. Sasō points out in the note to his essay that even when Mizoguchi turned "ideological" in his writing, he never carried that ideology unchanged (*sono mama*) into his films.[42] This, of course, leaves open the possibility that the ideology found other forms of expression. Unfortunately, *Aa furusato*, the film that Mizoguchi was working on when he wrote this essay, no longer survives. It was widely panned by critics, so much so that the actress Yamada Isuzu (1917–2012) went out of her way to visit a disconsolate Mizoguchi to try to convince him that the film had been treated unfairly.[43] Although critics blamed the story structure more than anything else, it may also be the case that at some level, perhaps even unconscious, the conspicuous use of regional dialect was off-putting or even threatening to the representatives of cultural homogeneity who demolished the film. That they were more forgiving of the "otherness" in films such as *Naniwa erejī* and *Gion no shimai* may have been as much a function of Kansai's cultural capital and prestige relative to Yamagata (Kansai was the cradle of Japanese civilization, after all) as to those films' greater narrative and/or aesthetic accomplishments.

Throughout his writings on the subject, Mizoguchi uses the term "scent of the soil" (*tsuchi ni nioi*) to refer to what he wants to convey through his films, and this conflation of two invisible media, sound and scent, was confirmed by his screenwriter Yoda Yoshikata:

> From what I saw, Mizoguchi found the musicality of the Kansai dialect I wrote (the full-flavored Kyoto dialect, that is—simply adding an Osaka accent wasn't enough) extremely interesting and was captivated by the sticky, body odor–like quality that emanated from it. "You have to make people come alive! You have to make them so vivid you can practically smell their body odor."[44]

These repeated references to the sense of smell suggest that Mizoguchi's idea of realism was quite visceral, very much a matter of embodiment. It was certainly that, but elsewhere in his writings we are reminded that he was just as interested in social and economic realism. In an essay published in the May 1936 issue of *Ōru Shōchiku* about the making of *Naniwa erejī*, Mizoguchi wrote: "Recently people have been going on about 'realist cinema.' I'm certainly not against the pursuit of realism in the world of cinema. I think that in *Naniwa erejī* I pointed my camera, in a fairly realistic way, at the spirit and wit residing in the inner lives of contemporary women."[45]

It is, in Mizoguchi's view, precisely the accurate representation of language that captures this broader social reality:

> In order to create charged moments, no matter what, you need the nuances conveyed by Kansai dialect, that is, the language of Osaka.
>
> Compared with Kyoto dialect, which is also a branch of the larger Kansai dialect, Osaka dialect is not entirely without a hint of garishness. If you make a single misstep (in nuance or delivery), there's a good chance that it will result in *niwaka*-style buffoonery.[46] So, in this film, I went to great pains to get that right. Using pure Osaka dialect, I want to portray the modern women of Osaka—who until now haven't been taken up much as a subject—as well as their modern landscapes. Of course, there have been quite a few films that capture the spirit of Osaka, but those have mainly been demimonde love stories and tales of common folk; I think films that take the mechanized culture of contemporary Osaka as their background, that portray a modern Osaka, are still uncommon.[47]

There is a tension in Mizoguchi's thinking concerning the relationship between language and the "mechanized culture of contemporary Osaka." That tension is played out most vividly in the film itself, in which the protagonist, Ayako, works as a telephone operator. Nagato Yōhei notes that this is a significant narrative choice. As we've seen, the labor of telephone operation soon became a starkly gendered one, as it became clear that such labor was not merely technical but also affective. Men were gradually phased out of the job, both because their voices didn't carry as well across phone lines and because their gruffer manner of speaking didn't correspond to the kind of affective "service" that telephone users (who were mostly male) had grown to expect.[48] The telephone thus became the site where spoken language, "mechanized culture," gender, and other social and economic realities intersected.

JIDAIGEKI KOTOBA

By the time talkies started being produced in Japan, the project of language unification and modernization was, in theory at least, well advanced. A standard vernacular, based on Tokyo dialect, had been established, and most written discourse had been simplified in order to be intelligible to literate readers without any further special training in the Japanese and Chinese classics. Newspapers and other print media helped consolidate this standardization, whose foundations could be found in the compulsory educational curriculum, while radio broadcasts helped reinforce the *sounds* of the standard vernacular in the ears of listeners. Indeed, radio announcers received training in pronunciation to ensure that they didn't unwittingly revert to their regional accents. While language reform could never be perfectly completed, for most practical purposes, the standard spoken and written languages were intelligible throughout the archipelago.

Before the creation of an invented language for period film, popular writers had to invent a language for period fiction. The rise of popular literature in modern Japan has received increasing scholarly attention, though not enough given the magnitude of the phenomenon. The term *taishū bungaku* (mass literature) began to be used in the late Taishō period (1912–1926) to designate relatively affordable paperback editions of novels in popular genres. In the context of the time, *taishū bungaku* was largely synonymous with *jidai shōsetsu* (period novels), although genres such as detective fiction also were popular. In the beginning, these genres were categorized as *tsūzoku shōsetsu* (popular novels),[49] and only in around 1930 were the two streams consolidated (or the distinctions blurred) into a single conception of popular literature under the *taishū bungaku* moniker. Even then, *jidai shōsetsu* were, on the whole, the most popular and best-selling genre under the umbrella.

The most successful of the pioneering authors of the genre included Nakazato Kaizan (1885–1944), whose serialized magnum opus *Daibosatsutoge* (Great Bodhisattva Pass, 1913–1941) was adapted for film five times (the most famous adaptation being the last, *Sword of Doom*, directed by Okamoto Kihachi in 1966); Naoki Sanjūgo (1891–1934), after whom Japan's premiere popular fiction prize is named; and Yoshikawa Eiji (1892–1962), who of the three is still the most translated and best known outside Japan.

Of a slightly later generation, the most popular writer in the genre by far was Yamamoto Shūgorō (1903–1967). Dozens of his works were adapted for the screen, particularly in the postwar period, including two that served as the basis for Kurosawa Akira's *Tsubaki Sanjūrō* (*Sanjuro*, 1962) and *Akahige* (*Red Beard*, 1965).

The first talkie *jidaigeki* appears to be *Akagaki Genzō*, produced by Teikoku Kinema Engei, directed by Watanabe Shintarō and written by Ueshima Ryō, released on April 29, 1931. The film is one of no fewer than sixteen bearing this title, as it is the name of a prominent character in *Chūshingura*. Whether this was in fact the first sound *jidaigeki* is in some doubt, however, because according to Kurokigawa Takashi, the first sound *jidaigeki* were the dubbed *Onna Kunisada* (release date unknown), the sync-sound *Ikinokotta Shinsengumi* (The surviving Shinsengumi, May 20, 1932) by Kinugasa Teinosuke (1896–1982), and the half-dubbed *Tabi wa aozora* (Journey to the blue sky, July 14, 1932) directed by Inagaki Hiroshi (1905–1980).[50]

Kurokigawa argues that what distinguishes *jidaigeki* from *gendaimono*, or films set in contemporary times, is the dynamic range of the emotions expressed. Retaining those emotional extremes is the task of sound *jidaigeki*, and the three films he had seen so far had failed, in his opinion, to accomplish that. The reason was that the *sound* in these films lacked dynamic range—it was either too quiet or too loud, without variation. He also complains about the musical accompaniment, which, he felt, needed to be more contrapuntal, more in conflict, with the image (echoing, I believe, Soviet theory on this score). In regard to this he held up Shōchiku's *Kuma no yattsu kiri jiken* (Kumajirō's killing spree, released May 13, 1932), directed by Saitō Torajirō.

Kurokigawa never addresses the question of historical usage directly. In the question of *jidaigeki* dialogue more broadly, he takes his cue from "Tōkī jidaigeki no daiarōgu: Toku ni haiyū no tachiba kara" (Period Talkie Dialogue: Especially from the Actor's Perspective) by the director and screenwriter Kiyose Eijirō (1902–1941).[51] Kiyose wrote this before ever trying to direct a talkie *jidaigeki* himself, although not before the earliest such attempts, as he does not mention *Akagaki Genzō* and *Nakayama shichiri*. Like Kurokigawa, Kiyose also does not mention the problem of historical language. He makes the case that dialogue in period films must be standardized because the actors in these films would be coming from different backgrounds: some would be kabuki stars; some would come from *kengeki* sword-fighting plays or other genres (such as *fushigeki*, a simplified kabuki-style drama based on stories from the *naniwabushi* repertoire); while others would be newcomers or amateurs. His concern here was not so much the lines—that is, the language—but how the performers would deliver them.

Not until the period from 1934 to 1936 was this issue addressed explicitly. The earliest mention that I could find was in a roundtable discussion in *Kinema junpō* with the *jidaigeki* director Itō Daisuke (1898–1981). Itō was without question one of the most important directors and screenwriters of the prewar era; he directed ninety-one films and wrote the screenplays for nearly two hundred. Most of these were *jidaigeki*, and a significant number were critical or commercial successes or both. In 1927, three of the films in *Kinema junpō*'s Best Ten were his. With the conversion to talkies, however, he was widely considered to have lost his stride. Itō's first sound film was *Tange Sazen Part 1* in 1933, and this inaugurated what came to be called a "slump" that, in many tellings of it, lasted all the way to 1948.

In the roundtable, Itō points out that the abilities of the actors are indeed decisive in writing dialogue for period films:

> ITŌ DAISUKE: We have actors gathered from all over Japan, and thanks to their regional accents, most of their pronunciation is terrible. I would go so far as to say that there are almost no Japanese who can pronounce standard Japanese. For example, . . . [*transcription stopped*]
>
> . . .
>
> HAZUMI TSUNEO: Concerning lines: In this film you use a lot of contemporary language, such as *otōsan*, *okudari asobasarenu desu yo*, and so on. This, of course, is not done in kabuki or even in *shinkokugeki*. The word *inchiki* even appears. Was this all done intentionally?
>
> ITŌ: Yes, I did it intentionally based on the scene and the actor.
>
> HAZUMI: Is that really acceptable?
>
> ITŌ: This film is "new *kōdan*" style, so it's all right, though if you look at it from the standards of *kōdan* or look at it very seriously, you can't be that slipshod with your usage. If you're making a true *jidaigeki*, you can't take that attitude. But if you modernize the language as Kinugasa [Teinosuke] had his screenwriter Ōishi do in *Chūshingura*, that's a completely different way of thinking.

HAZUMI: The language in that film was awful. It just went from one extreme to another.

KOBAYASHI ISAMU: He even has Chobi Yasu say, "Sōtō na mono da."

ITŌ: I don't want the stenographer to take this down (please cut this out to protect the actors' reputations): Even if you want an actor to say a certain thing, there are times when you need to adjust the dialogue to suit the actor.

. . .

KISHI MATSUO: For talkie dialogue, don't you need to create words especially for talkies and depend on those?

ITŌ: I think it's especially true for *jidaigeki* that you need to create such words.[52]

Although he wrote frequently about historical veracity in period films, Itō wrote less frequently about the creation of a new language for talkies. What he did write, though, exhibited such a wealth of knowledge and went into such detail that I think the relative absence of such writings is not because Itō wasn't interested in questions of historical usage but because he knew so much about historical usage that writing period dialogue came very naturally to him.

The most direct and extensive discussion of the problem of period dialogue appears in *Eiga kyakuhon kōseiron* (On screenplay composition, 1935) by the critic Yasuda Kiyoo (dates unknown).[53]

At present, instead of using words that are accurate to the period, we employ words that bring out the feeling of a period film. Such words bring together all the different periods that period films might represent, and all the different social classes within them. In the Edo period under feudalism—most period films don't treat the periods before the Edo—each of the social classes (samurai, peasants, craftsmen, merchants) used their own respective languages. To represent all of their speech accurately, even in just a single talkie, would not be that easy. What we need to consider here is that cinema is, above all, an art, even if a commercial one. Thus it makes no sense to try to recreate every period and every social class's language just as they were. This is so for exactly the same reason that it isn't suitable to use everyday spoken language, exactly as it is, in a contemporary piece.[54]

Yasuda captures here what I think came to be the consensus view on the use of dialogue in period films—that feeling or flavor is more important than accuracy. *Jidaigeki* dialogue became a hybrid of, generally, modern grammatical forms with a lexicon that was stripped of foreign loanwords and modern (Meiji and after) Sino-Japanese neologisms, sprinkled with some archaic (or archaic-sounding, even if they weren't actually used during the period depicted) words, especially pronouns, copulas, titles, and period-specific objects. This particular formula retains relatively easy intelligibility (at least once the meanings of the archaisms have been learned or inferred) while still imparting period flavor. At the same time, it doesn't bog down the dialogue in a heteroglossia so rich that could only be appreciated by a historical linguist.

Yasuda also notes that even many of the surviving examples of Tokugawa-period speech that were set down in print are not representative of the way people actually spoke then. The closest examples, he suggests, are to be found in the humorous *sharebon* (books of wit and fashion) popular literary genre, which were gradually transformed into the quasi-melodramatic *ninjōbon* (sentimental fiction) genre. If one looks at the language in kabuki or bunraku theater, however, the gulf between them and the everyday vernacular of the age was great indeed. As Yasuda writes, "There's no doubt that people in the past already unconsciously believed that there had to be a difference between art and reality."[55] Thus he finds in traditional theater a historical precedent for the practice he endorses of using language in historical dramas that has a historical feeling instead of being accurate.

Similar sentiments are expressed in this roundtable discussion published in the September 1, 1935, *Kinema junpō*:

KISHI MATSUO: In terms of *jidaigeki* dialogue, you use language fairly similar to that in contemporary films, so it must not be too difficult.
INOUE KINTARŌ: It's extremely difficult. We're groping in the dark.
KISHI: I suppose it largely depends on the person.
INOUE: It does, but nobody watching or making the films today has ever seen a real samurai. I think most of what we know comes from kabuki. There's definitely a tendency to borrow from that.
KISHI: The actual historical samurai language was probably different.
INOUE: And there were different varieties of samurai language.

KISHI: If it became natural to hear contemporary speech in *jidaigeki*, could you limit yourself to just that?

INOUE: It no longer seems that unnatural for a woman in a *jidaigeki* to say, "Sō desu wa," but for a man who is thrusting a sword to say, "Sō ja nai yo" would still be strange. But it's gradually becoming less so.[56]

Yasuda brings up the question of gendered language as well. Miyako Inoue has examined how *onna kotoba* (women's language) has become a pillar of a certain contemporary linguistic ideology, one that many Japanese today have come to believe has been a timeless part of the Japanese language.[57] Yasuda, writing in 1935, was close enough to the origins of *onna kotoba* to know that it was, in fact, a relatively recent innovation. "Even if we set aside the differences based on class, the most vexing problem remains: women's language. Women's language is simply *too new* to impart that period feeling, and even in terms of elocution, it's too close to real language as it is spoken today."[58]

This is one point on which subsequent writers of period drama seem to have parted ways with Yasuda; the ideology of a timeless women's language had to be enforced, which in turn led to the retrojection of that very modern invention into dialogue set in the past, something still discernible in period dramas to this day. Screenwriters squared this circle by inventing an archaically inflected women's language, which, once the base period-drama language had taken shape, necessitated only some minor adjustments.

Much as it did for Itō Daisuke, the conversion to sound presented a difficult challenge to the *jidaigeki* genre as a whole. In a roundtable discussion among Inagaki Hiroshi, Kinugasa Teinosuke, and Yamanaka Sadao (1909–1938) published in *Eiga no tomo* in January 1936, Kinugasa expresses discontent with the whole genre:

KINUGASA TEINOSUKE: But somehow when I'm shooting a contemporary piece, it feels real. *Jidaigeki* aren't pure. You've got the hair tied in a *chonmage* and actors saying, "Sō de gozansu," and "Sayō de gozaru ja"—it just doesn't hold together. The make-up, the lines—they're a lot different than before, but still . . .

YAMANAKA SADAO: It's true. When I see a *habutae* tied around the actor's head, and all that garish makeup, I sometimes think, "Is this what the films we make are all about?"

KINUGASA: Don't you feel there's something holding *jidaigeki* back? I feel one can do things more freely and expansively in contemporary pieces. But shooting a *chonmage* charade day after day...
YAMANAKA: Now that you mention it, I *would* like to try shooting a contemporary piece.
INAGAKI HIROSHI: I'd like to keep focusing in *jidaigeki* for a while, but the day is gradually coming when *jidaigeki* directors will try their hands at contemporary films.[59]

Besides the fascinating question of what a contemporary piece by a talent like Yamanaka might have looked like, this exchange does speak, I think, to a new crisis of authenticity in *jidaigeki*, one that became more apparent with the introduction of sound and the necessity for historically inflected dialogue. As the discourses of realism became more prominent in film circles, everything about the genre, from the makeup to the dialogue, was scrutinized and caused, Kinugasa at least, exasperation and even borderline disgust. I am also tempted to speculate that the triumph of Yamanaka's final film, *Ninjō kamifūsen* (*Humanity and Paper Balloons*, 1937), was due in no small part to the fact that it was a *jidaigeki* that felt very much like a work of contemporary social drama, and that perhaps this conversation played some role in that. Yamanaka never was able to direct a contemporary film before his untimely death, but *Ninjō kamifūsen* was the next best thing.

CONTRARY MOTIONS

The introduction of sound cinema might, in one sense, be considered the last major milestone of the electrical sounding of twentieth-century culture. There would be subsequent innovations, of course: commercially viable magnetic tape recording, stereo sound, vinyl LP records, and so on. These were all, however, improvements on existing paradigms of sound reproduction and transmission. None of them could really be said to have created new art forms, something that arguably didn't happen again until the widespread adoption of digital sound manipulation in the late twentieth century. The introduction of sound cinema, then, is a bookend in a series of developments that began with the telephone and phonograph in

1876 and 1877, respectively. In the Japanese context, both bookends were imbricated in questions of language, and in both cases new languages had, for lack of a better word, to be invented. The telegraph, telephone, and phonograph precipitated the emergence of an imagined community of audible speech, a nation-state of orality, that demanded the creation of a language that could be understood in every corner of its homeland and, subsequently, in its empire. At the other end of this period, the introduction of the talkie demanded the creation of an imagined shared history, an imagined spoken "bygonese"[60] for this imagined community, and sound film was the medium in which that creative process, as idiosyncratic and ad hoc as it may have been, played out. Although this language was never learned well enough to be used by anybody other than screenwriters and period-drama actors, it was learned well enough by film audiences that they would be able to follow along. It was, in effect, a standardized vernacular in the microcosm of the historical imaginary. Yet, as we have seen with Mizoguchi's use of dialect, sound cinema was also a site of centrifugal motion running counter to this centripetal motion of retrospective standardization, and while that centrifugal motion was by no means as powerful as the other, it did render the cultural and ideological uses of the new medium very productively ambiguous.

CODA-*OKE*

I would have liked to write other books alongside this one, with one about the role of auditory media in Japan's colonial empire probably at the top of the list. Scholars in a host of disciplines have begun to explore the range of cultural production in Japan's colonies, and Daqing Yang has written a meticulous historical study of telecommunications in the empire.[1] But much work remains to be done on the sonic dimensions of Japan's colonial project. I also would have liked to pursue questions of sound technology in a comparative transnational context, particularly in relation to Germany, a nation whose twentieth-century history offers striking parallels with Japan's and where radio drama is probably more highly valued as cultural (and as literary) production than anywhere else. Though one is a European power and the other an Asia-Pacific power, I am not the first to note that Germany and Japan's modernities share more commonalities with each other than with those of their immediate neighbors. Instead of speaking of universal or, less ambitiously, trans-Atlantic modernities, we might want to start thinking of clusters of similarity and affinity. Although these topics are now tucked away, to borrow a title of George Steiner's, in the file of "my unwritten books," I hope that this work may help lay the groundwork for future such research, whether by myself or by others with similar interests.

I also hope that this work helps expand the boundaries of the disciplines that I have called home the longest, Japanese literary and film studies. As I noted earlier, radio drama occupies an important place in twentieth-century German literary history, but the genre is little more than a footnote (if it's noted at all) in the histories of modern Japanese literature. Such boundaries deserve rethinking, and work by colleagues in Japanese film has brought the sound studies revolution to that field as well.[2] I am glad to have contributed to that effort. Nonetheless, there are many other nested histories of sound waiting to be told in the shadows of Japanese cinema's grand narratives. In the meantime, however, I would like to conclude with one last mini-history of sound technology.

In his 2001 novel *Nihon bungaku seisuishi* (The rise and fall of Japanese literature),[3] Takahashi Gen'ichirō (1951–) imagines a fictional space in which the literary personages of Meiji-period (1868–1912) Japan collide with his contemporary, turn-of-the-millennium reality. Early in the book, for example, Natsume Sōseki asks Mori Ōgai if he knows where he might be able to find some Tamagotchi digital pets.[4] This time warp, or blended temporality, was an idea taken from the manga series *Botchan no jidai* (The era of *Botchan*) by Sekikawa Natsuo and Taniguchi Jirō.[5] It works wonderfully as both a source of absurd humor and a representation of the ways in which the past is always present—perhaps only as memory, or as something even more spectral, but never inconsequentially.

In a scene about halfway through the book, Shimazaki Tōson is out with one of his students in a karaoke box:

> When he had finished speaking, the young man, his face still distorted with pain, let the hand that had been holding the mike go limp. His eyes were still turned toward the old man. The voices of the innumerable people who were singing the innumerable songs of Japan blended into a single voice that made the whole karaoke building rumble and resonate. The two of them could feel it through the soles of their feet.
>
> A smile began to form on the old man's face. Silently he stared at the young man. Time passed.
>
> The old man suddenly rose to his feet and snatched the mike away from the young man.
>
> "May I? Utada Hikaru's 'Automatic.'"[6]

Japan as a karaoke center, a partitioned collective of heteroglossia.

The origins of the karaoke machine are shrouded in the ancient mists of the 1970s. Inoue Daisuke claims to have invented the idea for karaoke around 1971, but he never patented it. Clarion was the first industrial firm to begin producing the machines, but it also neglected to patent it. It was not until 1983 and 1986 that the first patents were filed, by Roberto del Rosario of the Philippines, based on his own designs dating back to 1975.[7]

The karaoke machine was not, strictly speaking, a new technology. Rather, like most inventions, it was a combination of existing technologies. It was also an open-ended invention, one that could be added to and improved on as new technologies, such as home video, became commercially viable. Karaoke machines today employ the latest digital technologies, and one can even sing along to karaoke online. Karaoke has become a global pastime, enjoyed even in villages from Laos to Louisiana. It has taken on different and specific cultural and social functions in every place it has been adopted. It has become the object of extensive historiography, ethnography, and theorization.[8]

After nearly a century of electrified voices being transmitted, replayed, and amplified, listeners decided that they wanted their own voices electrified. They wanted to situate themselves in the amplified auditory field. At first glance, this seems like an emancipatory movement. Karaoke is, after all, more personalized and participatory than the passive experience of simply listening to a recording or broadcast. But in Japan it coincides historically with the closure of certain radical political paths and the fading of certain emancipatory energies. The auditory-technological icon of the late 1960s was the bullhorn, a tool of assembly, protest, and collective action. But by the 1980s, that icon had been largely replaced by karaoke, a tool of depoliticized sociability and "self-expression." The irony of this was surely not lost on Takahashi when he wrote those words around 2000. He had been arrested as a student radical in November 1969 and sentenced to prison in February 1970, remaining there until August of that year. While in prison, he developed a form of psychosomatic aphasia that prevented him from speaking and writing, and it took him years to recover completely. His first novel was published in 1982.[9] In sum, his rehabilitation, his return to linguistic expression, followed a trajectory almost exactly coterminous with the rise of karaoke. Similarly, Takahashi's reemergence as a speaking, writing subject represented a move away from political protest and toward postmodern ventriloquism and play.[10]

In a late capitalist context in which reproduced and transmitted sounds are so ubiquitous that it often requires an act of will simply to remember that they are in fact mediated, karaoke affords an opportunity to be reminded that there are actual bodies—living, breathing, slowly dying—that generate the disembodied voices to which we have become accustomed. The many intermediate steps leading to this stage of saturation took place during the postwar period, outside the purview of this book, but these steps were, as I noted in chapter 6, merely enhancements and amplifications (in every sense) of the technical foundations established during the Meiji, Taishō (1912–1926), and early Shōwa (1926–1989) periods. To call the very first instance of reproduced sound a historical rupture or discontinuity would be correct but would not do justice to all that this event added to cultural production, introducing new dimensions (again, in every sense) to mediated experience. Reproduced voices, sounds, and music created their own spaces, their own topographies, succeeding even more than print in giving "airy nothing a local habitation and a name." I am even tempted to say that they were the original virtual reality and that only the arrival of a "true"—that is, a haptic and olfactory, in addition to visual and auditory—virtual reality will represent as profound a transformation of the ways in which we do culture.

NOTES

INTRODUCTION: ALL THAT IS SOLID MELTS INTO SOUND

1. This anecdote is recounted in several different sources, although some versions omit Komura's presence. One retelling replaces Komura with Kurino Shin'ichirō. The most reliable sources, based on the reminiscences and diaries of those present, include Komura. This encounter in Bell's laboratory is all the more remarkable because all three of the young Japanese students would go on to become three of the most important figures of Meiji Japan. Kaneko became minister of justice, among many other posts he held, and he was instrumental in resolving the Russo-Japanese War. Komura became minister of foreign affairs in the period leading up to and including the Russo-Japanese War, and he also played a key role in the Japan-Korea Annexation Treaty. Isawa became a foundational figure in the fields of Western music education, deaf education, and language education in Japan. He also helped found the Tokyo Music School (forerunner of the Tokyo National University of the Arts) and then exported his educational methods to Taiwan in the immediate aftermath of the first Sino-Japanese War. I first encountered the anecdote in Matsuda Hiroyuki's *Meiji terekomu monogatari: Jōhō tsūshin shakai no "genfūkei"* (Tokyo: Nihon keizai hyōronsha, 2001), 76, and I recount the story here more or less as told there. Another version may be found in Itō Takashi's *Nihon no kindai: Media to kenryoku*, vol. 14 (Tokyo: Chūō kōronsha, 1999), 100. For an excellent treatment of Visible Speech as well as Isawa's influential and multifaceted career, see Seth Jacobowitz, *Writing Technology in Meiji Japan: A Media History of Modern Japanese Literature and Visual Culture* (Cambridge, MA: Harvard University East Asia Center, 2015).
2. Martin Jay, *Downcast Eyes: The Denigration of Vision in Twentieth-Century French Thought* (Berkeley: University of California Press, 1993).
3. Jay, 6.

4. Jay, 10.
5. Mladen Dolar, "The Linguistics of the Voice" in *The Sound Studies Reader*, ed. Jonathan Sterne (New York: Routledge, 2012), 540.
6. The indispensable study of this process of inventing tradition in Japan remains Carol Gluck, *Japan's Modern Myths* (Princeton, NJ: Princeton University Press, 1985).
7. For helpful background information on modernism in Japan, see Roy Starrs, ed., *Rethinking Japanese Modernism* (Leiden: Brill, 2011).
8. Donald Richie, *A Hundred Years of Japanese Film: A Concise History, with a Selective Guide to Videos and DVDs*, 1st ed. (Tokyo: Kodansha International, distributed in the United States by Kodansha America, 2001), 28.
9. See, for example, Peter Childs, *Modernism* (London: Routledge, 2000).
10. For a contemporary example of this phenomenon in a radically different cultural and historical context, see Charles Hirschkind, *The Ethical Soundscape: Cassette Sermons and Islamic Counterpublics* (New York: Columbia University Press, 2006).
11. The ostensible "end" of the Cold War did lead to a negotiated reduction in the U.S. and Russian nuclear arsenals, but not to a truly rational course of universal disarmament. Indeed, nuclear proliferation among smaller nation-states continues to be a problem, and as of this writing in 2018 we seem on the brink of a new arms race between the United States and the Russian Federation.
12. The science of this kind cognitive restructuring is still somewhat speculative, but reflective readers who have lived through epochal shifts in the media ecology may have noticed it already in themselves. For an acute, if polemical, roundup of research for the general reader, see Nicholas Carr, *The Shallows: What the Internet Is Doing to Our Brains* (New York: Norton, 2010).
13. Michel de Certeau, *The Practice of Everyday Life*, trans. Steven Rendall (Berkeley: University of California Press, 1984).
14. Mladen Dolar, *A Voice and Nothing More* (Cambridge, MA: MIT Press, 2006), 39.
15. Andrew Parker argues that for Lacan, "the body as an object in the real world has no place" and that anatomy "only *figures* (it is a sham)" (quoted in Andrew Parker, *The Theorist's Mother* [Durham, NC: Duke University Press, 2012], 37).
16. Yoshimi Shun'ya, *"Koe" no shihon shugi: Denwa rajio chikuonki no shakaishi*, Kōdansha sensho mechie 48 (Tokyo: Kōdansha, 1995).
17. Jonathan Sterne, *The Audible Past: Cultural Origins of Sound Reproduction* (Durham, NC: Duke University Press, 2003).
18. Jacques Attali, *Noise: The Political Economy of Music*, trans. Brian Massumi (Minneapolis: University of Minnesota Press, 1985).
19. Karatani Kōjin, *Origins of Modern Japanese Literature*, ed. Brett de Bary (Durham, NC: Duke University Press, 1993).
20. See Hiromu Nagahara, *Tokyo Boogie-Woogie: Japan's Pop Era and Its Discontents* (Cambridge, MA: Harvard University Press, 2017). For a history of *enka* popular song, see Christine Yano, *Tears of Longing: Nostalgia and the Nation in Japanese Popular Song* (Cambridge, MA: Harvard University East Asia Center, 2003). For postwar

developments in Japanese popular music, see Michael K. Bourdaghs, *Sayonara Amerika, Sayonara Nippon: A Geopolitical Prehistory of J-Pop* (New York: Columbia University Press, 2012).
21. Michel Chion, *The Voice in Cinema*, trans. Claudia Gorbman (New York: Columbia University Press, 1999), 24.
22. Chion, 27 (italics in original).
23. Friedrich Kittler, *Discourse Networks, 1800/1900*, trans. Michael Metteer and Chris Cullens (Stanford, CA: Stanford University Press, 1990), 214.

1. VOCAL CORDS AND TELEPHONE WIRES: ORALITY IN JAPAN, OLD AND NEW

1. Louis Althusser, *Lenin and Philosophy, and Other Essays*, trans. Ben Brewster (New York: Monthly Review Press, 1971).
2. Paradoxically, this entails a translation process (from sound waves to electrical impulses, grooves on wax, or even to digital binary information, and then back again) that is far more complex and involved than the process of writing. This suggests that recording and transmission are themselves forms of writing, forms of translation, and some thinkers have seized on that analogy with great enthusiasm. At the same time, I think it would be an error to embrace this analogy too single-mindedly, to be content with the idea that "it's all writing in the end" and thereby lose sight of the very powerful phenomenological effects of reproduction and simulation.
3. See Guy L. Beck, *Sonic Theology: Hinduism and Sacred Sound* (Columbia: University of South Carolina Press, 1993).
4. Kawamura Minato, *Kotodama to takai* (Tokyo: Kōdansha, 2002), 15–16.
5. For an extensive consideration of these debates, see Susan L. Burns, *Before the Nation: Kokugaku and the Imagining of Community in Early Modern Japan* (Durham, NC: Duke University Press, 2003).
6. Kawamura, *Kotodama*, 14.
7. The founder of the Japanese postal service and early advocate of reforming the Japanese script along phonetic lines, Maejima Hisoka argued in 1866 that Chinese characters should be replaced by kana syllabic script. See Karatani Kōjin, *Origins of Modern Japanese Literature* (Durham, NC: Duke University Press, 1993), 45–48; and Seth Jacobowitz, *Writing Technology in Meiji Japan: A Media History of Modern Japanese Literature and Visual Culture* (Cambridge, MA: Harvard University East Asia Center, 2015), 44–47.
8. Spoken language may also be stolen, memorized, and regurgitated, but to learn how to speak and pronounce a foreign language or a dialect in one's native language so perfectly that one is mistaken to be a member of that community entails such a commitment of time and intellectual energy and resources that one becomes, in effect, an honorary member of that community.

9. Eiko Ikegami, *Bonds of Civility: Aesthetic Networks and the Political Origins of Japanese Culture, Structural Analysis in the Social Sciences* (Cambridge: Cambridge University Press, 2005), 314–15.
10. Maeda Ai, *Text and the City: Essays on Japanese Modernity*, ed. James A. Fujii (Durham, NC: Duke University Press, 2004), 229.
11. Maeda, 231.
12. Heinz Morioka and Miyoko Sasaki, *Rakugo, the Popular Narrative Art of Japan* (Cambridge, MA: Council on East Asian Studies, distributed by Harvard University Press, 1990).
13. Eric Rutledge, "Orality and Textual Variation in the *Heike Monogatari*: Part One, The Phrase and Its Formulaic Nature," in *Heike biwa: Katari to ongaku*, ed. Kamisangō Yūkō (Kasukabe: Hitsuji shobō, 1993).
14. Donald Richie, *A Hundred Years of Japanese Film: A Concise History, with a Selective Guide to Videos and DVDs* (Tokyo: Kodansha International, 2001), 20.
15. For an extended discussion of the growth of oral storytelling in the Meiji period, see John Scott Miller, "Japanese Oral Narrative in a Meiji Literary Context" (Ph.D. diss., Princeton University, 1988), chap. 2.
16. For the fullest discussion of shorthand in Japan, see Jacobowitz, *Writing Technology in Meiji Japan*.
17. See Hyōdō Hiromi, *"Koe" no kokumin kokka Nihon* (Tokyo: Nippon hōsō shuppan kyōkai, 2000).
18. Jeffrey A. Dym, *Benshi, Japanese Silent Film Narrators, and Their Forgotten Narrative Art of Setsumei: A History of Japanese Silent Film Narration* (Lewiston, NY: Edwin Mellen Press, 2003), 3.
19. Soeda Tomomichi, *Enka no Meiji Taishō shi*, Iwanami shinsho 501 (Tokyo: Iwanami shoten, 1963), 1–10.
20. Walter J. Ong, *Orality and Literacy: The Technologizing of the Word* (London: Routledge, 1982), 36–48.
21. Jonathan Sterne, *The Audible Past: Cultural Origins of Sound Reproduction* (Durham, NC: Duke University Press, 2003), 342.
22. Nakano Jun, *Nihonjin no nakigoe: Koe to iu media no kaikan* (Tokyo: NTT shuppan, 1993); Suzuki Matsumi, Suzuki Hajime, and Yoshida Yasushi, *Nihonjin no koe*, Yōsensha shinsho (Tokyo: Yōsensha, 2003).
23. Michel Chion, *The Voice in Cinema*, trans. Claudia Gorbman (New York: Columbia University Press, 1999), 5 (italics in original).
24. Some examples taken at random from the *Kōjien* dictionary: *uragoe* 裏声 (falsetto); *ubugoe* 産声 (first cry of a newborn baby); *urigoe* 売り声 (peddler's cry); *kakegoe* 掛け声 (a shout); *kazagoe* 風邪声 (the voice of somebody with a cold); *kanakirigoe* 金切り声 (shrill, piercing voice, lit. "a voice like cutting through metal"); *kisei* 奇声 (a strange voice); *kyōsei* 嬌声 (the excited or coquettish voices of women); *kowairo* 声色 (vocal mimicry, assumed voices); *shiokaragoe* 塩辛声 (hoarse, lit. "salty," voice); *shissei* 叱声 (rebuking voice); *seishitsu* 声質 (vocal quality, lit. "materiality of the voice"); *seichō* 声調 (tone of voice); *damigoe* (or *dakusei*) 濁声 (thick, gravelly voice); *tsukurigoe* 作り声 (feigned or

affected voice); *togarigoe* 尖り声 (harsh voice); *dosei* 怒声 (angry voice); *nakigoe* 泣き声 (crying voice); *namidagoe* 涙声 (tearful voice); *basei* 罵声 (booing, heckling); *hanagoe* 鼻声 (nasal voice, twang); *bansei* 蛮声 (loud, discordant voice); *bisei* 美声 (beautiful voice); *fukumigoe* 含み声 (muffled voice, lit., "voice held in one's mouth").

25. Diana Deutsch, "The Genesis of Absolute Pitch: Theories and Experimental Findings," *Journal of the Acoustical Society of America* 126, no. 4 (2009): 2278.
26. R. H. Robins, *A Short History of Linguistics*, 3rd ed. (London: Longman, 1990), 205, 222–24.
27. For example, Friedrich A. Kittler, *Gramophone, Film, Typewriter, Writing Science* (Stanford, CA: Stanford University Press, 1999); and Friedrich A. Kittler, *Discourse Networks, 1800/1900* (Stanford, CA.: Stanford University Press, 1990).
28. Ferdinand de Saussure, *Writings in General Linguistics* (Oxford: Oxford University Press, 2006), 104.
29. See Benedict R. Anderson, *Imagined Communities: Reflections on the Origin and Spread of Nationalism*, revised and extended (London: Verso, 1991).
30. Yoshimi Shun'ya, *"Koe" no shihon shugi: Denwa rajio chikuonki no shakaishi*, Kōdansha sensho mechie 48 (Tokyo: Kōdansha, 1995), 277–78.
31. Victor H. Mair, "Sound and Meaning in the History of Characters: Views of China's Earliest Script Reformers," in *Difficult Characters: Interdisciplinary Studies of Chinese and Japanese Writing*, ed. Mary S. Erbaugh (Columbus: National East Asian Languages Resource Center, Ohio State University, 2002).
32. For a fuller history of the development of the telegraphic code used in China, one which could have taken a very different direction, see Thomas S. Mullaney, *The Chinese Typewriter: A Global History of the Information Age* (Cambridge, MA: MIT Press, 2017).
33. Matsuda Hiroyuki, *Meiji terekomu monogatari: Jōhō tsūshin shakai no "genfūkei"* (Tokyo: Nihon keizai hyōronsha, 2001), 17–18.
34. Yoshimi, *"Koe" no shihonshugi*, 140.
35. Ōtsuka Toranosuke and Masuda Tamio, *Gokuhi denpō ni miru sensō to heiwa: Nihon denshin jōhōshi* (Kumamoto: Kumamoto shuppan bunka kaikan, 2002), 11.
36. "The telegraph sends communication over long distances by using electrical power. Since electricity was unknown to the Chinese of former times, it is obviously also something with which Japanese were not familiar. It is extremely difficult to explicate in a simple, concise way. For that reason, I won't go into the properties of electricity itself here but only summarize its actions and effects. If you run electricity through steel, it will create a magnetic pull that draws other iron or steel. If you cut off the electrical current, the magnetic field will be released. The telegraph uses this principle. You put an electrical contraption in one place, set up a steel contraption in another place, and connect them with a copper wire. If you send an electric current across the wire, the steel contraption will immediately sense it and magnetically draw other metal, regardless of the distance. It follows that if the current is cut off, the magnetic field will again be released. By alternating between current and no current in this fashion, you may move the metal component as you wish. Once the motive force of the metal component has been established, a stylus connected to that component can trace symbols on

a piece of paper, thereby transmitting communication. The speed of this is such that even ten million *ri* could be traversed in an instant. In order to spread out the cables for this, you will need to erect telegraph poles approximately 8 *shaku* high along the route of the cable every 30 or 40 *ken*. If you cover the cables with protection, you can also lay them under water. Right now in Western nations, these cables crisscross both land and sea like a spider's web. Important news can be relayed and conversations can be conducted across a thousand *ri*. It goes without saying that this is very useful for both official and private purposes. Westerners like to say that the invention of the telegraph has made the world a smaller place, and surely that is no exaggeration.

In the distant past, Westerners conveyed urgent messages by means of signals. In the 1600s they began to establish a system of signals by setting up stations on hills and using telescopes to read one another's signals. Near the end of the 1700s, this system was made even more elaborate and was in wide use across the West. In 1771 the Frenchman Le Sarge was the first to use electrical power to send messages. He built the first such device, after which the study of electricity progressed further, and the telegraph was improved further, but nobody thought to put it to widespread use. In 1837, the American Morse made a major discovery after five years of experimentation. Although he wanted to put his discovery to practical use, he lacked the funds to do so. After that, however, he applied for and received $30,000 from the United States government, and in 1844 he set up a wire between Washington, D.C. and Baltimore, a distance of 17 or 18 *ri*, so that messages could be sent between those two cities. This was the world's first telegraph line. The first underwater telegraph cable was laid in 1851 between Dover in England and the coast of France. Many underwater cables followed, and in 1858 a cable was laid down spanning the Atlantic Ocean between America and England. In Japanese measurements of distance, that is a distance of almost 1,000 *ri*. Although the laying of the cable was successful, it unfortunately didn't work, and so it is said that another attempt will be made soon." Fukuzawa Yukichi, *Seiyō jijō, shohen* (Tokyo: Shōkodō, 1866), 111–16.

37. Matsuda, *Meiji terekomu monogatari*, 14.
38. Nanette Twine, *Language and the Modern State: The Reform of Written Japanese* (London: Routledge, 1991), 112.
39. Yoshimi, *"Koe" no shihonshugi*, 142–43.
40. Stephen Kern, *The Culture of Time and Space, 1880–1918* (Cambridge, MA: Harvard University Press, 1983).
41. Nishibayashi Tadatoshi and Yūseishō teishin hakubutsukan, *Nihonjin to terefon: Meiji Taishō Shōwa no denwa sesōshi* (Tokyo: Teishin kyōkai, 1990), 11.
42. Matsuda, *Meiji terekomu monogatari*, 76–77. See also Nihon denshin denwa kabushiki kaisha, *Denwa 100-nen shōshi: The Story of Telephone* (Tokyo: Nihon denshin denwa kabushiki kaisha, 1990), 7.
43. Nishibayashi et al., *Nihonjin to terefon*, 11–12.
44. Fujii Nobuyuki, *Terekomu no keizaishi: Kindai Nihon no denshin denwa* (Tokyo: Keisō shobō, 1998), 68.
45. Nishibayashi et al., *Nihonjin to terefon*, 186.

46. Nishibayashi et al., 122.
47. Matsuda, *Meiji terekomu monogatari*, 202.
48. Quoted in Matsuda, 163.
49. Nishibayashi et al., *Nihonjin to terefon*, 25.
50. Quoted in Matsuda, *Meiji terekomu monogatari*, 162.
51. Quoted in Matsuda, 162–63.
52. Matsuda, 193–94.
53. Matsuda, 169.
54. The story of female telephone operators is central to the history of women's labor in modern Japan, but I can only allude to it here. See Yamanaka Ikuko, *Kōkandai ni ikita joseitachi* (Tokyo: Shin Nihon shuppansha, 1997).
55. *Tokyo Mainichi Shinbun*, May 23, 1918, quoted in Nihon denshin denwa kōsha, *Tōkyō no denwa: Sono gojūman kanyū made* (Tokyo: Denki tsūshin kyōkai, 1958), 429.
56. Nishimoto Ikuko, *Jikan ishiki no kindai: "Toki wa kane nari" no shakaishi*, shohan (Tokyo: Hōsei daigaku shuppankyoku, 2006), 237–38.
57. Nihon denshin denwa kabushiki kaisha, *Denwa 100-nen shōshi*, 68.

2. SOUND AND SENTIMENT

1. Akira Kurosawa, *Something Like an Autobiography* (New York: Vintage Books, 1983), 32–33. The title in Japanese can be translated as "toad oil," which carries some of the same connotations in Japanese as the English "snake oil."
2. For a thorough discussion of Schafer's ideas on soundscapes, see R. Murray Schafer, *The Soundscape: Our Sonic Environment and the Tuning of the World* (Rochester, VT: Destiny Books, 1993).
3. Walter J. Ong, *Orality and Literacy: The Technologizing of the Word* (London: Routledge, 1988), 31–32.
4. John Cage and Daniel Charles, *For the Birds* (Boston: M. Boyars, 1981), 94. See also John Cage, *Silence: Lectures and Writings* (Middletown, CT: Wesleyan University Press, 1961). Suzuki's presentation of Zen Buddhism has been subjected to considerable criticism by later scholars (see, for example, Dharmachāri Nāgapriya, "Poisoned Pen Letters? D.T. Suzuki's Communication of Zen to the West," *Western Buddhist Review* 5 [October 2010], http://www.westernbuddhistreview.com/vol5/suzuki-gentium.html [accessed May 1, 2018]), but what is important here is not its reliability so much as its reception in a particular historical moment.
5. Schafer, *The Soundscape*, 71–87. In acoustics, the technical definition of "noise" is sound composed of clashing frequencies that result in random, chaotic changes in frequency and/or amplitude.
6. For extensive discussion of the sound world of the *Man'yōshū*, see Takaoka-shi Man'yō rekishikan, *Oto no Man'yōshū* (Tokyo: Kasama shoin, 2002).

   It is also worth noting that attentiveness to sound is finely woven into the Japanese language itself. Japanese sound symbolism is unparalleled in its diversity and frequency of use. It can be divided into three categories: (1) phonomime or onomatopoeia (擬声語 *giseigo* or 擬音語 *giongo*); (2) phenomime (擬態語 *gitaigo*), or mimetic words to represent nonauditory phenomena; (3) Psychomime (also 擬態語 *gitaigo* or sometimes 擬情語 *gijōgo*), mimetic words to represent psychological states and bodily sensations.

Onomatopoeia is common in all languages, but phenomimes are far less common and psychomimes are so rare that they can safely be assumed to be unique to Japanese. This propensity to represent nonauditory phenomena, psychological states, and even abstractions through sonic mimesis suggests that the Japanese language has developed in ways that sonic mimesis has been considered just as legitimate a form of communication as semantic articulation. The value of sound as sound is affirmed within the language itself, the very place where we might expect primacy of the semantic to be relatively unquestioned. The cultural implications of this, I believe, are considerable.

7. Any discussion of premodern soundscapes in Japan must begin with Nakagawa Shin's landmark study, a marvelous and wide-ranging work that also addresses issues of the contemporary soundscape. See Nakagawa Shin, *Heiankyō oto no uchū: Saundosukēpu e no tabi* (Tokyo: Heibonsha, 1992).
8. According to Nakagawa, what was known as the *suzumushi* 鈴虫 (*Homoeogryllus japonicus*) in the Heian period is actually known today as the *matsumushi* 松虫, (*Xenogryllus marmorata*) (Nakagawa, *Heiankyō*, 67–68).
9. Murasaki Shikibu, *The Tale of Genji*, trans. Royall Tyler (New York: Viking, 2001), 712.
10. For a discussion of the musical culture of the pleasure quarters, see Tanaka Yūko, *Edo no oto* (Tokyo: Kawade shobō shinsha, 1988).
11. John Lawson Stoddard, *Japan* (Chicago: Belford, Middlebrook and Co., 1897), 101.
12. Henry Knollys, *Sketches of Life in Japan* (London: Chapman and Hall, 1887), 185–86.
13. Basil Hall Chamberlain, *Things Japanese: Being Notes on Various Subjects Connected with Japan for the Use of Travellers and Others* (London: J. Murray, 1905), 466.
14. Naitō Takashi, *Meiji no oto: Seiyōjin ga kiita kindai Nihon* (1791; Tokyo: Chūō kōron shinsha, 2005).
15. Edward Sylvester Morse, *Japan Day by Day: 1877, 1878–79, 1882–83* (Atlanta: Cherokee, 1990), 1.
16. Morse, 4.
17. Morse, 20.
18. Morse, 184.
19. Isabella Lucy Bird, *Unbeaten Tracks in Japan: An Account of Travels in the Interior Including Visits to the Aborigines of Yezo and the Shrines of Nikkō and Isé* (London: J. Murray, 1880), 90–91.
20. Bird, 97.
21. Jacques Attali, *Noise: The Political Economy of Music*, trans. Brian Massumi (Minneapolis: University of Minnesota Press, 1985), 26.
22. In a letter to Masaoka Shiki dated December 18, 1901, Sōseki writes: "Just think, I have moved again! Seven times in thirty-five years, in a search for quietness, I have changed my address, but it has always been in vain. This is certainly nothing to boast about! For my part, I have already moved from one boarding house to another five times since

I came to England!" Natsume Sōseki and Tsunematsu Ikuo, *Spring Miscellany and London Essays*. (Boston: Tuttle, 2002), 160.
23. Natsume and Tsunematsu, 130. Schopenhauer's essay "On Din and Noise" is available in many collections of his essays, including Arthur Schopenhauer, *Parerga and Paralipomena, Volume 2: Short Philosophical Essays*, trans. E. F. J. Payne (Oxford: Clarendon Press, 2000), 642–45.
24. Emily Ann Thompson, *The Soundscape of Modernity: Architectural Acoustics and the Culture of Listening in America, 1900–1933* (Cambridge, MA.: MIT Press, 2002), 116–17.
25. Paul A. Bell, *Environmental Psychology*, 5th ed. (Fort Worth, TX: Harcourt College Publishers, 2001), 147–56.
26. See, for example, Nakamura Kōsuke, *Kindai Nihon yōgakushi josetsu* (Tokyo: Tokyo shoseki, 2003).
27. Attali, *Noise*, 9–10 (italics in original).
28. Attali, 11. A recent example of music's prophecy in the realm of "economic organization" can be seen in the phenomenon of peer-to-peer file sharing and other forms of illegal downloading. Just as music was the herald of copyright and other forms of intellectual "property" laws in the eighteenth century, it is now intimating a new form of economic organization in which intellectual and creative work is decommodified.
29. Naitō, *Meiji no oto*, iii–iv.
30. See Nakamura, *Kindai Nihon yōgakushi*, 9–74.
31. Ury Eppstein, *The Beginnings of Western Music in Meiji Era Japan* (Lewiston, NY: Edwin Mellen Press, 1994).
32. Six months after the school opened and after Isawa had already returned to Japan, a group of local rebels killed all six of the Japanese teachers in the school in the Zhishanyan Incident. Isawa and the colonial government were not deterred, turning the six slain teachers into martyrs for the cause of Japanese-language education in the colonies. The first Shinto shrine in Taiwan was built on the site, and the slain teachers were still being commemorated forty-five years later. For example, in 1940, eight of the twelve issues of *Taiwan kyoiku* magazine had drawings of the Zhishanyan Shrine or photos of the slain teachers somewhere at the front of the magazine, if not on the cover. Through much of the Pacific War, the teachers were used as potent symbols of sacrifice for the empire.
33. Eppstein, *The Beginnings of Western Music*, 65.
34. Quoted in Nakamura Kōsuke, *Seiyō no oto, Nihon no mimi: Kindai Nihon ongaku to seiyō ongaku* (Tokyo: Shunjūsha, 2002), 301–2.
35. Nagai Kafū, *Kafū zenshū*, vol. 5 (Tokyo: Iwanami shoten, 1992–1995), 284.
36. Nagai Kafū, *Kafū zenshū*, vol. 7 (Tokyo: Iwanami shoten, 1992–1995), 133. In this passage Kafū refers repeatedly to the thoroughfares and music of *tōyō* ("the East," or "Asia") when, in the case of the music at least, he seems to be referring specifically to Japanese (and not Korean or Chinese, much less Indonesian) music. I have thus rendered the first instance as "Asia" and the second as "Japan."
37. Laird Addis, *Of Mind and Music* (Ithaca, NY: Cornell University Press, 1999), 72 (italics in original).

38. Note that the "spatial" aspect of this spatiotemporal essence refers to mental space, not actual physical space.
39. There is also something else at work in the human understanding of music as such. Our uniquely human understanding and appreciation of music, I believe, is rooted in the capacity to identify mentally with conspecifics, a capacity most thoroughly studied by the developmental psychologist Michael Tomasello in such works as *The Cultural Origins of Human Cognition* (Cambridge, MA: Harvard University Press, 1999). We do not hear music only as sound, we hear it as *humanly produced and ordered* sound and find ourselves identifying with the putative consciousness that produced it. This may be the reason why animals, even advanced primates, do not appear to be affectively moved by human music (although they can certainly be startled or calmed by it), or to dance to it.
40. It is interesting that the person credited with first successfully determining the exact ratios of twelve-tone equal temperament tuning was a prince of the Ming court named Zhu Zaiyu (朱載堉, 1536–1610), who published his findings in 1584. See Kenneth Girdwood Robinson and Erich F. W. Altwein, *A Critical Study of Chu Tsai-yü's Contribution to the Theory of Equal Temperament in Chinese Music* (Wiesbaden: Franz Steiner, 1980).
41. Although harmonic relationships are based in the acoustical properties of sound, they are by no means self-evident to listeners who have not internalized the idiom to some degree.
42. Gérard Genette. *Narrative Discourse: An Essay in Method* (Ithaca, NY: Cornell University Press, 1980).
43. Stephen Snyder, *Fictions of Desire: Narrative Form in the Novels of Nagai Kafū* (Honolulu: University of Hawai'i Press, 2000), 32.
44. Attali, *Noise*, 60.
45. Attali, 61.
46. Attali, 57.
47. For a discussion of musical life and compositional practice in wartime Japan, see Akiyama Kuniharu, *Shōwa no sakkyokukatachi: Taiheiyō sensō to ongaku* (Tokyo: Misuzu shobō, 2003).

3. THE GRAIN IN THE GROOVE: INSCRIBED VOICES, ECHOED TEMPORALITIES

1. The following list of Edison's imagined uses for the machine is taken from the standard history of the phonograph, Roland Gelatt, *The Fabulous Phonograph, 1877–1977*, 2nd rev. ed. (New York: Macmillan, 1977), 29.

    1. Letter writing and all kinds of dictation without the aid of a stenographer.
    2. Phonographic books, which will speak to blind people without effort on their part.

3. The teaching of elocution.
4. Reproduction of music.
5. The "Family Record"—a registry of sayings, reminiscences, etc., by members of a family in their own voices, and of the last words of dying persons.
6. Music boxes and toys.
7. Clocks that should announce in articulate speech the time for going home, going to meals, etc.
8. The preservation of languages by exact reproduction of the manner of pronouncing.
9. Education purposes; such as preserving the explanations made by a teacher, so that the pupil can refer to them at any moment, and spelling or other lessons placed upon the phonograph for convenience in committing to memory.
10. Connection with the telephone, so as to make that instrument an auxiliary in the transmission of permanent and invaluable records, instead of being the recipient of momentary and fleeting communication.

2. Kurata Yoshihiro, *Nihon rekōdo bunkashi* (Tokyo: Tōkyō shoseki, 1992), 17–18.
3. Komiyama Hiromichi, trans., *Kinsei ni daihatsumei: Denwaki-sogenki* (Tokyo: Kobunsha, 1880), info:ndljp/pid/846698.
4. Katō Michio, *Chikuonki no jidai* (Tokyo: Shopan, 2006), 106.
5. Kurata, *Nihon rekōdo bunkashi*, 13.
6. Edison's original vision was eventually vindicated not by the phonograph itself but by the later development of magnetic audio tape, which was quickly employed for all the practical uses that he had earlier enumerated.
7. As Jonathan Sterne points out, early phonograph cylinders were actually very fragile and the ones that still exist produce sounds that are often unintelligible. Once phonograph recordings became widespread commodities, they often proved to be only slightly less ephemeral than the fugitive sounds they were supposed to capture. Clearly, the rhetoric of permanence, of indestructibility, was premature with regard to the capacities of the technology at the time, but in any event, the technology did eventually catch up with the rhetoric. See Sterne, *The Audible Past: Cultural Origins of Sound Reproduction* (Durham, NC: Duke University Press, 2003), 287–333.
8. Lewis Mumford, *Technics and Civilization* (New York: Harcourt, 1963), 244.
9. Richard Osborne, *Vinyl: A History of the Analogue Record* (Burlington, VT: Ashgate, 2012), 90–91.
10. Kurata, *Nihon rekōdo bunkashi*, 34.
11. Katō, *Chikuonki no jidai*, 117–18.
12. Kurata, *Nihon rekōdo bunkashi*, 36.
13. See James Lastra, *Sound Technology and the American Cinema: Perception, Representation, Modernity, Film, and Culture* (New York: Columbia University Press, 2000).
14. Quoted in Kurata, *Nihon rekōdo bunkashi*, 47.

15. Quoted in Ozawa Emiko, *Edokko to Asakusa hanayashiki* (Tokyo: Shōgakkan, 2006), 187–88.
16. It is likely that the cylinders sounded much better when they were brand-new and not degraded by time, but even well-preserved cylinders do not approach anything like "high-fidelity."
17. Nishibayashi Tadatoshi and Yūseishō Teishin Hakubutsukan, *Nihonjin to terefon: Meiji Taishō Shōwa no denwa sesōshi* (Tokyo: Teishin kyōkai, 1990), 11–12.
18. Kurata, *Nihon rekōdo bunkashi*, 41–42.
19. The F. W. Horn Trading Company was named after its founder, Frederick Whitney Horn (dates unknown).
20. Nihon Koromubia kabushiki kaisha, "Our History," in *Koromubia gojūnenshi* (Tokyo: Nihon Koromubia, 1961).
21. "Nicchiku" was the common romanization at the time.
22. This ambiguity was also present in the original Berne Convention. The 1908 Berlin Revision to the convention extended rights to composers regarding the sound recording of their compositions, but it did not protect record companies' economic interests by prohibiting unlicensed reproductions of sound recordings. Such rights were not recognized internationally until the 1961 Rome Convention for the Protection of Performers, Producers of Phonograms, and Broadcasting Organizations.
23. Iizuka Tsuneo, *Rekōdo man no seiki: Kurofune raikō kara hibari zesshō made* (Tokyo: Aikusha, 2012), 176–77.
24. For an introduction to *naniwabushi* in English, see Hyōdō Hiromi and Henry D. Smith II, "Singing Tales of the Gishi: 'Naniwabushi' and the Forty-Seven Rōnin in Late Meiji Japan," *Monumenta Nipponica* 61, no. 4 (2006): 459–508, www.jstor.org/stable/25066463. An even more thorough history and critical analysis of the form, especially with regard to its connection to Gen'yōsha ultranationalism and pan-Asianism, can be found in Hyōdō Hiromi, *"Koe" no kokumin kokka Nihon* (Tokyo: Nippon hōsō shuppan kyōkai, 2000). For a discussion of Miyazaki Tōten's transformation from political activist to *naniwabushi* chanter, see Faye Yuan Kleeman, "Pan-Asian Romantic Nationalism: Revolutionary, Literati, and Popular Oral Tradition and the Case of Miyazaki Tōten," in *Sino-Japanese Transculturation: From the Late Nineteenth Century to the End of the Pacific War*, ed. Richard King, Cody Poulton, and Katsuhiko Endo (Lanham, MD: Lexington Books, 2012), 45–67.
25. Other *yose* entertainments included *rakugo* 落語 and *kōdan* 講談 narrative performance art, *manzai* 漫才 comedy duos, and *tejina* 手品 illusionists, among many others.
26. The *kōdan* narrator and *shinpa* acting pioneer Kawakami Otojirō, 1864–1911.
27. Peter Ganea, "Copyright History," in *Japanese Copyright Law: Writings in Honour of Gerhard Schricker*, ed. Peter Ganea et al. (The Hague: Kluwer Law International, 2005), 1–10.
28. Mitsui Tōru, "Copyright and Music in Japan: A Forced Grafting and Its Consequences," in *Music and Copyright*, ed. Simon Frith (Edinburgh: Edinburgh University Press, 1993), 127–28.

29. Fukuzawa Yukichi, *Seiyō jijō gaihen san-kan Fukuzawa Yukichi sanshū* (Tokyo: Shōkodō, 1872), http://hdl.handle.net/2027/keio.10811640418, 42.
30. Ganea, "Copyright History," 4.
31. Masuda Satoshi, *Sono ongaku no sakusha towa dare ka: Rimikkusu sangyō chosakuken* (Tokyo: Misuzushobō, 2005), 107.
32. Treaty of Commerce and Navigation Between Great Britain and Japan, 11. Accessed on May 1, 2018 at http://treaties.fco.gov.uk/docs/pdf/1894/TS0023.pdf.
33. Quoted in Tōru, "Copyright and Music in Japan," 130.
34. Tōru, 131–32.
35. Ganea, "Copyright History," 6.
36. Jacques Attali, *Noise: The Political Economy of Music*, trans. Brian Massumi (Minneapolis: University of Minnesota Press, 1985), 72.
37. Although *onpu* 音譜 today means "score" or "sheet music," at the time it meant "recording."
38. These were *Akagaki Genzo (tokkuri no wakare)*, 赤垣源蔵 (徳利の別れ); *Nanbuzaka koshitsu yuki no wakare*, 南部阪霽の別れ; *Oishi Oitachi (okusuri kenjō)*, 大石 生立 (御薬献上); *Murakami Kiken*, 村上喜劍; and *Masamune Takako den*, 正宗孝子伏.
39. This practice was called *shutchō rokuon* (出張録音, dispatch recording) and was largely the norm at this time, when Japan still lacked the know-how and equipment necessary to record high-quality masters.
40. Kurata, *Nihon rekōdo bunkashi*, 144–45. I was unable to find any record of the terms of the settlement. Nomi Yoshihisa says that although Sankōdō and Nicchiku were rivals, they both were heavily invested in producing content and had a common enemy in the pirates, making a settlement possible. See Nomi Yoshihisa, "Tōchūken Kumoemon jiken to Meiji-Taishō no fuhōkōi riron," *Gakushūin daigaku hōgakukai zasshi / Gakushūin daigaku hōgakukai hen* 44, no. 2 (2009): 192, n. 13.
41. Quoted in Nomi, "Tōchūken Kumoemon jiken," 199.
42. Nihon ongaku chosakuken kyōkai, *Nihon ongaku chosakukenshi*, vol. 1 (Tokyo: Nihon ongaku chosakuken kyōkai, 1990), 127–28.
43. Masuda, *Sono ongaku no sakusha towa dare ka*, 119.
44. Quoted in Nomi, "Tōchūken Kumoemon jiken," 204.
45. "When the piece is merely improvised and momentary, even if there happen to be new melodies contained therein, they cannot be the objects of copyright" (Sokkyōteki katsu shunkanteki sōsaku ni sugizaru toki wa sono onkyoku wa tamatama shinsenritu o hōgan suru mo chosakuken no mokuteki taru o ezu 即興的且瞬間的創作ニ過キサルトキハ其音曲ハ偶々新旋律ヲ包含スルモ著作権ノ目的タルヲ得ス) (Quoted in Nomi, "Tōchūken Kumoemon jiken," 206).
46. That is, *wagakuni koyū no ongaku* 我国固有ノ音楽 (our country's native music), *wagakuni tokuyū no ongaku* 我国特有ノ音楽 (our country's characteristic music), *wagakuni ni oite jūrai okonwaretaru teikyū ongaku no isshu taru naniwabushi* 我国ニ於テ従来行ハレタル低級音楽ノ一種タル浪花節 (one of the low-grade forms of music that has traditionally been performed in our country, *naniwabushi*).
47. Iizuka, *Rekōdo man no seiki*, 177.

48. Copyright protections of recordings were further strengthened by amendments in 1934 and 1939.
49. Nihon ongaku chosakuken kyōkai, *Nihon ongaku chosakukenshi*, 1:170.
50. Nihon ongaku chosakuken kyōkai, 1:169.
51. Hosokawa Shūichi, "Chosakuken seido to medeia no hensei: Nihon no shoki ongaku sangyō o jirei to shite," *Soshiorogos* 27 (2003): 249–68.
52. For a brief discussion of the *Purāge senpū* (プラーゲ旋風), see Ganea, "Copyright History," 7–9.
53. Masuda, *Sono ongaku no sakusha towa dare ka*, 124.
54. Richard Rogers Bowker, *Copyright: Its History and Its Law* (Boston: Houghton Mifflin, 1912), 212–13.
55. Attali, *Noise*, 98.
56. The 1909 Copyright Act was itself triggered by a number of factors, but one of the most important was the 1908 U.S. Supreme Court decision in *White-Smith Music Publishing Company v. Apollo Company*. In this decision, the Court ruled that makers of piano rolls for player pianos did not have to pay royalties to composers because the piano rolls were not directly perceptible as copies of the music. The 1909 act introduced a "compulsory license for the manufacture and distribution of such 'mechanical' embodiments of musical works." This decision was significant because it did not recognize the processes of translation by which a mechanical or other encoding (and this included phonograms proper) could recreate the work under copyright. The decision was later used as a precedent for the argument that computer software could not be copyrighted because software was not explicitly covered (for obvious reasons) in the 1909 act, which did introduce protections for piano rolls.
57. Masuda, *Sono ongaku no sakusha towa dare ka*, 117.
58. Quoted in Masuda, 117.
59. Hyōdō and Smith, "Singing Tales of Gishi," 479.
60. *Yomiuri shinbun*, December 16, 1912, 3.
61. He was not averse to commodifying his voice as long as he was the one doing it, as the title of his great-grandson's book attests: *Ore no nodo wa hitokoe senryō* 俺の喉は一声千両 (The voice in my throat is worth a thousand ryō). See Okamoto Kazuaki, *Ore no nodo ha hitokoe senryō: Tensai rōkyokushi Tōchūken Kumoemon* (Tokyo: Shinchōsha, 2014).
62. Nicchiku is said to have sold 500,000 of these records (Nomi, "Tōchūken Kumoemon jiken," 191), a truly astonishing number for the time and impressive even by today's standards.
63. Okamoto, *Ore no nodo wa hitokoe senryō*, 356. I quote Okamoto on this matter with caution, since he makes a number of factual errors in his account of the Kumoemon trial, including the amount that Kumoemon was paid (he writes that it was 1,000 yen instead of 15,000) and the nature of the case (he thinks it was about Kumoemon's breach of contract instead of about the pirated records).
64. *Yomiuri shinbun*, November 15, 1921, 4.

65. William Howland Kenney, *Recorded Music in American Life: The Phonograph and Popular Memory, 1890–1945* (New York: Oxford University Press, 1999), xix.
66. See Koizumi Kyōko, *Memorīsukēpu: Ano koro o yobiokosu ongaku* (Tokyo: Misuzushobō, 2013).

4. IMAGINING THE WIRELESS COMMUNITY

1. Yoshimi Shun'ya, *"Koe" no shihon shugi: Denwa rajio chikuonki no shakaishi*, Kōdansha sensho mechie 48 (Tokyo: Kōdansha, 1995), 198.
2. For the best single-volume history of early radio in Japan, see Takeyama Akiko, *Rajio no jidai: Rajio wa chanoma no shuyaku data* (Kyoto: Sekai shisōsha, 2002).
3. Japan Broadcasting Corporation, *Broadcasting in Japan: The Twentieth Century Journey from Radio to Multimedia* (Tokyo: NHK, 2002), 36.
4. Kuroda Isamu, *Rajio taisō no tanjō* (Tokyo: Seikyūsha, 1999), 11–16.
5. For an extensive discussion, see William McNeill, *Keeping Together in Time: Dance and Drill in Human History* (Cambridge, MA: Harvard University Press, 1995).
6. See, for example, Thomas Riedelsheimer's documentary film *Touch the Sound* (2004) about the percussionist Evelyn Gennie, who is nearly deaf.
7. Mary Ann Doane, "The Voice in the Cinema: The Articulation of Body and Space," in *Film Sound: Theory and Practice*, ed. Elisabeth Weis and John Belton (New York: Columbia University Press, 1985), 169. See also Guy Rosolato, "La voix: entre corps et langage," *Revue française de psychanalyse* 38 (1974): 75–94.
8. Tanizaki Jun'ichirō, *Childhood Years: A Memoir*, trans. Paul McCarthy (Ann Arbor: University of Michigan Press, 2017), 25.
9. Scientists call this the "functional hyper-connectivity of the senses." See Daphine Maurer, Laura C. Gibson, and Ferrinne Spector, "Synesthesia in Infants and Very Young Children," in *Oxford Handbook of Synesthesia*, ed. Julia Simner and Edward M. Hubbard (Oxford: Oxford University Press, 2013), 46–63.
10. Michel Chion, *The Voice in Cinema*, trans. Claudia Gorbman (New York: Columbia University Press, 1999), 24.
11. Mladen Dolar, *A Voice and Nothing More* (Cambridge, MA: MIT Press, 2006), 63.
12. Slavoj Žižek, *On Belief* (London: Routledge, 2001), 58.
13. I'm indebted to the second anonymous reviewer of the manuscript for pushing me to rethink my use of Lacanian discourses of vocality in ways that I think make the larger arguments in the book stronger and more unified.
14. Neil Verma, *Theater of the Mind: Imagination, Aesthetics, and American Radio Drama* (Chicago: University of Chicago Press, 2012).
15. Yamaguchi Makoto, "Supōtsu jikkyō no orariteii—shoki hōsō ni okeru yakyū hōsō no wahō ni tsuite," *Kansai daigaku shakaigakubu kiyō* 34, no. 3 (2003): 181–204. Also see Nihon hōsō kyōkai, *20 seiki hōsōshi* (Tokyo: NHK shuppan, 2001).
16. Takeyama, *Rajio no jidai*, 167.

17. Hashimoto Kazuo, *Nihon supōtsu hōsōshi* (Tokyo: Taishūkan shoten, 1992), 19.
18. Quoted in Yamaguchi, "Supōtsu jikkyō," 188.
19. Quoted in Yamaguchi, 189.
20. Quoted in Yamaguchi, 192.
21. Quoted in Yamaguchi, 192.
22. Quoted in Yamaguchi, 202.
23. Hibi Yoshitaka, "Koe no fukusei gijutsu jidai: 'supōtsu kūkan' to fukugō medeia jōkyō," in *Supōtsu suru bungaku: 1920–30 nendai no bunka shigaku*, ed. Hikita Masaaki, Hidaka Yoshiki, and Hibi Yoshitaka (Tokyo: Seikyūsha, 2009), 109–31.
24. Takeyama, *Rajio no jidai*, 186–87.
25. She died of pneumonia on August 2, 1931, three years to the day after winning the silver medal.
26. Quoted in Kuroda, *Rajio taisō*, 194–95.
27. For a fuller discussion of this recording, and the best discussion of the Maehata victory recordings in general, see Shiho Tetsuo, *SP rekōdo: Sono kagirinai miwaku no sekai* (Tokyo: Shopan, 2008),
28. *Yomiuri shinbun*, August 12, 1936, 7.
29. Hashimoto, *Nihon supōtsu hōsōshi*, 80.
30. Hashimoto, 79.
31. Quoted in Takeyama, *Rajio no jidai*, 211
32. Christian Leitz, *Nazi Foreign Policy, 1933–1941: The Road to Global War* (London: Routledge, 2004), 132–33.
33. Although the big Other, as I understand the concept, largely overlaps with the symbolic order in Lacan's thought, it has valences and dimensions that go beyond that order. Specifically, the big Other is also conditioned by the Real in the form of a traumatic alterity that makes true relationship impossible. This is what Lacan means when he says, "there is no big Other." When I suggest that Kasai Sansei at the 1936 Berlin Olympics is addressing the big Other, I mean not only the Symbolic Order but also that aspect of the Real that Žižek calls the "'traumatic bone in the throat' that contaminates every ideality of the symbolic, rendering it contingent and inconsistent" See Slavoj Žižek, "Holding the Place," in *Contingency, Hegemony, Universality: Contemporary Dialogues on the Left*, ed. Judith Butler, Ernesto Laclau, and Slavoj Žižek (London: Verso, 2000), 310.
34. John Durham Peters, *Speaking Into the Air: A History of the Idea of Communication* (Chicago: University of Chicago Press, 1999), 207.
35. Peters, 218–19.
36. Quoted in Takeyama, *Rajio no jidai*, 217.
37. Quoted in Hyōdō Hiromi, *"Koe" no kokumin kokka Nihon* (Tokyo: Nippon hōsō shuppan kyōkai, 2000), 229.
38. Hyōdō, 235.
39. Hyōdō Hiromi and Henry D. Smith II, "Singing Tales of the Gishi: 'Naniwabushi' and the Forty-Seven Rōnin in Late Meiji Japan," *Monumenta Nipponica* 61, no. 4 (2006): 460, www.jstor.org/stable/25066463.

40. Edward Seidensticker, *Kafū the Scribbler: The Life and Writings of Nagai Kafū* (Stanford, CA: Stanford University Press, 1965), 297.
41. Quoted in Yoshimi, *"Koe" no shihonshugi*, 7.
42. Max Picard, *The World of Silence*, The Humanist Library (Chicago: Regnery, 1952), 203–4.
43. Max Picard and Heinrich Hauser, *Hitler in Our Selves* (Hinsdale, IL: Regnery, 1947), 30.
44. Takeyama, *Rajio no jidai*, 116–38.
45. Yoshimi, *"Koe" no shihonshugi*, 264–66.
46. Dolar, *A Voice and Nothing More*, 118.
47. Quoted in Takeyama, *Rajio no jidai*, 157–58.

5. GHOSTLIER DEMARCATIONS, KEENER SOUNDS: EARLY JAPANESE RADIO DRAMA

1. The earliest radio plays of all were broadcast in the United States but, as Tim Crook writes, "American radio history is complex and chaotically documented. It would be a brave scholar who confidently asserted that the first U.S. radio drama had been identified with a particular date and on a certain radio station." Crook himself unearthed evidence that the very earliest experiments in radio drama took place in 1914 at KQW, the radio station run by Charles "Doc" Herrold. The transmission was of a stage play being performed in the auditorium of the Normal College (now San Jose State University), so doesn't qualify as a radio drama in the strictest sense, but it does have some claim to being the earliest documented transmission of a narrative drama over the radio. See Tim Crook, *Radio Drama: Theory and Practice* (London: Routledge, 1999), 5.
2. Quoted in Nishizawa Minoru, *Sōshiki rajio dorama to rajio dorama no "kotoba" kenkyū* (Tokyo: Fuji gurūpu, 2000), 35.
3. Nishizawa, 35.
4. Nishizawa, 23–25.
5. Nishizawa, 27.
6. Quoted in Nishizawa, 19.
7. Yuasa Atsushi, *Yumemiru shumi no Taishō jidai: Sakkatachi no sanbun fūkei*, Shohan (Tokyo: Ronsōsha, 2010), 145.
8. Takeyama Akiko, *Rajio no jidai: Rajio wa chanoma no shuyaku datta* (Kyoto: Sekai shisōsha, 2002), 232–233.
9. Quoted in Nishizawa, *Sōshiki rajio dorama*, 18.
10. Quoted in Nishizawa Minoru, *Rajio dorama no ōgon jidai* (Tokyo: Kawade shobō shinsha, 2002), 50.
11. Four of the five volumes can be found in the National Diet Library's Digital Collection: Vol. 1: info:ndljp/pid/1019083, vol. 2: info:ndljp/pid/1019084, vol. 3: info:ndljp/pid/1019086, and vol. 5: info:ndljp/pid/1019088.

Each volume of the series begins with the following statement of principles:

Resolved: In all matters relating to the broadcast of radio drama, for the time being the Playwrights' Union awaits the completion of a contract between each author and the Tokyo Broadcasting Station. However, before any broadcast is made the consent of the original author must be obtained.

Resolved: Said agreement between dramatist and broadcast station will include the matter of royalty fee for the broadcast scenario. The fee paid shall be the same regardless of whether the entire scenario is broadcast or only part.

Resolved: In the case of a radio adaptation, the rights of the original author take priority over those of the scenario author.

Resolved: In general, the Playwrights' Union will rely on the good faith of the Tokyo Broadcasting Station (in particular, broadcasting section head Hattori).

Resolved: The above encompasses the hope that all matters of broadcast direction, and any related matters that may arise in the future, can be settled through mutually favorable agreements between the appropriate authors, directors, and broadcasting stations.

Resolved: For the time being, the royalty fee for the broadcasting of one radio drama shall be 50 yen. Although radio drama broadcasting is in an early, trial phase, we have made it our policy to exchange clear memoranda of understanding from the start of this publication series so that the proper protocols may be widely known to others besides the principals involved.

12. Alan Beck, *The Invisible Play—BBC Radio Drama, 1922–1928* (A Sound Journal CD ROM Publication, 2000).
13. Quoted in Nishizawa, *Sōshiki rajio dorama*, 41.
14. Quoted in Yuasa, *Yumemiru shumi no Taishō jidai*, 189.
15. Nihon hōsō kyōkai, *Enueichikei hōsōgeki senshū* (Tokyo: Rajiosābisusentā, 1957), 311.
16. See Anke Birkenmaier, "'Proposition for a Radiophonic Art': Introduction," *Modernism/Modernity* 16, no. 2 (2009): 403–5.
17. Quoted in Nihon hōsō kyōkai, *Enueichikei hōsōgeki senshū*, 17.
18. Satomi Ton's *Aru fūfu* is interesting because in the preface to the piece, he instructs that all voices and sound effects must sound equally near the microphone, that no sounds should be heard approaching or moving away from it. Satomi describes this as sonic description from "multiple perspectives," a kind of acoustic Cubism, although logically it should sound more like a flattened acoustical perspective—that is, no perspective at all. No recording of the play survives, so it is impossible to judge how this worked in practice. Beyond this vague experiment in auditory perspective, however, nothing about the play itself goes beyond the conventions of chamber drama.
19. See Tsvetan Todorov, *The Fantastic: A Structural Approach to a Literary Genre*, trans. Richard Howard (Ithaca, NY: Cornell University Press, 1975).
20. Peter Lewis, "Radio Drama," in *The Cambridge Guide to Theatre*, ed. Martin Banham, new ed. (Cambridge: Cambridge University Press, 1995), 897.

5. GHOSTLIER DEMARCATIONS, KEENER SOUNDS   247

21. As Orson Welles's 1938 production of *The War of the Worlds* made clear, the power of radio to suggest unseen realities was so great as to fool at least some in the audience into believing that the events depicted (in the form of "news bulletins" for the first two-thirds of the hour-long, commercial-free broadcast) were actually taking place. Incidentally, the *War of the Worlds* panic had an interesting consequence three years later: When the Imperial Japanese Navy attacked Pearl Harbor on the morning of December 7, 1941, some of the Americans who heard the earliest radio bulletins of the attack assumed that it, too, was a hoax. See Gerald Nachman, *Raised on Radio: In Quest of the Lone Ranger, Jack Benny* . . . (New York: Pantheon Books, 1998), 445.
22. *Yomiuri shinbun*, September 5, 1925, 3.
23. *Asahi shinbun*, September 27, 1925, 11.
24. *Asahi shinbun*, November 29, 1925, 11.
25. *Asahi shinbun*, October 29, 1931, 7.
26. *Yomiuri shinbun*, April 11, 1941, 3.
27. Kobayashi Nobuhiko, *Nihon no kigekijin* (Tokyo: Shōbunsha shuppan, 1972), 13.
28. *Yomiuri shinbun*, November 29, 1931, 3. Markus Nornes also writes about this episode, in *Cinema Babel: Translating Global Cinema* (Minneapolis: University of Minnesota Press, 2007), 148.
29. Brian Niiya and the Japanese American National Museum, *Japanese American History: An A-Z Reference from 1868 to the Present* (New York: Facts on File, 1993), 247.
30. *Asahi shinbun*, December 3, 1931, 10; December 4, 1931, 7.
31. *Yomiuri shinbun*, August 31, 1935, 10.
32. *Yomiuri shinbun*, October 13, 1935, 3.
33. *Yomiuri shinbun*, September 8, 1892, 2.
34. Yamato Sadaji, *Otozukuri hanseiki: Rajio terebi no onkyō kōka* (Tokyo: Shunjūsha, 2005), 268–69.
35. For a fuller discussion of kabuki sound effects, see Fukuda Michiko, "A Study of Sound Effects in Kabuki (I)," *Ochanomizu University Studies in Arts and Culture* 49 (1996): 15–30.
36. Iwabuchi Toyō, *Watashi no onkyōshi: Kōka man no kiroku* (Tokyo : Shakai shisōsha, 1981), 147.
37. Yamato, *Otozukuri hanseiki*, 272.
38. Yamato, 272.
39. Yamato, 273–74.
40. *Yomiuri shinbun*, July 6, 1931, 7.
41. *Yomiuri shinbun*, July 25, 1930, 5.
42. Quoted in Yamato, *Otozukuri hanseiki*, 278–79.
43. *Asahi shinbun*, December 29, 1937, 10.
44. *Yomiuri shinbun*, May 18, 1971, 9.
45. Iwabuchi, *Watashi no onkyōshi*, 164.
46. Yamato, *Otozukuri hanseiki*, 329.
47. As Michel Chion writes, "Added value works reciprocally. Sound shows us the image differently than what the image shows alone, and the image likewise makes us hear

sound differently than if the sound were ringing out in the dark. However for all this reciprocity the screen remains the principal support of filmic perception" (Michel Chion, *Audio-Vision: Sound on Screen* [New York: Columbia University Press, 1994], 21).

48. Iwabuchi, *Watashi no onkyōshi*, 262.
49. Iwabuchi, 166.
50. Yamato, *Otozukuri hanseiki*, 190.
51. Yamato, 190.
52. Sasaki Norio, *Hassei eiga kantoku to kyakuhonron* (Tokyo: Ōraisha, 1931).
53. Kawabata Masao, "Gion tōkī," *Eiga jidai* 11, no. 1 (July 1931): 82–89.
54. Magami Gitarō, *Onga geijutsu no hōhōron* (Tokyo: Ōraisha, 1933).
55. Kaeriyama Norimasa, *Tōkī to tennenshoku eiga* (Tokyo: Nihonkyōzaieiga, 1931).
56. Hirata Masuo and Muramatsu Yoshinaga, *Tōkī no sekkei to seisakuhō* (Tokyo: Ryūshōkaku, 1933).
57. Nakagi Teiichi and Yoshida Masayoshi, *Saishin tōkī no seisaku to eisha no jissai* (Tokyo: Seikōdō, 1935).
58. Minawa joined Tōhō in 1942, and in 1971 established the Tōhō Kōka Shūdan (Tōhō Effects Group).
59. Nishimura Yūichirō, *Kurosawa Akira: Oto to eizō* (Tokyo: Tachikaze shobō, 1998), 238–40.
60. Akira Kurosawa, *Something Like an Autobiography* (New York: Vintage Books, 1983), 70.
61. The play can be found in Kurosawa Akira, *Taikei Kurosawa Akira, bekkan*, ed. Hamano Yasuki (Tokyo: Kōdansha, 2010).
62. Nagato Yōhei, *Eiga onkyōron: Mizoguchi Kenji eiga o kiku* (Tokyo: Misuzu shobō, 2014), 270–71.
63. Noël Burch, "On the Structural Use of Sound," in *Film Sound: Theory and Practice*, ed. Elisabeth Weis and John Belton (New York: Columbia University Press, 1985), 203–4.
64. *Asahi shinbun*, March 5, 1933, 7.
65. Chion, *Audio-Vision*, 22–23.
66. Iwabuchi, *Watashi no onkyōshi*, 260.
67. The only exception was Tōhō, which had an *onkyō kōkabu* (sound-effects department).
68. René Clair, "The Art of Sound," trans. Vera Traill, in *Film Sound: Theory and Practice*, ed. Elisabeth Weis and John Belton (New York: Columbia University Press, 1985), 93.

6. SOUND AND MOTION

1. See, for example, Richard Abel and Rick Altman, eds., *The Sounds of Early Cinema* (Bloomington: Indiana University Press, 2001); and Rick Altman, *Silent Film Sound* (New York: Columbia University Press, 2007). Exhibition practices in Japan were even more tilted in the direction of audition. For some examples of the earliest forms of sonic accompaniment, see Shuhei Hosokawa, "Sketches of Silent Film Sound in Japan: Theatrical Functions of Ballyhoo, Orchestras, and *Kabuki* Ensembles," in *The Oxford*

Handbook of Japanese Cinema, ed. Daisuke Miyao (New York: Oxford University Press, 2014), 288–305.
2. John Cage pointed out that no lived experience in or out of an anechoic chamber is ever completely silent. Even a silent film exhibited without narrative, musical, or sound-effects accompaniment would be viewed listening to the sounds of the audience and whatever could be heard of the projector and the world outside the exhibition venue. See John Cage, *Silence: Lectures and Writings* (Middletown, CT: Wesleyan University Press, 1961).
3. For an introduction to the *benshi*, see J. L. Anderson, "Spoken Silents in the Japanese Cinema; or, Talking to Pictures: Essaying the Katsuben, Contextualizing the Texts," in *Reframing Japanese Cinema: Authorship, Genre, History*, ed. Arthur Noletti and David Desser (Bloomington: Indiana University Press, 1992), 259–311. For a fuller history, see Jeffrey A. Dym, *Benshi, Japanese Silent Film Narrators, and Their Forgotten Narrative Art of Setsumei: A History of Japanese Silent Film Narration* (Lewiston, NY: Edwin Mellen Press, 2003).
4. For a concise yet comprehensive description of this phenomenon, see Chika Kinoshita, "Mise-en-Scène of Desire: The Films of Mizoguchi Kenji" (PhD diss., University of Chicago, 2007), 201–9.
5. Nagato Yōhei, *Eiga onkyōron: Mizoguchi Kenji eiga o kiku* (Tokyo: Misuzu shobō, 2014), 62–65.
6. Kikuchi Kiyomaro, *Nihon ryūkōka hensenshi: Kayōkyoku no tanjō kara J poppu no jidai e* (Tokyo: Ronsōsha, 2008), 26–29.
7. Kinoshita, "Mise-en-Scène of Desire," 63–193.
8. Many of these *benshi* recordings have survived, and some have been reissued in digital formats. See *Katsubenshū: Ryūkōka, eiga setsumeishū*, Koromubia Myūjikku Entateinmento, 2008; and *Natsukashi no katsuben: orijinaru SP genban ni yoru: Ryūkōka eiga setsumeishū*, Nippon Koromubia, 2000.
9. Satō Tadao, *Nihon eigashi*, vol. 1 (Tokyo: Iwanami shoten, 1995), 330.
10. The accents of the northeast, or Tōhoku, region, for example, generally had (and still have) more rustic and negative associations.
11. For the best survey of PCL's early days, see Johan Nordstrom, "'Toki wa P.C.L.': P.C.L. no ongakusei ga motarashita mono: P.C.L. reimeiki ni okeru ongakusei dōnyū to revyū eiga no hatten," *Engeki kenkyū: Engeki hakubutsukan kiyō* no. 37 (2014): 45–63. A complete filmography of PCL and Tōhō productions can be found in Stuart Galbraith, *The Toho Studios Story: A History and Complete Filmography* (Lanham, MD: Scarecrow Press, 2008).
12. Satō, *Nihon eigashi*, 1:333.
13. For insight into the film-theoretical discourses of the silent era, particularly the Pure Film Movement, see Aaron Gerow, *Visions of Modernity: Articulations of Cinema, Nation, and Spectatorship, 1895–1925* (Berkeley: University of California Press, 2010).
14. Donald Kirihara, "Reconstructing Japanese Film," in *Post-Theory: Reconstructing Film Studies*, ed. David Bordwell and Noël Carroll (Madison: University of Wisconsin Press, 1996), 503. I have not seen this figure corroborated elsewhere, and it should be taken as

a very rough estimate, as production figures were not recorded as precisely as they were after the war.

15. The National Diet Library's Digital Collections can be searched online at the URL http://dl.ndl.go.jp/, although most of the collection's content can be viewed only from dedicated terminals in Japan.
16. Magami Gitarō, *Onga geijutsu no hōhōron* (Tokyo: Ōraisha, 1933).
17. Heinz Umbehr and Hans H. Wollenberg, *Der Tonfilm: Grundlagen und Praxis seiner Aufnahme und Wiedergabe* (Berlin: Verlag der "Lichtbildbühne," 1930).
18. Walter B. Pitkin and William Moulton Marston, *The Art of Sound Pictures* (New York: D. Appleton, 1930).
19. Hans Kahan, *Dramaturgie des Tonfilms* (Berlin: M. Mattisson, 1930).
20. Peter Schulman writes: "In *L'homme standard* [Rageot] anticipated how technology would actually create more immobility even though people could travel further. For Rageot, the world was becoming increasingly cinematic and unreal. Transportation or other pleasures could be replaced within the imagination without any effort from the viewers. In fact, he describes a protocyberspace that Jean Baudrillard would later write about in the 1980s.... Rageot perceived a miniaturization of life as a result of people's shrinking field of vision. What he labeled *cinématisme* referred to a metamorphosis of the space around us. In the past, the village church was the all-powerful center of the villagers' actions; in the nineteenth century, new inventions such as steam and gas heat changed the way people thought about their surroundings by providing indoor warm temperatures all year long, or rapidly bringing distant cities together via train travel. Inventions such as the motion picture brought the world to individuals, who no longer searched for the world outside of their private realms" (Peter Schulman, *The Sunday of Fiction: The Modern French Eccentric* [West Lafayette, IN: Purdue University Press, 2003], 146–47).
21. In this context, "jazz" refers more specifically to big band swing.
22. Nakane Hiroshi, *Tōkī ongakuron* (Tokyo: Ōraisha, 1932), 22.
23. Leonid Sabaneev, *Music for the Films: A Handbook for Composers and Conductors* (London: Sir I. Pitman and Sons, 1935).
24. Kurt London, *Film Music; A Summary of the Characteristic Features of Its History, Aesthetics, Technique; and Possible Developments* (London: Faber and Faber, 1936).
25. Nakane, *Tōkī ongakuron*, 35.
26. Nakane, 31.
27. Nakane, 49–50.
28. Nakane, 84.
29. Nakane, 85.
30. I use this term with caution, as most scholarship today recognizes that none of the supposedly "vernacular" forms of writing with which we're familiar were fully accurate representations of language as it was actually spoken.
31. "Nearly six-thousand jidai-geki were made between 1908 and the end of the Pacific War. By 1911 period films accounted for 39 percent of the total film production. Their production peaked at 60 percent in 1918 and fluctuated slightly around 40 percent between

1920 and 1925, dropping only once to 32 percent in 1923, the year the Great Kanto Earthquake devastated Tokyo. From 1926 through 1940, production ranged from 46 percent to 56 percent, with a yearly mean of 51 percent" (Lisa Spalding, "Period Films in the Prewar Era," in *Reframing Japanese Cinema: Authorship, Genre, History*, ed. Arthur Noletti and David Desser [Bloomington: Indiana University Press, 1992], 131).

32. Multiple sources attest to this, but a good place to begin is Shindō Kaneto's documentary, *Kenji Mizoguchi: The Life of a Film Director* (1975).
33. Mizoguchi Kenji, *Mizoguchi Kenji chosakushū: The Complete Writings of Kenji Mizoguchi*, ed. Sasō Tsutomu (Tokyo: Omuro, 2013), 54.
34. Mizoguchi, 66–67.
35. Mizoguchi, 115.
36. Mizoguchi, 115.
37. Mizoguchi, 115.
38. Mizoguchi, 116.
39. Mizoguchi, 116.
40. Mizoguchi, 116–17.
41. An interesting comparison might be made with Kurosawa Akira's relationship with his older brother Heigo, who had a profound effect on Akira's intellectual development and committed suicide in 1933. For more on the relationship between the two brothers, see Paul Anderer, *Kurosawa's Rashomon: A Vanished City, a Lost Brother, and the Voice Inside His Iconic Films* (New York: Pegasus Books, 2016).
42. Mizoguchi, *Mizoguchi Kenji chosakushū*, 117.
43. "Basue no kan ni sagashita onshi no 'fuhyōsaku': Mizoguchi o nagusame ni iku Yamada," *Yomiuri shinbun*, October 12, 1938, 2.
44. Yoda Yoshikata, *Mizoguchi Kenji no hito to geijutsu* (Tokyo: Tabata shoten, 1970), 51.
45. Mizoguchi, *Mizoguchi Kenji chosakushū*, 95.
46. *Niwaka* was a form of improvised mimicry or impersonation popular in urban areas during the Tokugawa period.
47. Mizoguchi, *Mizoguchi Kenji chosakushū*, 96–97.
48. Nagato cites the work of Barbara Sato in this reading of telephone operators' labor. See Barbara Sato, *The New Japanese Woman: Modernity, Media, and Women in Interwar Japan* (Durham, N.C.: Duke University Press, 2003).

    Nagato uses the term "erotic service" to describe these brief, mediated encounters. While there was arguably an erotic dimension at play, to call them simply "erotic" seems to exclude a broader range of affective transactions that were both possible and likely (Nagato, *Eiga onkyōron*, 118).
49. Irena Powell, *Writers and Society in Modern Japan* (New York: Kodansha International, 1983), 120.
50. Kurokigawa Takashi, "Jidaigeki onga no susumu beki michi," *Kinema junpō*, September 1, 1941, 69.
51. Kiyose Eijirō, "Tōkī jidaigeki no daiarōgu: Toku ni haiyū no tachiba kara," *Eiga kagaku kenkyū*, September 1931, 95–104.
52. "Itō Daisuke o kakonde: Jidaigeki tōkī zadankai," *Kinema junpō*, January 1, 1934, 203.

53. Yasuda Kiyoo, *Eiga kyakuhon kōseiron* (Tokyo: Eiga hyōronsha, 1935).
54. Yasuda, 187–88.
55. Yasuda, 188.
56. "Eiga sakka 8-nin o yō shite: Nihon eiga no shōrai o kataru," *Kinema junpō*, September 1, 1935, 172.
57. See Miyako Inoue, *Vicarious Language: Gender and Linguistic Modernity in Japan* (Berkeley: University of California Press, 2006).
58. Yasuda Kiyoo, *Eiga kyakuhon kōseiron*, 188 (italics added).
59. Yamanaka Sadao, *Yamanaka Sadao sakuhinshū: Zen ikkan* (Tokyo: Jitsugyō no Nihonsha, 1998), 918–19.
60. I borrow the term from Bryony D. Stocker, "'Bygonese'—Is This Really the Authentic Language of Historical Fiction?," *New Writing: International Journal for the Practice and Theory of Creative Writing* 9, no. 3 (November 2012): 308–18.

CODA-*OKE*

1. Daqing Yang, *Technology of Empire: Telecommunications and Japanese Expansion in Asia, 1883–1945* (Cambridge, MA: Harvard University Asia Center), 2010.
2. See, for example, the work of Johan Nordstrom and Michael Raine.
3. Takahashi Gen'ichirō, *Nihon bungaku seisuishi* (Tokyo: Kōdansha, 2001).
4. Takahashi, 18.
5. Personal conversation with Takahashi Gen'ichirō, September 2002.
6. Takahashi, *Nihon bungaku seisuishi*, 376.
7. Zhou Xun and Francesca Tarocco, *Karaoke: The Global Phenomenon* (London: Reaktion Books, 2007), 19–30.
8. See, for example, Tōru Mitsui and Shūhei Hosokawa, eds., *Karaoke Around the World: Global Technology, Local Singing* (New York: Routledge, 2001).
9. Takahashi Gen'ichirō, *Sayonara, gyangutachi* (Tokyo: Kōdansha, 1982).
10. In more recent years, especially after the Tohoku earthquake/tsunami/meltdown triple disaster, Takahashi has taken a much more active role in public political debates. Interestingly, amplified progressive protest has also made a comeback, while right-wing sound trucks never went away. See Noriko Manabe, *The Revolution Will Not Be Televised: Protest Music After Fukushima* (New York: Oxford University Press, 2016).

BIBLIOGRAPHY

Abel, Richard, and Rick Altman, eds. *The Sounds of Early Cinema*. Bloomington: Indiana University Press, 2001.

Addis, Laird. *Of Mind and Music*. Ithaca, NY: Cornell University Press, 1999.

Akiyama Kuniharu. *Shōwa no sakkyokukatachi: Taiheiyō sensō to ongaku*. Tokyo: Misuzu shobō, 2003.

Althusser, Louis. *Lenin and Philosophy, and Other Essays*. Translated by Ben Brewster. New York: Monthly Review Press, 1971.

Altman, Rick. *Silent Film Sound*. New York: Columbia University Press, 2007.

Anderer, Paul. *Kurosawa's Rashomon: A Vanished City, a Lost Brother, and the Voice Inside His Iconic Films*. New York: Pegasus Books, 2016.

Anderson, Benedict R. *Imagined Communities: Reflections on the Origin and Spread of Nationalism*. London: Verso, 1991.

Attali, Jacques. *Noise: The Political Economy of Music*. Translated by Brian Massumi. Minneapolis: University of Minnesota Press, 1985.

Beck, Alan. *The Invisible Play—BBC Radio Drama, 1922–1928*. A Sound Journal CD ROM Publication, 2000.

Beck, Guy L. *Sonic Theology: Hinduism and Sacred Sound*. Columbia: University of South Carolina Press, 1993.

Bell, Paul A. *Environmental Psychology*. 5th ed. Fort Worth, TX: Harcourt College Publishers, 2001.

Bird, Isabella Lucy. *Unbeaten Tracks in Japan: An Account of Travels in the Interior Including Visits to the Aborigines of Yezo and the Shrines of Nikkō and Isé*. London: J. Murray, 1880.

Birkenmaier, Anke. "'Proposition for a Radiophonic Art': Introduction." *Modernism/Modernity* 16, no. 2 (2009): 403–5.

Bourdaghs, Michael K. *Sayonara Amerika, Sayonara Nippon: A Geopolitical Prehistory of J-Pop*. New York: Columbia University Press, 2012.

Bowker, Richard Rogers. *Copyright: Its History and Its Law*. Boston: Houghton Mifflin, 1912.
Burns, Susan L. *Before the Nation: Kokugaku and the Imagining of Community in Early Modern Japan*. Durham, NC: Duke University Press, 2003.
Cage, John. *Silence: Lectures and Writings*. Middletown, CT: Wesleyan University Press, 1961.
Cage, John, and Daniel Charles. *For the Birds*. Boston: M. Boyars, 1981.
Carr, Nicholas. *The Shallows: What the Internet Is Doing to Our Brains*. New York: Norton, 2010.
Certeau, Michel de. *The Practice of Everyday Life*. Translated by Steven Rendall. Berkeley: University of California Press, 1984.
Chamberlain, Basil Hall. *Things Japanese: Being Notes on Various Subjects Connected with Japan for the Use of Travellers and Others*. London: J. Murray, 1905.
Childs, Peter. *Modernism*. London: Routledge, 2000.
Chion, Michel. *Audio-Vision: Sound on Screen*. Translated by Claudia Gorbman. New York: Columbia University Press, 1994.
———. *The Voice in Cinema*. Translated by Claudia Gorbman. New York: Columbia University Press, 1999.
Clair, René. "The Art of Sound." Translated by Vera Traill. In *Film Sound: Theory and Practice*, edited by Elisabeth Weis and John Belton, 92–95. New York: Columbia University Press, 1985.
Crook, Tim. *Radio Drama: Theory and Practice*. London: Routledge, 1999.
Deutsch, Diana. "The Genesis of Absolute Pitch: Theories and Experimental Findings." *Journal of the Acoustical Society of America* 126, no. 4 (2009): 2278.
Dolar, Mladen. "The Linguistics of the Voice." In *The Sound Studies Reader*. Edited by Jonathan Sterne. New York: Routledge, 2012.
———. *A Voice and Nothing More*. Cambridge, MA: MIT Press, 2006.
Dym, Jeffrey A. *Benshi, Japanese Silent Film Narrators, and Their Forgotten Narrative Art of Setsumei: A History of Japanese Silent Film Narration*. Lewiston, NY: Edwin Mellen Press, 2003.
Eppstein, Ury. *The Beginnings of Western Music in Meiji Era Japan*. Studies in the History and Interpretation of Music 44. Lewiston, NY: Edwin Mellen Press, 1994.
Frith, Simon, ed. *Music and Copyright*. Edinburgh: Edinburgh University Press, 1993.
Fujii Nobuyuki. *Terekomu no keizaishi: Kindai Nihon no denshin denwa*. Tokyo: Keisō shobō, 1998.
Fukuda Michiko. "A Study of Sound Effects in Kabuki I." *Ochanomizu University Studies in Arts and Culture* 49 (1996): 15–30.
Fukuzawa Yukichi. *Seiyō jijō gaihen san-kan Fukuzawa Yukichi sanshū*. Tokyo: Shōkodō, 1872. http://hdl.handle.net/2027/keio.10811640418, 42.
———. *Seiyō jijō: Shohen*. Tokyo: Shōkodō, 1866. http://project.lib.keio.ac.jp/dg_kul/fukuzawa/flipper/F7-A02-01/book150.html, 111–16. Accessed September 1, 2017.
Galbraith, Stuart. *The Toho Studios Story: A History and Complete Filmography*. Lanham, MD: Scarecrow Press, 2008.
Ganea, Peter, ed. *Japanese Copyright Law: Writings in Honour of Gerhard Schricker*. The Hague: Kluwer Law International, 2005.

Gelatt, Roland. *The Fabulous Phonograph, 1877–1977*. 2nd rev. ed. New York: Macmillan, 1977.
Genette, Gérard. *Narrative Discourse: An Essay in Method*. Ithaca, NY: Cornell University Press, 1980.
Gerow, Aaron. *Visions of Modernity: Articulations of Cinema, Nation, and Spectatorship, 1895–1925*. Berkeley: University of California Press, 2010.
Gitelman, Lisa. *Always Already New: Media, History, and the Data of Culture*. Cambridge, MA: MIT Press, 2014.
———. *Scripts, Grooves, and Writing Machines: Representing Technology in the Edison Era*. Stanford, CA: Stanford University Press, 1999.
Gluck, Carol. *Japan's Modern Myths*. Princeton, NJ: Princeton University Press, 1985.
Hashimoto Kazuo. *Nihon supōtsu hōsōshi*. Tokyo: Taishūkan shoten, 1992.
Hikita Masaaki, Hidaka Yoshiki, and Hibi Yoshitaka, eds. *Supōtsu suru bungaku: 1920–30 nendai no bunka shigaku*. Tokyo: Seikyūsha, 2009.
Hirata Masuo, and Muramatsu Yoshinaga. *Tōkī no sekkei to seisakuhō*. Tokyo: Ryūshōkaku, 1933.
Hirschkind, Charles. *The Ethical Soundscape: Cassette Sermons and Islamic Counterrepublics*. New York: Columbia University Press, 2006.
Hosokawa Shūichi. "Chosakuken seido to medeia no hensei: Nihon no shoki ongaku sangyō o jirei to shite." *Soshiorogos* 27 (2003): 249–68.
Hyōdō Hiromi. *"Koe" no kokumin kokka Nihon*. Tokyo: Nippon hōsō shuppan kyōkai, 2000.
Hyōdō Hiromi, and Henry D. Smith II. "Singing Tales of the Gishi: 'Naniwabushi' and the Forty-Seven Rōnin in Late Meiji Japan." *Monumenta Nipponica* 61 no. 4 (2006): 459–508. www.jstor.org/stable/25066463.
Iizuka Tsuneo. *Rekōdo man no seiki: Kurofune raikō kara hibari zessho made*. Tokyo: Aikusha, 2012.
Ikegami, Eiko. *Bonds of Civility: Aesthetic Networks and the Political Origins of Japanese Culture, Structural Analysis in the Social Sciences*. Cambridge: Cambridge University Press, 2005.
Itō Takashi. *Nihon no kindai: Media to kenryoku*. Vol. 14. Tokyo: Chūō kōronsha, 1999.
Iwabuchi Toyō. *Watashi no onkyōshi: Kōka man no kiroku*. Tokyo: Shakai shisōsha, 1981.
Jacobowitz, Seth. *Writing Technology in Meiji Japan: A Media History of Modern Japanese Literature and Visual Culture*. Cambridge, MA: Harvard University East Asia Center, 2015.
Japan Broadcasting Corporation. *Broadcasting in Japan: The Twentieth Century Journey from Radio to Multimedia*. Tokyo: NHK, 2002.
Jay, Martin. *Downcast Eyes: The Denigration of Vision in Twentieth-Century French Thought*. Berkeley: University of California Press, 1993.
Kaeriyama Norimasa. *Tōkī to tennenshoku eiga*. Tokyo: Nihon kyōzai eiga, 1931.
Kahan, Hans. *Dramaturgie des Tonfilms*. Berlin: M. Mattisson, 1930.
Karatani Kōjin. *Origins of Modern Japanese Literature*. Edited by Brett de Bary. Durham, NC: Duke University Press, 1993.
Katō Michio. *Chikuonki no jidai*. Tokyo: Shopan, 2006.
Katsubenshū: Ryūkōka, eiga setsumeishū. Tokyo: Koromubia myūjikku entateinmento, 2008.
Kawamura Minato. *Kotodama to takai*. Tokyo: Kōdansha, 2002.

Kenney, William Howland. *Recorded Music in American Life: The Phonograph and Popular Memory, 1890–1945*. New York: Oxford University Press, 1999.

Kern, Stephen. *The Culture of Time and Space, 1880–1918*. Cambridge, MA: Harvard University Press, 1983.

Kikuchi Kiyomaro. *Nihon ryūkōka henshenshi: Kayōkyoku no tanjō kara J poppu no jidai e.* Tokyo: Ronsōsha, 2008.

Kinoshita, Chika. "Mise-en-Scene of Desire: The Films of Mizoguchi Kenji." Ph.D. diss., University of Chicago, 2007.

Kirihara, Donald. "Reconstructing Japanese Film." In *Post-Theory: Reconstructing Film Studies*. Edited by David Bordwell and Noël Carroll. Madison: University of Wisconsin Press, 1996.

Kittler, Friedrich A. *Discourse Networks, 1800/1900*. Translated by Michael Metteer and Chris Cullens. Stanford, CA: Stanford University Press, 1990.

———. *Gramophone, Film, Typewriter*. Translated by Geoffrey Winthrop-Young and Michael Wurtz. Stanford, CA: Stanford University Press, 1999.

Kleeman, Faye Yuan. "Pan-Asian Romantic Nationalism: Revolutionary, Literati, and Popular Oral Tradition and the Case of Miyazaki Tōten." In *Sino-Japanese Transculturation: From the Late Nineteenth Century to the End of the Pacific War*. Edited by Richard King, Cody Poulton, and Katsuhiko Endo, 45–67. Lanham, MD.: Lexington Books, 2012.

Knollys, Henry. *Sketches of Life in Japan*. London: Chapman and Hall, 1887.

Kobayashi Nobuhiko. *Nihon no kigekijin*. Tokyo: Shōbunsha, 1972

Koizumi Kyōko. *Memorīsukēpu: Ano koro o yobiokosu ongaku*. Tokyo: Misuzushobō, 2013.

Komiyama Hiromichi, trans. *Kinsei ni daihatsumei: Denwaki-sogenki*. Tokyo: Kobunsha, 1880. info:ndljp/pid/846698.

Kurata Yoshihiro. *Nihon rekōdo bunkashi*. Tokyo: Tōkyō shoseki, 1992.

Kuroda Isamu. *Rajio taisō no tanjō*. Tokyo: Seikyūsha, 1999.

Kurosawa, Akira. *Something Like an Autobiography*. Translated by Audie Bock. New York: Vintage Books, 1983.

———. *Taikei Kurosawa Akira, bekkan*. Edited by Hamano Yasuki. Tokyo: Kōdansha, 2010.

Lastra, James. *Sound Technology and the American Cinema: Perception, Representation, Modernity, Film and Culture*. New York: Columbia University Press, 2000.

Latour, Bruno. *Reassembling the Social: An Introduction to Actor-Network-Theory*. Oxford: Oxford University Press, 2005.

Leitz, Christian. *Nazi Foreign Policy, 1933–1941: The Road to Global War*. London: Routledge, 2004.

Lewis, Peter. "Radio Drama." In *The Cambridge Guide to Theatre*. Edited by Martin Banham. New ed. Cambridge: Cambridge University Press, 1995.

London, Kurt. *Film Music: A Summary of the Characteristic Features of Its History, Aesthetics, Technique; and Possible Developments*. London: Faber and Faber, 1936.

Maeda, Ai. *Text and the City: Essays on Japanese Modernity*. Edited by James A. Fujii. Durham, NC: Duke University Press, 2004.

Magami Gitarō. *Onga geijutsu no hōhōron*. Tokyo: Ōraisha, 1933.

Mair, Victor H. "Sound and Meaning in the History of Characters: Views of China's Earliest Script Reformers." In *Difficult Characters: Interdisciplinary Studies of Chinese and Japanese*

Writing. Edited by Mary S. Erbaugh. Columbus: National East Asian Languages Resource Center, Ohio State University, 2002.

Manabe, Noriko. *The Revolution Will Not Be Televised: Protest Music After Fukushima*. New York: Oxford University Press, 2016.

Marvin, Carolyn. *When Old Technologies Were New: Thinking About Electric Communication in the Late Nineteenth Century*. New York: Oxford University Press, 1988.

Masuda Satoshi. *Sono ongaku no sakusha towa dare ka: Rimikkusu sangyō chosakuken*. Tokyo: Misuzushobō, 2005.

Matsuda Hiroyuki. *Meiji terekomu monogatari: Jōhō tsūshin shakai no "genfūkei."* Tokyo: Nihon keizai hyōronsha, 2001.

Maurer, Daphne, Laura C. Gibson, and Ferrinne Spector. "Synesthesia in Infants and Very Young Children." December 1, 2013. doi:10.1093/oxfordhb/9780199603329.013.0003.

McLuhan, Marshall. *Understanding Media: The Extensions of Man*. Edited by W. Terrence Gordon. Corte Madera, CA: Gingko Press, 2003.

McNeill, William. *Keeping Together in Time: Dance and Drill in Human History*. Cambridge, MA: Harvard University Press, 1995.

Miller, John Scott. "Japanese Oral Narrative in a Meiji Literary Context." Ph.D. diss., Princeton University, 1988.

Mitsui, Tōru, and Shūhei Hosokawa. *Karaoke Around the World: Global Technology, Local Singing*. London: Routledge, 2001.

Miyako, Inoue. *Vicarious Language: Gender and Linguistic Modernity in Japan*. Berkeley: University of California Press, 2006.

Miyao, Daisuke, ed. *The Oxford Handbook of Japanese Cinema*. New York: Oxford University Press, 2014.

Mizoguchi, Kenji. *Mizoguchi Kenji chosakushū: The Complete Writings of Kenji Mizoguchi*. Edited by Sasō Tsutomu. Tokyo: Omuro, 2013.

Morioka, Heinz, and Miyoko Sasaki. *Rakugo, the Popular Narrative Art of Japan*. Harvard East Asian Monographs 138. Cambridge, MA: Council on East Asian Studies. Distributed by Harvard University Press, 1990.

Morse, Edward Sylvester. *Japan Day by Day:1877, 1878–79, 1882–83*. Atlanta: Cherokee, 1990.

Mullaney, Thomas S. The Chinese Typewriter: A Global History of the Information Age. Cambridge, MA: MIT Press, 2017.

Mumford, Lewis. *Technics and Civilization*. New York: Harcourt, 1963.

Murasaki Shikibu. *The Tale of Genji*. Translated by Royall Tyler. New York: Viking, 2001.

Nachman, Gerald. *Raised on Radio*. New York: Pantheon Books, 1998.

Nagahara, Hiromu. *Tokyo Boogie-Woogie: Japan's Pop Era and Its Discontents*. Cambridge: Harvard University Press, 2017.

Nagai Kafū. *Kafū zenshū*. Tokyo: Iwanami shoten, 1992.

Nāgapriya, Dharmachāri. "Poisoned Pen Letters? D. T. Suzuki's Communication of Zen to the West." http://www.westernbuddhistreview.com/vol5/suzuki-gentium.html. Accessed September 1, 2017.

Nagato Yōhei. *Eiga onkyōron: Mizoguchi Kenji eiga o kiku*. Tokyo: Misuzu shobō, 2014.

Naitō Takashi. *Meiji no oto: Seiyōjin ga kiita kindai Nihon*. Chūkō shinsho 1791. Tokyo: Chūō kōron shinsha, 2005.
Nakagawa Shin. *Heiankyō oto no uchū: Saundosukēpu e no tabi*. Tokyo: Heibonsha, 1992.
Nakagi Teiichi, and Yoshida Masayoshi. *Saishin tōkī no seisaku to eisha no jissai*. Tokyo: Seikōdō, 1935.
Nakamura Kōsuke. *Kindai Nihon yōgakushi josetsu*. Tokyo: Tōkyō shoseki, 2003.
———. *Seiyō no oto, Nihon no mimi: Kindai Nihon ongaku to seiyō ongaku*. Tokyo: Shunjūsha, 2002.
Nakane Hiroshi. *Tōkī ongakuron*. Tokyo: Ōraisha, 1932.
Nakano Jun. *Nihonjin no nakigoe: Koe to iu media no kaikan*. Tokyo: NTT shuppan, 1993.
Natsukashi no katsuben: Orijinaru SP genban ni yoru: Ryūkōka eiga setsumeishū. Tokyo: Nippon koromubia, 2000.
Natsume Sōseki. *Spring Miscellany and London Essays*. Translated by Sammy Tsunematsu. Boston: Tuttle, 2002.
Nihon hōsō kyōkai. *Enueichikei hōsōgeki senshū*. Tokyo: Rajio sābisu sentā, 1957.
———. *20 seiki hōsōshi*. Tokyo: NHK shuppan, 2001.
Nihon Koromubia kabushiki kaisha. "Our History." In *Koromubia gojūnenshi*. Tokyo: Nihon Koromubia, 1961.
Nihon ongaku chosakuken kyōkai. *Nihon ongaku chosakukenshi*. Tokyo: Nihon ongaku chosakuken kyōkai, 1990.
Nippon denshin denwa kabushiki kaisha. *Denwa 100-nen shōshi = The Story of Telephone*. Tokyo: Nippon denshin denwa kabushiki kaisha, 1990.
Nippon denshin denwa kōsha. *Tōkyō no denwa: Sono gojūman kanyū made*. Tokyo: Denki tsūshin kyōkai, 1958.
Niiya, Brian, and Japanese American National Museum. *Japanese American History: An A–Z Reference from 1868 to the Present*. New York: Facts on File, 1993.
Nishibayashi Tadatoshi and Yūseishō Teishin Hakubutsukan. *Nihonjin to terefon: Meiji Taishō Shōwa no denwa sesōshi*. Tokyo: Teishin kyōkai, 1990.
Nishimoto Ikuko. *Jikan ishiki no kindai: "Toki wa kane nari" no shakaishi*. Tokyo: Hōsei daigaku shuppankyoku, 2006.
Nishimura Yūichirō. *Kurosawa Akira: Oto to eizō*. Tokyo: Tachikaze shobō, 1998.
Nishizawa Minoru. *Rajio dorama no ōgon jidai*. Tokyo: Kawade shobō shinsha, 2002.
———. *Sōshiki rajio dorama to rajio dorama no "kotoba" kenkyū*. Tokyo: Fuji gurūpu, 2000.
Noletti, Arthur, and David Desser, eds. *Reframing Japanese Cinema: Authorship, Genre, History*. Bloomington: Indiana University Press, 1992.
Nomi Yoshihisa. "Tōchūken Kumoemon jiken to Meiji-Taishō no fuhōkōi riron." *Gakushūin daigaku hōgakukai zasshi / Gakushūin daigaku hōgakukai hen* 44, no. 2 (2009): 183–222.
Nordstrom, Johan. "'Toki wa P.C.L.': P.C.L. no ongakusei ga motarashita mono: P.C.L. reimeiki ni okeru ongakusei dōnyū to revyū eiga no hatten." *Engeki kenkyū: Engeki hakubutsukan kiyō*, no. 37 (2014): 45–63.
Nornes, Markus. *Cinema Babel: Translating Global Cinema*. Minneapolis: University of Minnesota Press, 2007.

Okamoto Kazuaki. *Ore no nodo wa hitokoe senryō: Tensai rōkyokushi Tōchūken Kumoemon.* Tokyo: Shinchōsha, 2014.
Ong, Walter J. *Orality and Literacy: The Technologizing of the Word.* London: Routledge, 1982.
Osborne, Richard. *Vinyl: A History of the Analogue Record.* Burlington, VT: Ashgate, 2012.
Ōtsuka Toranosuke, and Masuda Tamio. *Gokuhi denpō ni miru sensō to heiwa: Nihon denshin jōhōshi.* Kumamoto: Kumamoto shuppan bunka kaikan, 2002.
Ozawa Emiko. *Edokko to Asakusa hanayashiki.* Tokyo: Shōgakkan, 2006.
Parker, Andrew. *The Theorist's Mother.* Durham, NC: Duke University Press, 2012.
Peters, John Durham. *Speaking into the Air: A History of the Idea of Communication.* Chicago: University of Chicago Press, 1999.
Picard, Max. *Hitler in Our Selves.* Translated by Heinrich Hauser. Hinsdale, IL: Regnery, 1947.
———. *The World of Silence, the Humanist Library.* Chicago: Regnery, 1952.
Pitkin, Walter B., and William Moulton Marston. *The Art of Sound Pictures.* New York: D. Appleton, 1930.
Powell, Irena. *Writers and Society in Modern Japan.* Tokyo; New York: Kodansha International, 1983.
Richie, Donald. *A Hundred Years of Japanese Film: A Concise History, with a Selective Guide to Videos and DVDs.* New York: Kodansha International, 2001.
Robins, R. H. *A Short History of Linguistics.* 3rd ed. London: Longman, 1990.
Robinson, Kenneth Girdwood, and Erich F. W. Altwein. *A Critical Study of Chu Tsai-yü's Contribution to the Theory of Equal Temperament in Chinese Music.* Wiesbaden: Franz Steiner, 1980.
Rosolato, Guy. "La voix: entre corps et langage." *Revue française de psychanalyse* 38 (1974): 75–94.
Rutledge, Eric. "Orality and Textual Variation in the *Heike monogatari*: Part One, the Phrase and Its Formulaic Nature." In *Heike biwa: Katari to ongaku.* Edited by Kamisangō Yūkō. Kasukabe: Hitsuji shobō, 1993.
Sabaneev, Leonid. *Music for the Films: A Handbook for Composers and Conductors.* London: Sir I. Pitman and Sons, 1935.
Sasaki Norio. *Hassei eiga kantoku to kyakuhonron.* Tokyo: Ōraisha, 1931.
Sato, Barbara. *The New Japanese Woman: Modernity, Media, and Women in Interwar Japan.* Durham, NC: Duke University Press, 2003.
Satō Tadao. *Nihon eigashi.* Tokyo: Iwanami shoten, 1995.
Saussure, Ferdinand de. *Writings in General Linguistics.* Oxford: Oxford University Press, 2006.
Schafer, R. Murray. *The Soundscape: Our Sonic Environment and the Tuning of the World.* Rochester, VT: Destiny Books, 1993.
Schulman, Peter. *The Sunday of Fiction: The Modern French Eccentric.* West Lafayette, IN: Purdue University Press, 2003.
Seidensticker, Edward. *Kafū the Scribbler: The Life and Writings of Nagai Kafū.* Stanford, CA: Stanford University Press, 1965.
Shiho Tetsuo. *SP rekōdo: Sono kagirinai miwaku no sekai.* Tokyo: Shopan, 2008.

Snyder, Stephen. *Fictions of Desire: Narrative Form in the Novels of Nagai Kafū*. Honolulu: University of Hawai'i Press, 2000.
Soeda Tomomichi. *Enka no Meiji Taishō shi*. Iwanami shinsho 501. Tokyo: Iwanami shoten, 1963.
Starrs, Roy, ed. *Rethinking Japanese Modernism*. Leiden: Brill, 2011.
Sterne, Jonathan. *The Audible Past: Cultural Origins of Sound Reproduction*. Durham, NC: Duke University Press, 2003.
Stocker, Bryony D. "'Bygonese'—Is This Really the Authentic Language of Historical Fiction?" *New Writing: International Journal for the Practice and Theory of Creative Writing* 9, no. 3 (2012): 308–18.
Stoddard, John Lawson. *Japan*. Chicago: Belford, Middlebrook and Co., 1897.
Suzuki Matsumi, Suzuki Hajime, and Yoshida Yasushi. *Nihonjin no koe*. Tokyo: Yōsensha, 2003.
Takahashi Gen'ichirō. *Nihon bungaku seisuishi*. Tokyo: Kōdansha, 2001.
———. *Sayonara, gyangutachi*. Tokyo: Kōdansha, 1982.
Takaoka-shi Man'yō rekishikan. *Oto no "Man'yōshū."* Tokyo: Kasama shoin, 2002.
Takeyama Akiko. *Rajio no jidai: Rajio wa chanoma no shuyaku data*. Kyoto: Sekai shisōsha, 2002.
Tanaka Yūko. *Edo no oto*. Tokyo: Kawade shobō shinsha, 1988.
Tanizaki Jun'ichirō. *Childhood Years: A Memoir*. Translated by Paul McCarthy. Ann Arbor: University of Michigan Press, 2017.
Thompson, Emily Ann. *The Soundscape of Modernity: Architectural Acoustics and the Culture of Listening in America, 1900–1933*. Cambridge, MA: MIT Press, 2002.
Todorov, Tsvetan. *The Fantastic: A Structural Approach to a Literary Genre*. Translated by Richard Howard. Ithaca, NY: Cornell University Press, 1975.
Tomasello, Michael. *The Cultural Origins of Human Cognition*. Cambridge, MA: Harvard University Press, 1999.
Treaty of Commerce and Navigation Between Great Britain and Japan. http://treaties.fco.gov.uk/treaties/treatyrecord.htm?tid=8828.
Twine, Nanette. *Language and the Modern State: The Reform of Written Japanese*. London: Routledge, 1991.
Umbehr, Heinz, and Hans H. Wollenberg. *Der Tonfilm: Grundlagen und Praxis seiner Aufnahme und Wiedergabe*. Berlin: Verlag der "Lichtbildbühne," 1930.
Verma, Neil. *Theater of the Mind: Imagination, Aesthetics, and American Radio Drama*. Chicago: University of Chicago Press, 2012.
Weis, Elisabeth, and John Belton, eds. *Film Sound: Theory and Practice*. New York: Columbia University Press, 1985.
Yamaguchi Makoto. "Supōtsu jikkyō no orariteii—shoki hōsō ni okeru yakyū hōsō no wahō ni tsuite." *Kansai daigaku shakaigakubu kiyō* 34, no. 3 (2003): 181–204.
Yamanaka Ikuko. *Kōkandai ni ikita joseitachi*. Tokyo: Shin Nihon shuppansha, 1997.
Yamanaka Sadao. *Yamanaka Sadao sakuhinshū: Zen ikkan*. Tokyo: Jitsugyō no Nihonsha, 1998.
Yamato Sadaji. *Otozukuri hanseiki: Rajio terebi no onkyō kōka*. Tokyo: Shunjūsha, 2005.

Yang, Daqing. *Technology of Empire: Telecommunications and Japanese Expansion in Asia, 1883–1945*. Cambridge, MA: Harvard University Asia Center, 2010.

Yano, Christine. *Tears of Longing: Nostalgia and the Nation in Japanese Popular Song*. Cambridge, MA: Harvard University East Asia Center, 2003.

Yasuda Kiyoo. *Eiga kyakuhon kōseiron*. Tokyo: Eiga hyōronsha, 1935.

Yoda Yoshikata. *Mizoguchi Kenji no hito to geijutsu*. Tokyo: Tabata shoten, 1970.

Yoshimi Shun'ya. *"Koe" no shihon shugi: Denwa rajio chikuonki no shakaishi*. Kōdansha sensho mechie 48. Tokyo: Kōdansha, 1995.

Yuasa Atsushi. *Yumemiru shumi no Taishō jidai: Sakkatachi no sanbun fūkei*. Tokyo: Ronsōsha, 2010.

Zhou, Xun, and Francesca Tarocco. *Karaoke: The Global Phenomenon*. London: Reaktion Books, 2007.

Žižek, Slavoj. "Holding the Place." In *Contingency, Hegemony, Universality: Contemporary Dialogues on the Left*. Edited by Judith Butler, Ernesto Laclau, and Slavoj Žižek. London: Verso, 2000.

——. *On Belief*. London: Routledge, 2001.

INDEX

Aa furusato (Mizoguchi), 214, 215
accents, 174, 198, 249n10
acousmêtre, 19
Addis, Laird, 75–76
Akagaki Genzō (Watanabe), 218
Akahige (*Red Beard*) (Kurosawa), 218
Akutagawa Ryūnosuke, 169
Alexandrov, Grigori, 204
Althusser, Louis, 22
Among the Man-Eaters (Antoine), 208
Anderson, Benedict, 28, 35, 36
Andrievskii, Aleksander, 200
anime, 173, 176, 185
Anti-Comintern Pact, 142
Antoine, André-Paul, 208
Aoyama Sugisaku, 175
Araki Toratarō, 98–99
Ararezake (Saitō), 44
architecture, and sound, 67–68
arms race, 10, 230n11
"Art of Sound, The" (Clair), 191
Art of Sound Pictures, The (Pitkin and Marston), 200
Aru fūfu (Satomi Ton), 246n18
Asahi Records, 138

Asahi shinbun, 84, 128, 174, 175, 177, 189
Asahi supōtsu, 128
Atatakaki tochi nite (Enchi), 172
Attali, Jacques, 64–65, 68–69, 80–81, 96, 105–6
Audible Past, The (Sterne), 13
auditory culture, 2–3
auditory discourse, 22–24
automata, 44

Bakhtin, Mikhail, 79
BBC, 154
Beikoku Chikuonki Shōkai, 91
Bell, Alexander Graham, 1–2, 44, 71, 85, 229n1
Bell, Alexander Melville, 35, 71
Benjamin, Walter, 19
Benkei tai Ushiwaka (Masaoka), 176
benshi (film narrators), 25, 28, 34, 177, 193, 197, 249n8
Berliner, Emile, 85
Berne Convention for the Protection of Literary and Artistic Works (1887), 94, 95, 99–100, 104–5, 240n22
Bēsubōru, 132

big Other, 142, 153, 244n33
Bird, Isabella, 63–64
Birkenmaier, Anke, 166
Bizet, Georges, 207
Blake, Clarence, 44
Blüthgen, Victor, 156, 180
body, 120–21, 124–26
Bokutō kidan (*A Strange Tale from East of the River*) (Nagai), 147–48
Botchan no jidai (Sekikawa and Taniguchi), 226
Bowker, Richard Rogers, 105
bullhorn, 227
Bungaku zasshi, 84
Bungei shunjū, 143
Bungei shunjū ōru yomimono, 132
bunraku, 93, 146
Burch, Noël, 188

Cage, John, 55, 249n2
Carlyle, Thomas, 65, 150
Certeau, Michel de, 11
Chamberlain, Basil Hall, 60
chanbara (sword-fighting films), 187
Chikamatsu monogatari (*A Story from Chikamatsu*) (Mizoguchi), 188
Chikara to onna no yo no naka (Masaoka), 176
Chinese language: and orality, 24; and telegraph, 39; and vocalized reading, 26; and written Japanese, 24, 39, 72, 231n7
Chion, Michael, 19–20, 30, 31, 125, 190, 208, 247–48n47
chirimen (crepe paper books), 90
chongare (ballad form), 144
Chūjō Yūjirō, 89–90
Chūō kōron, 157
Chūshingura, 110, 146–47, 218
cinema. *See* film
cinématisme, 201
Clair, René, 191, 207
Cold War, 10, 230n11
colonialism. *See* Japanese colonialism; Western colonialism

Columbia Phonograph Company, 90
Coppola, Francis Ford, 191
copyright: and music, 94, 98, 100–101; and recording companies, 91; and Western culture, 93–96, 99. *See also* sound recording copyright
Copyright Act (1899), 91, 95, 97, 101
Copyright Act (1909), 242n56; 1971 amendment, 106
Copyright, Its History and Its Law (Bowker), 105
courtship, 33
Crook, Tim, 245n1
Culture of Time and Space, The (Kern), 41
Cusy, Pierre, 166

Daibosatsutoge (Nakazato), 217
Daichi wa hohoemu (radio drama), 156
Daiseigakuritsukō (Udagawa), 70
Danchōtei nichijō (Nagai), 148–49
Danger (Hughes), 154–55, 162
Derrida, Jacques, 3, 15
detethering, 13, 230n15
dialect, 25, 71, 174, 177; and film, 210–11, 213–16
dialogue: and dialect, 210–11; and operetta, 207; and period film, 218–21; and radio drama, 156, 164, 168; and sound film transition, 209–10, 222–23. *See also* film
Dictaphone, 182
Doane, Mary Ann, 121
documentaries, 207–8
Dolar, Mladen, 4–5, 12, 125, 151
Dōshi no hitobito (Yamamoto), 170
Downcast Eyes (Jay), 3
Dramaturgie des Tonfilms (Kahan), 200
dubbing, 176–78
Dym, Jeffrey, 28

ear phonoautograph, 44
Edison, Thomas, 83, 84, 85, 86, 238–39n1, 239n6
education, 71–72, 237n32
Eichmann, Adolf, 151

INDEX 265

Eiga hyōron, 192
Eiga jidai, 186
Eiga kagaku kenkyū, 186, 203
Eiga kyakuhon kōseiron (Yasuda), 220–21
Eiga no tomo, 222–23
Eiga ōrai, 212
Eiga to shihonshugi (Iwasaki), 203
Eijigoroshi (Yamamoto), 170
Eisenstein, Sergei, 201, 203, 204, 211, 212
Enchi Fumiko, 172
enka (popular song genre), 28–29
Enoken no seishun suikoden (*Romantic and Crazy*), 198–99
Enomoto Ken'ichi, 199
Enomoto Takeaki, 39, 86
Eppstein, Ury, 71
Ewing, James Alfred, 84

fantastic, 171, 172
February 26 Incident (1936), 140
Feet First (Lloyd), 177
film: anime, 173, 176, 185; *benshi*, 25, 28; as collective dreaming, 155; and dialect, 210–11, 213–16; Japanese production extent, 249–50n14; and Nagata Mikihiko, 160; and *naniwabushi*, 28; and nonverbal communication, 34; and PCL, 198–99; period, 210, 218–23, 250–51n31; and sound effects, 181, 184–88, 190, 191, 193, 248n67; and sound recording, 196–97, 249n8; and spoken Japanese, 198, 209–11, 212–16. *See also* film music; film theory
film music, 202–9; and cross-pollination, 208–9; and documentaries, 207–8; and naturalism, 203–4; opera, 206–7; operetta, 207; and sound film transition, 204–5
Film Music (London), 203
film theory, 199–202, 250n20. *See also* film music
"500-yen" dramas, 168–71, 169t
Forty-Seven Righteous Samurai of Akō, 146–47
Foucault, Michel, 121

4'33" (Cage), 55
Four Hours to Kill!, 177
Fox Film, 176–77
Fūfu (Nagata), 157
Fujiwara Yoshie no furusato (Mizoguchi), 196, 201
Fukuchi Gen'ichirō, 84
Fukuda Sōkichi, 190–91
Fukuzawa Yukichi, 39, 93–94, 233–34n36
Furukawa Roppa, 176
Futocchō (Sawa), 175
F. W. Horn Trading Company, 90, 91, 240n19

Gakugei shirin, 84
Gama no abura (*Something Like an Autobiography*) (Kurosawa), 52–53, 235n1
game theory, 9–11, 12, 14
Gan (Mori), 79–80
Geijutsu Eigasha, 185
Gekidan Kaze, 183
Gekiryū (Mafune), 164
genbun itchi (unification of speech and writing), 15
Gendarm Möbius (Blüthgen), 156, 180
Genenger, Martha, 136, 137
Genette, Gérard, 79
Gen'yōsha, 92, 240n24
Germinet, Gabriel, 166
gidayū (musical narrative genre), 27
Gion (Nagata), 157
Gion no shimai (*Sisters of the Gion*) (Mizoguchi), 210, 212
"Gion tōki" (Kawabata), 186
Gion yawa (Nagata), 157
Godzilla (Honda), 187
Goikō (Mabuchi), 23
Gosho Heinosuke, 184, 197–98, 201, 202

Hadaka no machi (Mafune), 164
Hagiwara Kyōjirō, 172
haikai poetics, 33, 57–58
hanashimono, 26. *See also* storytelling

266 INDEX

Handbook of Phonetics (Sweet), 35
hanken. *See* copyright
Hankenhō (Copyright Law), 94
Hanken jōrei (Copyright Statute) (1887), 94
Harada Jun, 174
harmony, 77–81, 238n41
Hasegawa Takejirō, 90
Hashido Shin, 129
Hassei eiga kantoku to kyakuhonron (Sasaki), 186, 200
"Hassei eiga kigyō no taisei" (Ishimaki), 200–201
Hatoyama Ichirō, 102, 106
Hatoyama Kazuo, 95
Hattori Yoshio, 159, 160–61, 175
Hayashi Nikuta, 166
health, 67
Hearn, Lafcadio, 62, 63
Hegel, G. W. F., 12
Heian period, 33, 56
heikyoku (narrative genre), 25, 27
Henry, Joseph, 37
Hibi Yoshitaka, 132
hi-fi soundscapes, 56
Higashiyama Chieko, 175
hiragana, 38
Hirata Masuo, 186
Hirohito. *See* Shōwa emperor
Hitler, Adolf, 151
Hitomi Kinue, 134, 244n25
Hitori musuko (*The Only Son*) (Ozu), 197
Hollywood, 191, 208
Honda Ishirō, 187
Hongō Shuntairō, 167–68
Horn, Frederick Whitney, 91, 102, 240n19
Hōsō, 138
Hosokawa Shūichi, 103
Hughes, Richard, 154–55
Hyōdō Hiromi, 28, 107, 146–47

Ibsen, Henrik, 163, 179
Ibuka Masaru, 198
Ichikawa Danjurō IX, 87

Ichikawa Sadanji II, 163, 179
identity, and orality, 24–25, 231n8
Iijima Tadashi, 201
Ikegami, Eiko, 25
Ikinokotta Shinsengumi (Kinugasa), 218
illusion, 189
imagined community, 28, 42, 113, 116
improvisation, 101, 241n45
Inagaki Hiroshi, 218, 222
India, 70
industrialization, 45, 66, 67, 75. *See also* modernity
inner voice, 21
Inokawa Koji, 27
Inokuma Teiji, 118, 120
Inoue Daisuke, 227
Inoue Kaoru, 85–86
Inoue Masao, 180
interior monologue, 171–72
International Federation of the Phonographic Industry, 112
internet, 51, 237n28
Inukai Tsuyoshi, 116
Isawa Shūji, 1–2, 71–72, 229n1, 237n32
Ishikawa Takuboku, 73, 79
Ishimaki Yoshio, 200–201
Islam, 121
Itachi (Mafune), 164
Itō Daisuke, 219–20, 222
Itō Hirobumi, 86
Itō Noboru, 186
Iwabuchi Toyō, 180, 184, 185, 189, 190
Iwasaki Akira, 200, 201, 203

Japan Day by Day (Morse), 62–63
Japanese colonialism, 71, 92, 120, 140, 214–15, 225, 237n32
Japanese nationalism/militarism: and *naniwabushi*, 146–47; and radio, 120, 126, 140–44; and radio drama, 155–56; and sports broadcasting, 139, 140, 142; and Western music, 81–82. *See also* Japanese colonialism; state formation

Japanese oral traditions: and materiality of voice, 31–32; nonverbal communication in, 34; performance in, 32–33, 232–33n24; and residual orality, 25; and sound recording, 85; storytelling in, 26–29
Jay, Martin, 3
Jazz Singer, The (film), 193
jidaigeki (period drama), 210, 218–23, 250–51n31
jidai shōsetsu (period novels), 217
jidō denwa (automatic phones), 48
Jiji shinbun, 88
Jiji shinpō, 160
jikkan hōsō (broadcasts that feel live), 135, 137–38
jissha eiga (actuality films), 207
Jiyū Gekijō (Free Theater), 163, 179
Jiyū minken undō (Freedom and People's Rights Movement), 29
JOAK (Tokyo Broadcasting Station): and introduction of radio, 114; and radio drama, 154, 157, 158t, 160–61, 168–71, 169t; and sound effects, 182–83, 184–85, 189; and sports broadcasting, 129, 130, 134, 136
JOBK (Osaka Broadcasting Station), 116, *117*, 127–28, 184–85
JOCK (Nagoya Broadcasting Station), 116
JODK (Seoul/Keijō Broadcasting Station), 127
John Gabriel Borkman (Ibsen), 163, 179
jōruri (musical narrative genre), 27
Josei, 159–60
Jūjiya, 90–91

kabuki: and language, 213, 221; and radio, 110, 146; and sound effects, 179, 180; and sound recording, 87, 89, 109–11
Kaen no tsuzumi (Nagata), 160
Kaeriyama Norimasa, 181, 186
Kahan, Hans, 200
Kamo no Mabuchi, 23–24
Kanashiki henro (Nagata), 162–63, 174
kana syllabaries, 38, 39, 40–41, 72

Kaneko Kentarō, 2, 43–44, 229n1
Kanwa kyūdaiko, 129–30
karaoke, 226–28
Karatani Kōjin, 15, 21, 37
Kasai Sansei, 133–34, 136–37, 138–40, *141*, 142
katakana, 38, 72
katarimono (ballad recitation), 27
Katayama Sen, 90
Katō Takaaki, 116
katsudō benshi. See *benshi*
Katsuragawa Hoshū, 70
Kawabata Masao, 186, 189
Kawabata Yasunari, 172
Kawakami Otojirō, 179, 240n26
Kawamura Minato, 23, 24
kawaraban (commercial broadsheets), 29
Kemuyama Jirō, 182
Kenney, William Howland, 111–12
Kern, Stephen, 41
Kido Shirō, 176
Kikuchi Kan, 129, 161, 169–70, 196
Kimura Hajime, 182, 184, 185
Kinema junpō, 192, 200, 203, 219, 221–22
Kinoshita, Chika, 196
Kinsei ni daihatsumei: Denwaki-sogenki, 84
Kinugasa Teinosuke, 218, 222–23
Kiri hitoha (Tsubouchi), 156, 157
Kiri no naka (Yamamoto), 169, 170–71, 172
Kishida Kunio, 181
Kittler, Friedrich, 20, 36
Kiyose Eijirō, 218–19
Kleeman, Faye Yuan, 72
Knollys, Henry, 60
Kobayashi Tokujirō, 155, 160, 180, 183
kōdan, 25, 27–28, 130, 240n26
Kōda Rohan, 79
Koe no shihonshugi (Yoshimi), 13
Koizumi Kyōko, 112
Kokoro (Natsume), 41–42
kokugaku (national learning), 23–24
Kokuikō (Mabuchi), 23
Kokumin Bungeikai, 164
kokutai. See state formation

Komura Jutarō, 2, 229n1
Komura Kin'ichi, 163
kotodama shinkō, 23–24
kowairo (vocal timbre, mimicry), 87–88, 89
Kōzu Senzaburō, 84
Kubota Mantarō, 161, 163
kudoki singers, 29
Kumakawa Masao, 176
Kuma no yattsu kiri jiken (Saitō), 218
Kume Masao, 129, 130–31, 132, 161
Kumoemon record case (Kumoemon onpu jiken), 96–101, 102, 107–9, 241n38, 241n39, 241n40, 241n45, 241n46, 242n61, 242n62, 242n63
Kunikada Doppo, 44
Kurata Yoshihiro, 83
Kurino Shin'ichirō, 229n1
Kuroda Isamu, 120
Kurokawa Seiichirō, 94
Kurokigawa Takashi, 218
Kurosawa Akira, 52–53, 55, 187, 191, 199, 235n1, 251n41
Kurosawa kyokubadan (Hongō), 168
Kyakuhon gakufu jōrei (Script and Music Statute), 94
Kyōyama Kyōansai, 144

Lacan, Jacques, 12, 13, 31, 121, 124, 125–26, 142, 230n15, 244n33
Langer, Susanne, 75
language: and period fiction, 217–18; and period film, 218–23; and radio drama, 168; and state formation, 35–36, 215; vs. voice, 32. *See also* literature; spoken Japanese; written Japanese
Lastra, James, 87, 190
Lea, Gordon, 166
Lewis, Peter, 171–72
linguistic communities, 24–25
linguistics, 34–35
literature: and harmony, 78–80; and multidimensionality, 33; naturalism, 20–21, 79; New Perceptionism, 21, 172; period fiction, 217–23; and soundscapes, 56, 57–58; telegraph in, 42–43; telephone in, 44; and vernacular, 221
liveness, 128–29, 130, 132–33, 134, 135, 143
Ljubljana school of psychoanalysis, 12–13
Lloyd, Harold, 177
lo-fi soundscapes, 56
London, Kurt, 203
Lubitsch, Ernst, 207
Lucas, George, 191
Lyrophone, 91, 96

Machida Kashō, 161
McLuhan, Marshall, 8, 154
Madamu to nyobo (*The Neighbor's Wife and Mine*) (Gosho), 176, 184, 197–98, 201, 202
Maedi Ai, 25–26
Maehata Hideko, 136, 137, 138–39, 142
Maejima Hisoka, 24, 39, 86, 231n7
Mafune Yutaka, 164–65, 183, 189
Magami Gitarō, 200
mail, and telephone, 48
Manabi no akatsuki, 83
Manchurian Incident (1931), 134
manga, 226
Man Who Came Back, The (Walsh), 176–77
Man'yōshū, 56, 235–36n6
manzai (comedy genre), 25, 26
Marston, William, 200
Martinville, Édouard-Léon Scott de, 83
Marxism, 12, 214
Masaoka Kenzō, 176
Mascagni, Pietro, 207
Mason, Luther Whiting, 71, 72
mass media, 11, 35–36
Masuda Satoshi, 94, 99–100, 104
Masutani Rin, 198
materiality: Lacan on, 12–13, 230n15; of media, 8, 9, 11; of sound, 61, 88; of voice, 12–13, 26, 30, 32
Matsuda Hiroyuki, 39, 46
Matsumoto Saburō, 90
Matsumoto Takeichirō, 90, 91

Matsuo Bashō, 33, 57–58
Matsuuchi Norizō, 129–31, 132, 133, 135
media: distinctive nature of, 7–8, 9; materiality of, 8, 9, 11; and neuroplasticity, 11, 230n12
media ecology, 14, 34, 230n15
Megata Tanetarō, 71
Meiji emperor, 86
Meiji no oto: Seiyōjin ga kiita kindai Nihon (Naitō), 62
Meiji period: copyright, 94; *naniwabushi*, 92–93, 146; soundscapes, 59–60, 61–64, 67–68; storytelling, 27–28; telegraph network, 39–40; and time synchronization, 120; vocalized reading, 25–26; Western commercial treaties, 93, 94, 95; and Western culture, 6, 70–71, 82; Western visitors, 59–60, 61–64. *See also* state formation
Mekura no kōrikashi (Nagata), 175
memorization, 27
memory, 111–13, 121, 124
Mikawaya Baisha, 107
militarism. *See* Japanese nationalism/militarism
Miller, John Scott, 27
mimicry, 33
Minawa Ichirō, 187, 191
Ministry of Communications (Teishinshō), 115, 116, 120, 128, 136–37, 175
Mio (Nagata), 157
Mitsui Tōru, 104
Miyazaki Tōten, 92
Mizoguchi Kenji, 187–88, 196, 201, 210–16
Mizuno Rentarō, 95
Mizutani Yaeko, 180
modernity: and auditory culture, 2–3; Japanese cultural logic of, 6–7; and noise, 66, 67, 150; as plural, 6; and speed, 201–2; and telephone, 47. *See also* industrialization
Momotarō no umiwashi (*Momotarō's Sea Eagles*) (Seo), 185

Moriari Arinori, 86
Mori Iwao, 200, 201, 203
Mori Ōgai, 72, 73, 79–80, 163
Morita Akio, 198
Morocco (Sternberg), 206
Morse, Edward S., 62–63
Morse, Samuel, 37
Motoori Norinaga, 23–24
Moussinac, Léon, 203
Mumford, Lewis, 85
Münsterberg, Hugo, 155
Muramatsu Yoshinaga, 186
Murata Kakuko, 167
Murata Minoru, 164
Murch, Walter, 191
music: commodification of, 81, 108; and consciousness, 75–76, 238n39; and copyright, 94, 98, 100–101; and cultural conservatism, 60–61, 69–70; and digital media, 103–4, 237n28; Japanese, 59–61, 65, 74–75, 101, 237n36, 241n46; karaoke, 226–28; power of, 68–69, 76, 81; as prophecy, 69, 237n28; and radio drama, 162, 174; and reverberation, 66; and speed, 202, 250n21. *See also* film music; sound recording copyright; Western music
Music for the Films (Sabaneev), 203
Mutsu Munemitsu, 86

Nadare (Mafune), 164, 183, 189
Nagai Kafū, 72–75, 79, 147–49, 150, 237n36
Nagasaki Eizō, 163
Nagata Hideo, 157, 161, 175
Nagata Mikihiko, 159; and amateur playwrights, 167; background of, 157; exposure to radio, 159–60; and JOAK, 160; and Radio Drama Research Group, 161, 162–63; and Tanizaki, 172; and voice acting, 173, 174, 175
Nagato Yōhei, 193, 196, 216
nagauta (musical narrative genre), 26–27
Nagoya Broadcasting Station (JOCK), 116

Naitō Takashi, 62, 69–70
Nakagi Teiichi, 186
Nakamura Hyōzō IV, 180
Nakamura Utaemon, 157
Nakamura Yoshikoto, 45
Nakane Hiroshi, 202–9
Nakano Jun, 31
Nakazato Kaizan, 217
Nakazawa Ken, 176–77
naniwabushi: disdain for, 101, 241n46; origins of, 144–46; and radio, 144, 146–47; and residual orality, 25; and sound recording, 28, 91–92, 109; and storytelling, 27, 28. See also Kumoemon record case
Naniwa erejī (*Osaka Elegy*) (Mizoguchi), 210–11, 212, 214, 215, 216
Naoki Sanjūgo, 217
nationalism. See Japanese nationalism/militarism
Natsume Sōseki, 41–42, 44–45, 47, 65, 150, 236–37n22
naturalism: and film, 204–5; and film music, 203–4; and harmony, 80–81; literary, 20–21, 79; and sound effects, 179. See also realism
NBC, 134–35
neuroplasticity, 11, 230n12
newspapers: and language standardization, 217; and oral traditions, 29; and radio, 114–15; and sound recording, 84; and telephone, 45, 46
New Perception school (*shinkankakuha*), 21, 172
Nicchiku (Nihon Chikuonki Shōkai), 91, 96–97, 102, 240n21, 241n40, 242n62. See also Kumoemon record case
Nichibei Chikuonki Kabushiki Kaisha, 91
Nihon bungaku seisuishi (Takahashi), 226
Nihon Chikuonki Shōkai. See Nicchiku
"Nihon eiga tenkōroku" (Mori), 201
Nihon kaiki (return to Japan), 75
ninjōbon (sentimental fiction), 221

Ninjō kamifūsen (*Humanity and Paper Balloons*) (Yamanaka), 223
Nippon Hōsō Kyōkai (NHK): formation of, 116; and radio drama, 160, 175, 182; and radio exercise, *119*, *122*; and sound effects, 184–85; and sports broadcasting, 134, 135, 136; and state formation, 118
Nishimoto Ikuko, 48–49
Nishimura Gyōson, 173–74
Nishino Teruo, 175
Nishiwaki Junzaburō, 172
Nishizawa Minoru, 156
niwaka (improvised mimicry), 216, 251n46
Noise: The Political Economy of Music (Attali), 13, 64–65, 96
noise: acoustics definition of, 235n5; and modernity, 66, 67, 150; radio as, 147–50; and rationalism, 81; and soundscapes, 56, 64–65; and space, 67; and Western culture, 65–66, 236–37n22
Nomi Yoshihisa, 100, 241n40
nonverbal communication, 33–34

Obana Sen'ichi, 90
objet petit a, 31, 151–52
Occupation of Japan, U.S., 82, 120, 126, 187
ocularphobic discourses, 3
Oda Mikio, 134
Odoriko nikki (Yakura), 198
Ogasawara Nagayoshi, 160
Okamoto Kazuaki, 108, 242n63
Okamoto Kihachi, 217
Ōkawabata, 163
Olympic Games (1932), 134–40, *141*, 142
Ong, Walter J., 7, 29–30, 54–55, 76
Onga geijutsu no hōhōron (Andrievskii), 186, 200
Ongaku kigeki—horoyoi jinsei, 198
"Ongaku oyobi onkyōka ni kan suru kōsatsu" (Itō), 186
Ongaku to bungaku, 202
Onna Kunisada, 218

onomatopoeia, 236n6
opera, 206–7
orality: and identity, 24–25, 231n8; residual, 7, 25; rhetorical patterns in, 29–30
orientalism, 59
Origins of Modern Japanese Literature (Karatani), 15
Ōru Shōchiku, 216
Osaka Broadcasting Station (JOBK), 116, *117*, 127–28, 184–85
Ōsaka mainichi shinbun, 115
Osanai Kaoru: background of, 163–64; and early radio drama, 154; and Mizoguchi, 211, 212; and Radio Drama Research Group, 161; and sound effects, 179–80, 181, 182, 183
Ōshima Hiroshi, 142
Ōtaguro Motoo, 202
Ōtani Iwao, 187–88
Ōtei Kinshō, 88
Ōtsuki Gentaku, 70
Ōya Ichijirō, 167
Ozu Yasujirō, 197

paralanguage, 34, 63
Paramount, 177
Parker, Andrew, 230n15
Pascal, Blaise, 121
PCL (Photo Chemical Laboratory), 177, 185, 198–99
Perry, Matthew, 38, 93
Peters, John Durham, 142–43
phenomimes, 236n6
phonetics, 35
phonocentrism, 15, 20, 21, 24, 34–35, 40
Photo Chemical Laboratory (PCL), 177, 185, 198–99
photography, 87, 94
Picard, Max, 149–50
pitch-accent languages, 32
Pitkin, Walter, 200
Playfair, Nigel, 154
political protest, 227, 252n10

postmodernism, 228
Principles of Phonetics (Sievers), 35
print culture, 131–33, 199
privacy, 68
psychomimes, 236n6
psychophysics, 20
Pudovkin, Vsevolod, 201, 203, 204
Pure Film Movement, 181

radio, 114–21, 140–53; and emperor's voice, 19, *115*, 150–53; Japanese introduction of, 114–18, *117*, 158t; and Japanese nationalism/militarism, 120, 126, 140–44; and kabuki, 110, 146; and language standardization, 217; listener preferences, 144, 145t, 146, 147t; and *naniwabushi*, 144, 146–47; as noise, 147–50; and Pearl Harbor attack, 247n21; radio exercise, 118–21, *119*, 122–23, 126; and state formation, 116, 118, 121, 134, 140; World War II surrender, 19, *115*, 152–53, *153*. *See also* sports broadcasting
radio drama, 154–78; and amateur playwrights, 167–68, 171, 175; American, 245n1; auditory perspective in, 246n18; and darkness, 154–55; "500-yen" dramas, 168–71, 169t; and Hattori Yoshio, 159, 160–61; how-to manuals, 166; Japanese introduction of, 156–57, 158t, 159–62; and Kurosawa, 187; and modernism, 171–72; and Nagata Mikihiko, 157, 159–60, 161, 162–63, 167, 172; and Osanai Kaoru, 163–64; and Radio Drama Research Group, 161–62, 163, 164, 172, 173, 174, 182; and sound effects, 156, 163, 164–66, 179–81, 183–84, 188–89, 190; and sound recording, 162–63; and supernatural, 171, 172; and voice acting, 173–78
Radio Drama and How to Write It (Lea), 166
Radio Drama Research Group (Rajio Dorama Kenkyūkai), 161–62, 163, 164, 172, 173, 174, 182
Rageot, Gaston, 201, 250n20

railroads, 41
Rajio Dorama Kenkyūkai (Radio Drama Research Group), 161–62, 163, 164, 172, 173, 174, 182
Rajio dorama no tsukurikata, narabi ni rajio doramashū (Hayashi Nikuta), 166
Rajio dorama sōsho, 162, 245–46n11
rajio taisō (radio exercise), 118–21, *119*, *122–23*, 126
rakugo (storytelling genre), 25, 26, 27–28, 34, 109
rangaku (Dutch studies), 70
realism: and film, 190, 207, 209, 211, 215–16, 223; and sound effects, 178. See also naturalism
Recording Industry Association of America, 106
recording/transmission process: and modernity, 3; and oral traditions, 27; as writing, 231n2
Reimei (Osanai), 181, 184, 193, 196
Reiraku (Nagata), 157
Reishō (Nagai), 74, 237n36
residual orality, 7, 25
reverberation, 66, 78–79
Ribbentrop, Joachim von, 142
Richie, Donald, 7, 27
rōdoku (type of vocalized reading), 26
Rojō no reikon (*Souls on the Road*) (Murata), 164
rōkyoku. See *naniwabushi*
Rome Convention for the Protection of Performers, Producers of Phonograms, and Broadcasting Organizations (1961), 240n22
Rosario, Roberto del, 227
rōshō (type of vocalized reading), 26
Rosolato, Guy, 124, 230n15
Russo-Japanese War, 90, 92
Rutledge, Eric, 27

Sabaneev, Leonid, 203
Sacco, Christiane, 31

Saishin tōkī no seisaku to eisha no jissai (Nakagi Teiichi and Yoshida Masayoshi), 186
Saitō Ryokuu, 44
Saitō Torajirō, 218
Sakazaki Dewa no kami (Yamamoto), 170
Sakuma Shōzan, 38
Sankōdō, 90, 96, 241n40. See also Kumoemon record case
San'yūtei Encho, 28
Sasaki Ken'ichi, 100
Sasaki Norio, 186, 200
Sasō Tsutomu, 211, 215
Sato, Barbara, 251n48
Satō Tadao, 198
Satomi Ton, 161, 246n18
Satsuma biwa (instrument and genre), 86
Saussure, Ferdinand de, 35
Sawa Katsuzō, 175
Schafer, R. Murray, 54, 56, 58
Schopenhauer, Arthur, 65, 150
Schulman, Peter, 250n20
science fiction, 187
Seimei o moteasobu otoko futari (Kishida), 181–82
Seiyō jijō (Fukuzawa), 39, 233–34n36
Seiyō jijō gaihen (Fukuzawa), 93
Sekiguchi Jirō, 175
Sekikawa Natsuo, 226
Seo Mitsuyo, 185
Seoul/Keijō Broadcasting Station (JODK), 127
sharebon (fiction genre), 221
shaseiki, 90. See also sound recording
Shashin hanken jōrei (Photo Copyright Statute) (1876), 94
Shashin jōrei (Photograph Statute), 94
Shimaura Seiji, 138
Shimazaki Tōson, 72, 79
Shimizu Kō, 200, 201
Shindō Seiichi, 118, 120
Shinengei, 160
shingeki theater, 170, 179–80, 181–82

shinkankakuha (New Perception school), 21, 172
shinpa theater, 179, 180, 240n26
Shinseinen, 167
Shinshichō, 169–70
Shinshisō, 163
Shin-Tōkyō, 175
Shinya no kyaku (Hongō), 168
Shiomi Yō, 175
shishōsetsu (I-novel), 21, 79
shizenshugi (naturalism), 21
Shōchiku, 160, 163, 176, 184, 218
shōtenbon (accent manuals), 32
Shōwa emperor, 19, *115*, 118, 134, 150–53, *153*
Shōwa period, 111, 146. *See also* Shōwa emperor
Shūkan Asahi, 129, 130
Shunkinshō (A Portrait of Shunkin) (Tanizaki), 172
Shuppan jōrei (Publishing Statute) (1869), 94
Sievers, Eduard, 35
sight as privileged, 53–54
silence, 54–55, 249n2
Silverman, Kaja, 31
Smith, Henry, 107, 146–47
Snyder, Stephen, 79, 80
"Sobuēto dōmei ni okeru tōkīron" (Yamanouchi), 201
social Darwinism, 121
sodoku (reading for sound only), 26
Sōmatō (Hongō), 168
sound: attentiveness to, 56–58, 235–36n6; and body, 120–21, 124–26; centrality of, 5; evanescence of, 54–55, 76; historical/cultural conditionality of, 5–6; materiality of, 61, 88; and natural world, 56–57, 189; and space, 66–68, 76, 88, 124, 238n38; tyranny of, 53, 58, 67. *See also* music; soundscapes
sound effects, 178–92; and film, 181, 184–88, 190, 191, 193, 248n67; and illusion, 189; and kabuki, 179, 180; and radio drama, 156, 163, 164–66, 179–81, 183–84, 188–89, 190;

radio-film transition, 184–85; and *shingeki* theater, 179–80, 181–82; and sound recording, 182–83, 189; terms for, 178, 190–91
sound film transition, 248n1, 249n2; as bookend of sound technology, 223–24; and dialogue, 209–10, 222–23; discourse on, 192–93; early sound film experiments, 194–96t; and film music, 204–5; Mizoguchi on, 211–12; and sound recording, 196–97
sound recording, 83–93, 109–13; anthropomorphization of, 89; early fragility of, 239n7; fidelity of, 89, 240n16; and film, 196–97, 249n8; invention of, 83, 85, 238–39n1; Japanese companies, 90–91, 108–9, 111, 240n19; Japanese domestic production of, 89–90; Japanese introduction of, 83–89; and Japanese oral traditions, 85; Japanese term for, 90; and kabuki, 87, 89, 109–11; and listening communities, 111–13; and memory, 111–13; and *naniwabushi*, 28, 91–92, 109; and radio drama, 162–63; and sound effects, 182–83, 189; and sports broadcasting, 131, *132*, 137–38, *141*, 143–44; and writing, 83, 105–7. *See also* sound recording copyright
sound recording copyright: and Berne Convention, 99–100, 104–5, 240n22; and digital storage/delivery, 103–4, 237n28; and disdain for *naniwabushi*, 101, 241n46; France, 105–6; and improvisation, 101, 241n45; Kumoemon record case, 96–101, 102, 107–9, 241n38, 241n39, 241n40, 241n45, 241n46, 242n61, 242n62, 242n63; laws, 91, 102–3, 106, 242n48, 242n56; and Western culture, 99, 104–5; Whirlwind Plage, 103; and writing, 105–7
soundscapes: and architecture, 67–68; evanescence of, 54; hi-fi vs. lo-fi, 56; memories of, 52–53; and noise, 57, 64–65; premodern, 55–58; urban environments, 67–68; and Western visitors, 58–60, 61–64
sound studies, 13

space, 66–68, 76, 88, 124, 238n38
Speaking into the Air (Peters), 142–43
speed, 202, 250n21
Spielberg, Steven, 191
spoken Japanese: accents, 174, 198, 249n10; attentiveness to sound in, 235–236n6; and colonialism, 71, 214–15, 237n32; dialect, 25, 71, 174, 177, 210–11, 213–16; and film, 198, 209–11, 212–16; *kowairo*, 87–88, 89; paralanguage, 34, 63; standardization of, 114, 217. *See also* voice
sports broadcasting, 126–40; and big Other, 142, 244n33; early, 127–28; and Japanese nationalism/militarism, 139, 140, 142; and liveness, 128–29, 130, 132–33, 134, 135, 143; and print culture, 131–33; and sound recording, 131, *132*, 137–38, *141*, 143–44; styles of, 128–31, 133; Summer Olympics (1932), 134–40, *141*, 142; and transcription, 128, 132–33, 138
Stalin, Joseph, 151
state formation, 22; and language, 35–36, 215; and *naniwabushi*, 28; and radio, 116, 118, 121, 134, 140; and telegraph, 40, 41–42; and voice, 20, 36–37. *See also* Japanese nationalism/militarism
Steiner, George, 225
Sternberg, Josef von, 206
Sterne, Jonathan, 13, 30, 239n7
Stoddard, John Lawson, 60
storytelling, 7, 25, 26–29, 126
Strauss, Richard, 207
Sturgeon, William, 37
Subaru, 157
Sudō Sadanori, 179
Sumidagawa (Hongō), 167–68
Summer Olympics (1932), 134–40, *141*, 142
supernatural, 171, 172
Suzuki, D. T., 55, 235n4
Suzuki Matsumi, 31
Sweet, Henry, 35
Sword of Doom (Okamoto), 217
synesthesia, 125

Tabi wa aozora (Inagaki), 218
Taii no musume (radio drama), 156, 157, 180
Tainter, Charles Sumner, 85
Taishō emperor, 116, 118
Taishō period, 28, 53–55, 111, 155–56
taishū bungaku (mass literature), 217
Takahashi Gen'ichirō, 226–27, 252n10
Takeyama Akiko, 118, 133, 139, 140, 151, 160–61
Tale of the Heike, The, 25, 27
Tamura Akiko, 175
Tanaka Kinuyo, 198
Tanaka Saburō, 203
Tange Sazen Part 1 (Itō), 219
Taniguchi Jirō, 226
Tanizaki Jun'ichirō, 49, 80, 124, 157, 172
Tankō no naka, 154–55
Tanomogi Shinroku, 136
Tayama Katai, 79
tea ceremony, 33
technological development: determinism discourse, 9, 11, 14; and game theory, 9–11; and social conditioning, 11–12; universalism discourse, 14
Teikoku Kinema Engei, 218
Teishinshō (Ministry of Communications), 115, 116, 120
telegrams, 48
telegraph, 37–43; Chinese introduction of, 38; invention of, 37–38; Japanese introduction of, 38–39, 233–34n36; in literature, 42–43; and state formation, 40, 41–42; and written Japanese, 40–41
telephone, 42–51; anthropomorphization of, 43, 89; female operators, 48, *49*, *50*, 216, 235n54, 251n48; greetings, 49; Japanese introduction of, 42–46; in literature, 44; and temporal disorder, 47–49, 51; *yobidashi denwa*, 46–47
Tenshōdō, 90
theater: multidimensional nature of, 33; narrative element, 27; and radio drama,

163–64, 166; residual orality in, 25; *shingeki*, 170, 179–80, 181–82; *shinpa*, 179, 240n26; and sound effects, 179. *See also* radio drama
Theater of the Mind (Verma), 127
Théâtre radiophonique (Cusy and Germinet), 166
Thompson, Emily, 66
Tie shan gongzhu (film), 177
time: commodification of, 45; disorder in, 45, 47–49, 51; and evanescence of sound, 54–55, 76; and sound recording, 111–13; synchronization of, 41, 120; tyranny of clock time, 47
Tōchūken Kumoemon, 91–93, 146. *See also* Kumoemon record case
Todorov, Tsvetan, 171
Tōhō Company, 199
Tōkī igo (Iijima), 201
"Tōkī jidaigeki no daiarōgu" (Kiyose), 218–19
"Tōkī to musan kaikyū" (Iwasaki), 201
"Tōkī no kotoba to butaigeki no serifu to" (Mizoguchi), 212
Tōkī no sekkei to seisakuhō (Hirata and Muramatsu), 186
"Tōkī no shōrai" (Shimizu), 201
Tōkī ongakuron (Nakane), 203–8
Tōkīron (Ishimaki et al.), 200
Tōkī to tennenshoku eiga (Kaeriyama et al.), 186
Toki Zenmaro, 138
Tokugawa Musei, 176, 177
Tokugawa period, 25, 28–29, 71, 213, 221
Tokyo Broadcasting Station. *See* JOAK
Tōkyō Hōsō Gekidan (Tokyo Broadcast Acting Company), 175
Tōkyō kōshinkyoku (Mizoguchi), 196
Tōkyō mainichi shinbun, 115
Tōkyō nichinichi shinbun, 84, 87, 115
Tōkyō Onpu Kaisha, 96, 97
Tomoda Kyōsuke, 175
tonal languages, 32

Der Tonfilm (Umbehr), 200
totalitarianism, 142, 150, 151–52
transcription, 128, 132–33, 138
translation, 22–23, 95, 104–5, 200
Tsubaki Sanjūrō (*Sanjuro*) (Kurosawa), 187, 218
Tsubouchi Shōyō, 156
Tsuchihashi Haruo, 184
Tsuchihashi Takeo, 184
Tsuda Sen, 84
Tsukiji Shōgekijō (Tsukiji Little Theater), 179–80
tsūzoku shōsetsu (popular novels), 217
20 seiki hōsōshi (NHK), 127

Uchida Hyakken, 47
Uchiyama Rizō, 160
Uchū senkan Yamato (*Space Battleship Yamato*), 178
Udagawa Yōan, 70
Ueda Akinari, 24
Ueda Bin, 72, 79
Uemura Yasuji, 198
Ueshima Ryō, 218
Ukiyodoko shōkei (Kubota), 169
Umbehr, Heinz, 200
Unbeaten Tracks in Japan (Bird), 63–64
undō suketchi ("sports sketch" recordings), 131, 132, 135, 138
Uotani Tadashi, 128–29, 130–31, 133
urban environments, and noise, 67–68

Verdi, Giuseppe, 207
Verma, Neil, 127
vernacular, 21, 22, 114, 209–10, 217, 221, 250n30
Virilio, Paul, 201
Visible Speech, 1, 35, 71
Visible Speech (Bell), 1, 35
vocalized reading, 25–26
voice: acting through, 173–78; and auditory culture, 4–5; aura of, 19; and body, 121, 124–26; disembodied, 19–20; and identity,

30, 174; *kowairo*, 87–88, 89; vs. language, 32; materiality of, 12–13, 26, 30, 31–32; and memory, 121, 124; as *objet petit a*, 31, 151–52; performance of, 32–33; plasticity of, 30–31; and pleasure, 47, 121, 124; power of, 19–20; and sound recording, 111; and state formation, 20, 36–37; transience of, 5, 19
Voice and Nothing More, A (Lacan), 12

Wada Sei, 180, 181–82, 185
Wagner, Richard, 207
waka poetics, 78
Wakare no Urashima (radio drama), 156
Walsh, Raoul, 176
War of the Worlds, The (Welles), 247n21
Watanabe Shintarō, 218
Welles, Orson, 247n21
Werdermann, Richard. *See* Kumoemon record case
Western colonialism, 59, 61
Western commercial treaties, 93, 94, 95
Western culture: and copyright, 93–96, 99, 104–5; Meiji embrace of, 6, 70, 71, 82; and noise, 65–66, 236–37n22; phonocentrism in, 34–35; and theater, 179. *See also* Western music
Western music: backlash against, 81–82; harmony in, 77–79, 80–81, 238n41; Japanese embrace of, 68, 70–71, 72–74, 75, 82, 237n36; twelve-tone equal temperament tuning, 77, 238n40; and Western visitors, 61
Western visitors: and music, 59–60; and soundscapes, 58–60, 61–64
Whirlwind Plage, 103
White-Smith Music Publishing Company v. Apollo Company (United States), 242n56
women: and language, 222; and radio drama, 172, 174; as telephone operators, 48, 49, 50, 216, 235n54, 251n48
"Work of Art in the Age of Mechanical Reproduction, The" (Benjamin), 19

World War II: declaration of surrender, 19, 115, 152–53, *153*; and film, 185; and radio, 247n21. *See also* Occupation of Japan, U.S.
writing: vs. auditory discourse, 22–24; recording/transmission process as, 231n2; and sound recording, 83, 105–7. *See also* written Japanese
written Japanese: and Chinese, 24, 39, 72, 231n7; kana syllabaries, 38, 39, 40–41; simplified style, 39; and standardization of vernacular, 21, 22, 35–36, 217; and state formation, 35–36; and telegraph, 40–41

Xavier, Francis, 70

Yabe Kenjirō, 168
Yakyū, 131–32
Yamada Isuzu, 215
Yamada Kōsaku, 174, 203
Yamaguchi Jun, 185
Yamaguchi Makoto, 127, 128
Yamamoto Shūgorō, 218
Yamamoto Teru, 136
Yamamoto Yūzō, 161, 169–71, 172
Yamanaka Sadao, 222, 223
Yamano Ichirō, 177
Yamanouchi Hikaru, 200, 201
yamato kotoba (Japanese language), 24
Yamato Sadaji, 179, 185, 189
Yanagita Kunio, 214
Yang, Daqing, 225
Yano Jirō, 84
Yasuda Kiyoo, 220–21
yobidashi denwa (telephone summons), 46–47
Yoda Yoshikata, 210–11, 215
Yōjimbō (Kurosawa), 187
yojō (overtones), 78
Yōki na kōjo (Kurosawa), 187
Yokomitsu Riichi, 172
Yokoyama Shin'ichirō, 90
yomimono (storytelling genre), 27

Yomiuri shinbun, 109, 173
yose (variety entertainment halls), 89, 92, 109, 240n25
Yoshida Masayoshi, 186
Yoshida Naramaru II, 108, 242n62
Yoshii Isamu, 161, 163
Yoshikawa Eiji, 217

Yoshimi Shun'ya, 13, 36
Yuji Tomio, 137–38

Zen Buddhism, 55, 121, 235n4
Zhishanyan, 71, 237n32
Zhu Zaiyu, 238n40
Žižek, Slavoj, 12, 31, 125

STUDIES OF THE WEATHERHEAD EAST ASIAN INSTITUTE
COLUMBIA UNIVERSITY

Selected Titles

(Complete list at: http://www.columbia.edu/cu/weai/weatherhead-studies.html)

The Invention of Madness: State, Society, and the Insane in Modern China, by Emily Baum. University of Chicago Press, 2018.

Idly Scribbling Rhymers: Poetry, Print, and Community in Nineteenth-Century Japan, by Robert Tuck. Columbia University Press, 2018.

Forging the Golden Urn: The Qing Empire and the Politics of Reincarnation in Tibet, by Max Oidtmann. Columbia University Press, 2018.

The Battle for Fortune: State-Led Development, Personhood, and Power among Tibetans in China, by Charlene Makley. Cornell University Press, 2018.

Aesthetic Life: Beauty and Art in Modern Japan, by Miya Mizuta Lippit. Harvard University Asia Center, 2018.

China's War on Smuggling: Law, Economic Life, and the Making of the Modern State, 1842–1965, by Philip Thai. Columbia University Press, 2018.

Where the Party Rules: The Rank and File of China's Authoritarian State, by Daniel Koss. Cambridge University Press, 2018.

Resurrecting Nagasaki: Reconstruction and the Formation of Atomic Narratives, by Chad Diehl. Cornell University Press, 2018.

China's Philological Turn: Scholars, Textualism, and the Dao in the Eighteenth Century, by Ori Sela. Columbia University Press, 2018.

Making Time: Astronomical Time Measurement in Tokugawa Japan, by Yulia Frumer. University of Chicago Press, 2018.

Mobilizing Without the Masses: Control and Contention in China, by Diana Fu. Cambridge University Press, 2018.

Post-Fascist Japan: Political Culture in Kamakura after the Second World War, by Laura Hein. Bloomsbury, 2018.

China's Conservative Revolution: The Quest for a New Order, 1927–1949, by Brian Tsui. Cambridge University Press, 2018.

Promiscuous Media: Film and Visual Culture in Imperial Japan, 1926–1945, by Hikari Hori. Cornell University Press, 2018.

The End of Japanese Cinema: Industrial Genres, National Times, and Media Ecologies, by Alexander Zahlten. Duke University Press, 2017.

The Chinese Typewriter: A History, by Thomas S. Mullaney. MIT Press, 2017.

Forgotten Disease: Illnesses Transformed in Chinese Medicine, by Hilary A. Smith. Stanford University Press, 2017.

Borrowing Together: Microfinance and Cultivating Social Ties, by Becky Yang Hsu. Cambridge University Press, 2017.

Food of Sinful Demons: Meat, Vegetarianism, and the Limits of Buddhism in Tibet, by Geoffrey Barstow. Columbia University Press, 2017.

Youth for Nation: Culture and Protest in Cold War South Korea, by Charles R. Kim. University of Hawaii Press, 2017.

Socialist Cosmopolitanism: The Chinese Literary Universe, 1945–1965, by Nicolai Volland. Columbia University Press, 2017.

Yokohama and the Silk Trade: How Eastern Japan Became the Primary Economic Region of Japan, 1843–1893, by Yasuhiro Makimura. Lexington Books, 2017.

The Social Life of Inkstones: Artisans and Scholars in Early Qing China, by Dorothy Ko. University of Washington Press, 2017.

Darwin, Dharma, and the Divine: Evolutionary Theory and Religion in Modern Japan, by G. Clinton Godart. University of Hawaii Press, 2017.

Dictators and Their Secret Police: Coercive Institutions and State Violence, by Sheena Chestnut Greitens. Cambridge University Press, 2016.

The Cultural Revolution on Trial: Mao and the Gang of Four, by Alexander C. Cook. Cambridge University Press, 2016.

Inheritance of Loss: China, Japan, and the Political Economy of Redemption After Empire, by Yukiko Koga. University of Chicago Press, 2016.

Homecomings: The Belated Return of Japan's Lost Soldiers, by Yoshikuni Igarashi. Columbia University Press, 2016.

Samurai to Soldier: Remaking Military Service in Nineteenth-Century Japan, by D. Colin Jaundrill. Cornell University Press, 2016.

The Red Guard Generation and Political Activism in China, by Guobin Yang. Columbia University Press, 2016.

Accidental Activists: Victim Movements and Government Accountability in Japan and South Korea, by Celeste L. Arrington. Cornell University Press, 2016.

Ming China and Vietnam: Negotiating Borders in Early Modern Asia, by Kathlene Baldanza. Cambridge University Press, 2016.

Ethnic Conflict and Protest in Tibet and Xinjiang: Unrest in China's West, coedited by Ben Hillman and Gray Tuttle. Columbia University Press, 2016.

One Hundred Million Philosophers: Science of Thought and the Culture of Democracy in Postwar Japan, by Adam Bronson. University of Hawaii Press, 2016.

Conflict and Commerce in Maritime East Asia: The Zheng Family and the Shaping of the Modern World, c. 1620–1720, by Xing Hang. Cambridge University Press, 2016.

Chinese Law in Imperial Eyes: Sovereignty, Justice, and Transcultural Politics, by Li Chen. Columbia University Press, 2016.

Imperial Genus: The Formation and Limits of the Human in Modern Korea and Japan, by Travis Workman. University of California Press, 2015.

Yasukuni Shrine: History, Memory, and Japan's Unending Postwar, by Akiko Takenaka. University of Hawaii Press, 2015.

The Age of Irreverence: A New History of Laughter in China, by Christopher Rea. University of California Press, 2015.

The Knowledge of Nature and the Nature of Knowledge in Early Modern Japan, by Federico Marcon. University of Chicago Press, 2015.

The Fascist Effect: Japan and Italy, 1915–1952, by Reto Hofmann. Cornell University Press, 2015.

Empires of Coal: Fueling China's Entry into the Modern World Order, 1860–1920, by Shellen Xiao Wu. Stanford University Press, 2015.

GPSR Authorized Representative: Easy Access System Europe, Mustamäe tee 50, 10621 Tallinn, Estonia, gpsr.requests@easproject.com

www.ingramcontent.com/pod-product-compliance
Lightning Source LLC
Chambersburg PA
CBHW021937290426
44108CB00012B/869